Disabling Policies?
A comparative approach to education policy and disability

Disability, Handicap and Life Chances
Series Editor: Len Barton

Disability, Handicap and Life Chances Series

Disabling Policies?
A comparative approach to education policy and disability

Gillian Fulcher
Monash University, Australia

The Falmer Press
(A member of the Taylor & Francis Group)
London, New York and Philadelphia

UK   The Falmer Press, Falmer House, Barcombe, Lewes, East Sussex, BN8 5DL

USA   The Falmer Press, Taylor & Francis Inc., 242 Cherry Street, Philadelphia, PA 19106–1906

© G. Fulcher 1989

First published 1989

British Library Cataloguing in Publication Data

Fulcher, Gillian
  Disabling policies? : a comparative approach to education policy and disability.
  1. Handicapped children. Education
  I. Title
  371.9
  ISBN 1–85000–315–7
  ISBN 1–85000–316–5 pbk

Library of Congress Cataloging-in-Publication Data

Fulcher, Gillian
  Disabling policies? : a comparative approach to education, policy and disability/Gillian Fulcher.
  p. cm. – (Disability, handicap, and life chances series)
  Bibliography: p.
  Includes index.
  ISBN 1–85000–315–7. – ISBN 1–85000–316–5 (pbk.)
  1. Handicapped children – Education – Cross-cultural studies.
  2. Handicapped children – Education – Government policy – Cross-cultural studies. I. Title. II. Series: Disability, handicap, and life chances.
  LC4015.F85 1989
  371.9–dc19

  89–1242
  C I P

Typeset in 10½/13 Bembo by
Bramley Typesetting Limited, 12 Campbell Court, Bramley, Basingstoke, Hants. RG26 5EG

Printed in Great Britain by BPCC Wheatons Ltd, Exeter

Contents

To Adam

Acknowledgments

While writing this book has seemed mainly a solitary, demanding yet enjoyable task, I have received a great deal of help. I am grateful firstly, to my mother and to Monash University Special Research Grants Committee for making available some research assistance, thus making the project viable; secondly, to Dianne, Teena and Janet, all three of whom in their different ways gave excellent assistance and whose willingness and efficiency were very encouraging.

I am grateful for the constructive help Len Barton has given me on specific issues relating to the manuscript and for his general encouragement to get the book published.

I thank Monash main library Interlibrary Loan librarians who obtained a great deal of material for me and Vivienne Nash who was very helpful; also the members of the committee who carried out the Victorian Ministerial Review of Educational Services for the Disabled in 1983–4, and for whom I acted as main policy analyst. It was this experience, and events since, which drove me to write the book. In helping sort out its ideas I thank students at Monash between 1984 and 1988 for their interest and constructive criticism.

To my friends I owe a great deal. To Robin, for his practical help, especially in fitting out a study for the computer age, to Eve for her practical and unflagging support, to Tony, and Colleen who was always so very encouraging. Also, Les, my grateful thanks. My thanks, too, to others who respected my involvement, and finally, to Adam, who turned eighteen while this was being written, and without whose interest and word-processing abilities I might never have finished the thing. It was he who told me which chapters were too long, too short, too packed with quotes – judgements with which you may agree.

I would like to thank J. Hansen of the Ministry of Education, Copenhagen, for permission to include Tables 3.1 and 3.3 and Figures 3.1 and 3.2, adapted from Hansen (1984) *Handicap and Education; The Danish*

Acknowledgments

Experience, and for Tables 3.2, 3.4 and 3.5 adapted from Pedersen (1982) *Some Statistics on Special Education;* the authors for Table 3.6 which is adapted from Dahl, Tangerud and Vislie (1982) *Integration of Handicapped Pupils;* Unesco for Tables 3.7 and 3.8 and Figure 3.4, adapted from Unesco (1987) *A Case Study on Special Education in Norway;* the Australian Association of Special Education for Figure 4.2, adapted from Ysseldyke (1986) 'Current US Practice in Assessing' in the *Australian Journal of Special Education;* the Education Department of Victoria for permission to use Tables 6.1, 6.2 and 6.3; James Carrier and the University of Chicago Press for Table 4.4 and Pro-Ed, Texas, for Tables 4.1 and 4.2 (Gerry, 1985), Table 4.3 (Forness, 1985) and for Table 6.4, The Australian Government Publishing Service (1987) *Schooling in Australia.*

Gillian Fulcher
Queenscliff, 1988

Series Editor's Preface

Our knowledge and understanding of other societies, their systems of education, educational policies, perspectives on and provisions for disabled people is often ill-informed and inadequate. This book is therefore important in that the writer, using her experience gained from 'being the main policy analyst and report writer for the Victorian Ministerial Review of Educational Services for the Disabled', combined with her skills as a researcher, provides a serious examination of important developments and key issues in relation to integration, or mainstreaming, within five countries including her own.

The author discusses the nature of policy and the different forms policy takes. A particular concern is 'Why certain policies fail?'. The role of discourse as a means of both articulating and legitimating different policies is a crucial aspect of the analysis. This is part of a more general interest in examining the objectives of specific groups concerning integration, including the institutional conditions under which they attempt to satisfy their objectives. From this perspective the question of power is fundamental, particularly in terms of how some groups control and disable others within the realities of unequal social relations.

A serious critique is offered of the role of professionalism in relation to disabled people and specifially that form of professional discourse which celebrates the 'individual gaze' on the part of such experts. Problems are thus located within the child or in C. Wright Mills' (1970) terms, the issues are seen as 'personal troubles', rather than 'public' ones. This has led to the underplaying of political considerations, particularly the centrality of choice and control for disabled people.

Traditional distinctions between theory and practice, policy and implementation, are seriously questioned and viewed by Fulcher as politically misleading. Policy is to be understood as being created at all levels, which results in a critical analysis being offered of those existing theories which provide an overly deterministic view of the social world. Such theories, the author maintains, fail to grasp the complexity of the processes of policy making. As part of a framework in which the dynamic interplay between structural and interactional factors can be understood and explained, the writer introduces the notion of 'arenas' which are to be seen as forums within which struggles over meaning and action take place.

The question of integration is to be approached through an examination of the different objectives that groups hold and the means through which they seek to realize them. These objectives are always part of some wider social theory of the world, including what it is like, or should be like. Integration is, therefore, a controversial issue and involves struggles between competing allegiances and interpretations. For the author of this book much of the discourse on integration is a discourse of exclusion, in which, she maintains, discipline and control are central interests. The way in which particular policies are disabling in themselves is thus a topic of perennial concern.

This book is highly informative, and the strong comparative emphasis raises serious questions about the ways in which we are both ethnocentric and dogmatic in our views on the subject of disability and integration. We too often believe that our priorities, views and policies are the proper, the *only* ones, and therefore they must be right. The writer of this book has provided us with an extremely readable and challenging perspective. Many questions are raised and new agendas are set for further research and discussion.

I hope this book is widely read and that it will provide a powerful impetus for future work on policy and practice.

Mills, C.W. (1970) *The Sociological Imagination*, Harmondsworth, Penguin.

Len Barton
Bristol 1989

List of Tables and Figures

List of Tables and Figures

Introduction

This book is about integration or mainstreaming policies. Its specific concerns are how we can develop a better deal for those schoolchildren who are (in increasing numbers) called 'disabled' or handicapped, and for their teachers. Moving towards that aim requires us to think about more general questions, especially What is the nature of government policy? and Why do some well-intentioned democratic policies (such as *some* of those policies called integration and mainstreaming) frequently fail? If we can answer these general questions – which are difficult but central – we should be able to develop better integration or mainstreaming policies, ones which are more successful than those that a number of Western governments have issued in recent years.

The book's concerns are thus both general, to do with the nature of government policy, and specific to education policy on disability. Dealing with these concerns means clarifying what we mean by policy, practice, integration, mainstreaming, etc. How I reached the definitions and the view of policy the book argues for, draws in part on the experiences which led to the book's concerns. Central to these experiences was a year's work, out of academia, as the main policy analyst and report writer for the Victorian Ministerial Review of Educational Services for the Disabled. None of my previous work or personal experiences prepared me for the intensely political process involved in producing the report. Both in Review meetings and outside them, vigorous struggles took place between Committee members and their associates in attempts to influence the Committee's decisions and the content of the position papers the writing team put forward for its consideration. The writing team was inevitably embroiled in these politics; it, too, became divided. Behind these struggles lay the different objectives of the various factions in the Review: perhaps the strongest, or most frequent, division here was between teacher union representatives and the lone parent representative, but alliances shifted according to the issue. Yet the report, since it was a report of the two-year-old Victorian Labour government whose wider policy was consensus in decision-making, was presented, both to the

Minister and later by him, as a consensus report. This, despite the intense struggles in Review meetings: for instance, the two Extension Notes inserted in the report (by the parent representative and a union representative) just ten minutes before it was presented to the Minister.

Further surprises lay ahead when, some two months later, the Minister issued *Integration in Victorian Education* (1984). The report was widely regarded, in Victoria and elsewhere in Australia, as democratic and controversial, if not radical, and as a strong attack on professionals in special education because its guiding principle was that all children have a right to a regular education, a phrase the Minister was careful to qualify in his statements about the report by mentioning resource provision.

The conflict this report produced in various educational forums or arenas was vigorous, marked and prolonged: it continues. Professional associations issued policy statements which explicitly or covertly rejected the report's proposals. Committees on integration were established in a whole range of settings (part of the Review's recommendations): in schools, Regional offices, teacher unions, parent groups, etc. Meetings on integration proliferated. At one, I became alarmed by the turn of the debate; by the way in which language the Review had suggested might democratize education for these children (help increase their participation in regular schools, for instance), such as 'integration child' (not a term the Review had suggested but certainly consistent with its vocabulary), was in fact being used against these schoolchildren, to marginalize them. Thinking I might have misunderstood her, I asked one teacher what the term integration child meant: '*Watch him!*' was the reply. Nor was this an isolated instance of language being deployed for certain ends. The somewhat clumsy concept of 'problems in schooling', which appeared in the report as a term suggesting *schools* owned or had produced 'learning' problems, was quickly deployed as a new deficit term: official posters appeared in numerous rooms advertizing activities concerning *children* with impairments, disabilities or problems in schooling. Here language was being used to reinforce the individual deficit approach which has characterized both the conceptual apparatus and practice (the discursive practices)[1] of special education in Western countries since its inception.

The conflict increased. 'Integration children' were suddenly discovered in regular classrooms;[2] some schools demanded extra resources from their Regional Board which they claimed were necessary for them to go on teaching particular children, and when the resources weren't granted, some of these schools attempted to suspend the student. The bureaucracy issued memoranda: one sought to direct schools not to exclude students on this basis but another memorandum established a new form of exclusion: regular schools might now enrol a student who sought entry but if they lacked the resources claimed necessary to teach that student, the school could put that student 'on hold': 'delayed admission' became official policy and the policy of *some* schools.

Watching these counter effects and the emergence of new educational practices, such as delayed admission and new uses of suspension, made me ask what had gone wrong: was Victoria such a peculiarly undemocratic place or were similar things happening in other places or countries where governments had already issued integration policies, such as the US, England, Denmark and Norway? While I gathered material to research these policies and their effects, I also began to read the literature: the social science literature on social policy in general, and on education policy, as well as the educational literature on policy.

Finding a model

In this literature I sought a model, a theoretical platform, which might provide an understanding of policy and its failure. But the literature was evasive, though voluminous, and varied widely in its theoretical bases.[3] Little of it conveys a political sense of the struggles involved in formulating policy (the concept of policy as the allocation of scarce values seemed especially remote from the Review's activities) nor of the *politics* of implementing policy, because clearly this was of the essence of what was going on in Victoria in schools, Regional offices, etc., wherever integration was the topic. In assessing the literature, I was struck by the generally apolitical view of policy and by the lack of insight to be gained from the frequent assertion that there are 'gaps' between policy and practice, or between rhetoric and practice. The statement (in respectable journals) that policy is like the layers of an onion was a diversion but surely they couldn't be serious? There were certainly gaps between the theoretical standpoints in this literature and my practical experience of processes in the Review and in educational settings since the 1984 report: between the theory about all this and its empirical reality.

The discrepancy between the literature and the political reality I saw, encouraged me to be sceptical of most of the conceptual and theoretical platforms the literature offered. I was impressed (but unconvinced) by the dichotomies the literature drew: the distinctions the authors made between policy and practice, policy and implementation, theory and practice and by the almost non-existent discussion about the relationship between policy and the social theory which guided it.[4]

I reflected first, on the division between policy and 'implementation', a distinction which derives from a top-down model of policy (only government makes it and its bureaucracies implement it). Instead of a clear division, I saw only similarities between what took place in Review meetings and processes in other settings where integration was debated, settings like teacher union meetings, Regional committees, in-service seminars for teachers and parents, school meetings, etc.: these I shall call *arenas*, meaning forums within which issues are debated, struggles ensue and decisions are made.

Whether in the Review or in other arenas, the same processes were at work: debate took place, language was used in particular senses to persuade others (so that for one person integration meant what another would describe as segregation) and decisions were reached. These processes, though in different arenas, were identical analytically: in each, a struggle occurred between contenders of competing objectives, contenders put their point of view; in each arena discourse (how the issues were talked about) was deployed as tactic (Macdonell's point, 1986), to persuade others to the speaker's view.

I saw that *how* language is used *matters*. It was the instrument of power.[5] The discourses deployed various themes, styles of statements and inherently different objectives.[6] For instance, asserting that integration had always been with us (because some children with disabilities were in regular schools already) is to use integration in a particular sense and this was part of an argument to dissuade others from writing a 'radical' report which might change existing special education practices. Another contender, whose objective was to change the way special education was organized, used integration in a different sense, to refer to increasing the participation of all children in the social and educational life of regular schools. This person would therefore argue that such practices (some disabled children in regular schools), whilst they co-existed with extensive practices of segregation (special

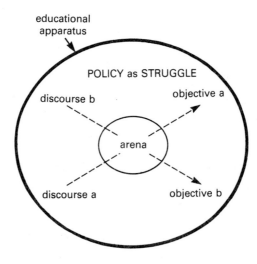

Figure 1: A political model of policy based in a theory of discourse

schools, units, support centres, withdrawal classes, etc.) was *not* integration and what was needed was a new *direction* for the education of children with disabilities; this contender deployed the alternative definition of integration just outlined. Hence, integration meant different things: these differing definitions had nothing to do with mistakes or misconceptions of what integration really is: the definitions constituted quite different objectives. How one talked about the issues revealed the politics of integration (to change or maintain the *status quo*?) and the nature of the competing discourses.

In these arenas, these struggles culminated in decisions. Decisions were the product of these arenas and as such constituted the attainment of an objective (however transitory). Both the product of the Review's activities (decisions and ultimately a report) and the products of other arenas (decisions about school 'policy', regulations, directions for action, etc.): all these products were equally 'policy'.

The degree of conflict and consensus over all this might vary, but the processes and the products were the same. The actual content of the objective might also vary: in Review meetings the objectives concerned the content of a particular point of view to be put, or recommendation to be included, in the report. In arenas where senior bureaucrats and teacher union representatives met together, the objectives for the senior bureaucrats were generally how to contain the politics of integration so that the most powerful players (the Minister, the Cabinet as the primary source of funds, teacher unions and the Party) were appeased. For teacher union representatives, the objective was how to maintain or improve the working conditions of their members, that is, how to prevent teachers having to teach either more students in their classroom than existing ratios required, or those students some teachers found difficult and whom they could presently exclude. In schools, objectives varied according to the principal's position on integration, his/her style of leadership and who the particular players were. Some principals might have democratic aims and seek to include more children called disabled, but others would see the integration debate as an opportunity for gaining more resources (staff and/or funds, for example) for their schools. (While this might sound like a cynical reading, several principals, outside the arena in which they made resources demands, openly admit this was their tactic.)

Thus all of these activities in these different arenas not only shared the process of struggle but each *made* 'policy'. The traditional framework with its top-down model of policy (government makes it and its bureaucracies implement) was clearly false: if by policy we mean the capacity to make decisions and act on them (power is implied here, so this is a political model), whether that action means producing a report, setting up school rules, directions for action, or making demands on Regional offices for resources, policy is made *at all levels*.

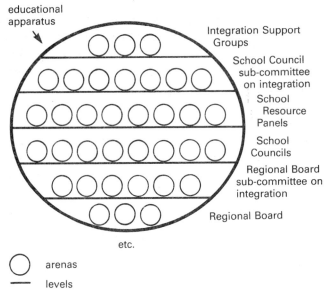

Figure 2: *Some examples of policy levels and arenas in the Victorian educational apparatus*

'Levels' is a useful concept:[7] broadly, it refers to arenas with equivalent autonomy or those operating in roughly equal institutional conditions: in Victoria, School Council arenas are one level, while their sub–Committees on integration (the way some Victorian schools chose to organize decision making on integration) were another, and Enrolment Support Groups another; Regional Boards are a higher level and so on. Levels then refer to levels of institutional conditions in an education system (though I shall replace the term system later).

So if policy is made at all levels, government policy in the form of a report (or even law: see chapters 3 and 4) may have widespread effects, as the 1984 Victorian report did, in the sense of initiating debate and conflict at other levels (Offe's insight (1984)) but to describe what happens at these other levels as implementation is politically misleading and analytically mistaken. But clearly, distinguishing between policy and implementation serves political purposes, since it suggests to people that governments are in charge. This, of course, is why government and bureaucrats retain this language since it occludes the real politics involved and presents bureaucrats as merely 'administrators': it constitutes a discourse of persuasion, of maintaining the view that only politicians hold real power. This is important to politicians in modern democracies since it is a popularly held view that these are democracies precisely because the people's vote is seen as giving a mandate to a particular politician to take part in government, in ruling them. Suggesting that policy is made at all levels, that rule in local arenas (by dominant players in Schools Councils, by teacher unions, by teachers) is just that, may challenge democratic principles. Whether or not it does this will depend on whether local government (used in a broad sense) is a high level policy decision and thus consistent with democratic principles but rule at local, level *against* government level policy, is inconsistent with the notion that the government is in charge. But clearly there *is* policy which countermands government policy, including integration. Evidence of this has already been cited, for instance in marginalizing children as 'integration child' and in instituting 'delayed admission'. Further evidence derives from research on Victorian School Councils written policies on integration: these showed a number of departures from the 1984 report.[8]

These findings, that policy is made at all levels, means that struggles about 'integration' are replayed in the range of arenas: what policy is made in say a School Council, or in a particular Regional Board, cannot be predicted from a knowledge of, say, national level written policy. The evidence cited above shows that power is diffused throughout the Victorian educational apparatus. In some educational apparatuses, for instance, in England, power may be more centralized, particularly under the more recent legislation (the Education Reform Act, 1988), but the extent to which the evidence fits this belief is discussed in chapter 5.

The struggles in formulating policy in these different arenas suggests that policy is clearly the outcome of political states of play (Fulcher, 1986b). Contenders with competing objectives deployed particular discourses: some argued some children have handicaps and ought to be taught by specialists outside regular classrooms while others put the view that regular teachers need to have broader curriculum strategies so that they can teach a wider range of children. What was happening was that discourse was deployed as tactic (Macdonell, 1986). In each arena, the contender(s) who won in this struggle, 'made' policy. This was the outcome of the *practical* activity in an arena. Thus struggles, discourses, personal ploys, intrigues, alliances, etc. constituted the *practical* activity of all these arenas.

All educational encounters as producing policy

The model of policy as struggle between contenders of competing objectives, where language – or more specifically, discourse – is used tactically, I then saw was relevant to other less obviously political and policy encounters. In classrooms, the teacher's decision to call a child an integration child (or by one of the more obviously derogatory disability labels), to include or exclude a student, is clearly a struggle, sometimes easily won, sometimes not: whether that means changing the curriculum to include a student, or persuading unwilling parents to agree to exclusion, or calling in a psychologist to 'assess' a student. Similarly, the encounters between parent and teacher can appropriately be seen as struggle to achieve particular objectives or about how to achieve them: the resulting decision and subsequent action are policy.

Implicit in seeing these different encounters and their products (reports, debate over means, exclusion, etc.) as policy is the idea that policy takes different forms. Thus government reports or law, a teacher's decision, or a style of pedagogy, can equally be called policy, as the exercise of power, that is, the capacity to make decisions and act on them. Here Macdonald's (1981) distinctions were useful. He distinguishes between *written* policy (reports, statutes, regulations, law, whether these derive from government, schools, Regional Boards or School Councils, etc.), *stated* policy: what we say we do (again, whether this is a bureaucrat, politician or teacher, etc.) and *enacted* policy: what the teacher does in the classroom (includes or excludes) or whether the government does redeploy specialists a report recommends should be redeployed. As Macdonald notes, these levels or types of policy may be inconsistent (1981:103). But clearly, identifying these levels and their potential discrepancies takes us further analytically than claiming a gap between rhetoric and practice.

This model of policy as political states of play illustrates what others have claimed, that all educational practices are political (for example, Barton (1987)). Thus, for instance, *where* or *how* or *what* to teach is never merely *technical*: the moral and political dimensions in this judgment precede their substantive technical implications. For instance, nothing follows technically from the fact that a 13-year-old cannot read; the options here include sending him/her to help teach 6-year-olds to read: the method called peer tutoring (this works, see Quicke (1986)) or sending that student elsewhere to be taught by specialists in reading or psychological methods. Each of these options involves political, moral and technical dimensions.

Theory *and* practice

Dissolving the distinction between policy and implementation, or policy and practice, invited me to think about the other distinctions the literature was making. As I reflected on the distinction often drawn between theory and practice, I also reflected on the role that discourse played in these policy struggles. While this was clearly deployed as tactic, it became obvious that discourse also constituted a *theoretical basis* for attaining an objective. Discourses articulate the world in certain ways: they 'identify' 'problems', perspectives on those problems and thus 'solutions'. For instance, the notion that some children have handicaps divides the school population into those with and those without handicaps: it constructs the notion of normal and abnormal, of belonging here or elsewhere, it leads to the view that specialist teachers are necessary for some children and this view suggests or articulates a particular range of objectives for special education: such as identifying 'difference', separate career structures, a focus on disability and so on. We can call this a divisive discourse: it is a close companion of professionalism, which I shall discuss later. An alternative view comes from the discourse that children are firstly *pupils* (the Danish discourse, chapter 3): this provides a different theory and articulation: it unites the school population, it identifies what children share, it provides an objective of including all children in regular schools and directs us to a particular means for achieving that, it invites us to focus on pedagogy. This is an inclusive discourse.

Thus each of these competing discourses contains a social theory of how this bit of the social world works and ought to work: children differ and they should be selected on the basis of their differences and sent to 'appropriate' settings versus children share the characteristics of pupil, each seeks to learn and this means teachers need to be as competent as possible pedagogically. Each discourse therefore proposes a different 'solution' to the issues in a debate on integration: crudely put, the divisive discourse theorizes problems as belonging to the child and as therefore 'needing' extra resources, whereas the inclusive discourse suggests the school has a responsibility to treat all children firstly as pupils, and therefore to concentrate on *pedagogical* solutions to do with curriculum which all teachers might use.

Discourse, as containing a theory which informs practice, means that we act on the basis of our ideas about how something works and what we want to achieve. This understanding of discourse dissolves the widely made distinction that theory is somehow different or separate from practice. Not only is practice (every aspect of social life) always theoretically (or discursively) based but theory, when we mean by that a practical activity some people engage in for its own sake (how does this bit of the social world work?), is always about practice and is itself a practical activity: people engage in doing it. While theoretical endeavour (how does that bit of the social world work?) is always a *practical* task (even if that means merely (?) sitting down with paper and pen), accurate theory is even more engaged with practice: it accurately explains how particular practices work.

Having put policy in a political framework, as struggle around various objectives, in which discourse is both tactic and theory (how you set out to achieve something depends on how you see it working), and having dissolved distinctions between policy and practice and theory and practice, the next task was putting all this in a wider theory of social relations or rather, explicating the implicit theory of social relations I was using. Again I consulted the literature for the theoretical bases underpinning the various discussions of 'policy'. It was here that the literature became unwieldy. It was easy to dismiss both traditional administrative approaches (policy is what government makes and *it* rather than the actions of ordinary people is all important, and only it holds real power) as well as those sociologists for whom 'policy' disappears in their theoretical focus on the class struggle (as the only struggle that matters). But the choice was still alarmingly broad. It ranged from various formulations of the 'state' as controlling policy (for a variety of ends), to the crisis in capitalism being the key constraint on policy, to the motives of individuals as formative on educational practices. The literature included the view that education was part of social policy (for instance, Finch, 1984)[9] as well as the apparent view that education policy is a separate issue.

Three contributions I had been drawing on offered further insights, either on policy and/or on locating it in a wider set of social relations. Each was useful and potentially reconcilable with the other two, despite the fact that at some levels they were consistent. Firstly, Offe's (1984) structuralist view contained useful insights, particularly his view that state social policy is concerned both with controlling or institutionalizing the production of wage labour[10] (who will or won't become a wage labourer: schools obviously do this via keeping students out of the labour force and by credentialling some students and not others); also relevant was his view that state social policy's role is, amongst other things, to initiate conflict at other levels of state apparatuses, and that the outcomes of state social policy depend on the social relations of power.

Secondly, Hindess's position, particularly his 1986 paper, had been useful in formulating the political model of policy I discussed above. In this paper, Hindess outlines his view that policy is made at all levels and that the institutional conditions in which policy is implemented (a concept he retains) are crucial issues. He puts this in a wider model of social life as consisting of *social actors* carrying out discursive social practices, that is, practices based on the discourses available to them: the view I have argued for above, though so far I have referred to players rather than social actors. Hindess's notion of social actors is crucial (because this is where he departs from the two traditional models of structural and humanistic social theory) both to his general framework and to the arguments on policy and who makes it. For Hindess, social actors are not only human individuals but also those groups that have the capacity for reaching decisions and acting on them: for instance, unions, committees, etc. He thus excludes concepts of class and capitalism from being considered as factors which influence or determine policy,[11] because neither class nor capitalism are social actors since neither can make decisions. Hindess argues that political struggles cannot be reduced to the class struggle, nor to crises in capitalism, though struggles between *capitalists* (as social actors) and others may be important (but not all-important). Here he both argues against classic concepts in social theory (class and capitalism) and against what he calls a reductionist view that one level of policy determines others. Such a view is implicit in conceptual frameworks which refer to class or capitalism. Hindess argues that no level of policy determines policy at other levels: national policy, for instance, may have widespread effects but it does not determine what Regional officers, or teachers or bureaucrats produce as their policies. For instance, legislation, despite the popular view that it underpins Ministerial portfolios or action by government departments in providing services, may be ignored, or may contain classic escape clauses, and other bases of action such as bureaucratic power may be more powerful in establishing practices: for instance, 'delayed admission' in the Victorian education apparatus is not a term which appears in legislation.

In sum, a number of Hindess's concepts had been useful: his notion of social actors, of social life as constituted by discursive practices and the 'social' as consisting of complex sets of interconnected practices, of policy being made at all levels and of institutional conditions of policy. Hindess's framework directs us to examine the discourses which inform people's utterances and practices in education. Two opposing discourses have already been mentioned: the divisive discourse about schoolchildren and an inclusive discourse. These are close companions of two other opposing discourses, professionalism and democratism. These are discussed below: they provide an alternative, but closely related, way of analyzing exclusive and inclusive discourses in education.

Thirdly, Mehan's work, in which he argues that social life, including special education practices, consists of *practical* projects had been useful, despite an epistemological clash between his and Hindess's position. Mehan's view that we should locate responsibility for special education placements with the enactment of routine procedures in institutions draws on Weber's ideas and is thus opposed at the level of what constitutes reality to Hindess's view that assigning responsibility is politically crucial, and that we should locate responsibility for decisions with *social actors*. Thus Hindess's concepts and Mehan's view that social life, including special education practices, consists of *practical* projects, allied with dissolving the distinctions I've argued should be dissolved, and seeing discourse as theory as well as tactic, suggests a model of policy located in the following wider theory of social relations.

A political model of policy in a wider model of social life as social practices

Policy is the product, whether written (laws, reports, regulations), stated or enacted (for example, pedagogic practice), of the outcome of political states of play in various arenas. In these arenas there are struggles between contenders of competing objectives, either about objectives or about how to achieve them: in these struggles discourse is deployed as tactic and theory. Social life may be theorized as consisting of *practical* activities, which are *theoretically* based, and in each of which *social actors* struggle to attain their objectives. This means *practical* activities are simultaneously *theoretical or technical, moral* and *political*. In other words, discursive practices are theoretically, politically and morally informed (that is what and how, where and why we should teach this): technical aspects (this is how we should do this) may enter, but no discursive practice (such as a judgment about a child's functioning) is ever purely technical. It is located in a moral system of values and in a political system which has established an hierarchy of values – a normative order: for instance, children by this age should be able to do this and if they can't they should be labelled and possibly sent elsewhere.

From a theoretically purist stance, policy is merely an instance of a discursive practice, that is, an action – whether a report, or a teaching style – which is based in a discourse. From this stance, policy loses its separateness from other social practices: should it then drop out of our array of concepts? As an everyday term it is worth retaining to a degree, since it directs (if somewhat evasively and inaccurately) our attention to certain kinds of actions in certain kinds of arenas, those which belong to what we can loosely call officialdom. But the evasiveness of policy, the woolliness of the term, is of its essence politically: when we can't grasp an idea in clear terms we can't grapple with it. This is why I wrestled with the term conceptually, theoretically and politically: because all theories and their concepts have political implications or platforms or agendas: if you see capitalism as evil then the agenda is to change it: if you see policy as made at all levels, then the agenda includes struggling with policy in a range of arenas at all levels.

As Hindess argues, a discursive practices model of social life seeks to overcome the dilemma the structural and humanistic alternatives have presented for sociology and for political action. One of the ways in which it does this for the purposes of this book, is to avoid conflating structural position (such as teacher or parent or bureaucrat) with a set of ideas: in contrast to the reductionist view (your being determines your consciousness), social actors may have a variety of discourses available to them. Not all teachers use a divisive discourse about schoolchildren (what I shall call later a discourse in disability), nor do parents uniformly adopt a democratic discourse about their children's rights to a regular education, nor do professionals inevitably adopt professionalism: the discourse which asserts that experts know best. Which discourse someone deploys is a matter to be established by research empirically rather than by deduction from a structural model, which is clearly inaccurate empirically.

Saying that theory informs policy, that policy is a form of practice, that political, moral and sometimes technical aspects inhere in all practices, whether educational or other, extends Hindess's discussion of policy as discursive practice. Emphasizing the role of discourse in education policy practices is consistent with recent discussion about how to analyze educational policy (for example, Codd (1988)).

Objectives and their sources

All of this raises the issue of where, in which context, social actors acquire their objectives and the discourses they deploy. These issues Hindess does not address. In this context, given the focus on 'education policy and disability', the notion of *state apparatus* becomes important: this is the official site where practical activities organized around a notion of disability in education are carried out. State apparatuses are an important concept for two reasons. It is in state apparatuses that significant struggles occur about specific objectives (Culley and Demaine, 1983): Western education apparatuses, for instance, have historically been the site of struggles to integrate or segregate schoolchildren well before official policies using these terms appeared. Furthermore, it is in state apparatuses that the institutional conditions are established which both provide institutionalized bases for particular discourses (such as a discourse about education and disability) and which provide the power bases for realizing particular objectives. For instance, separate career structures for special teachers, specific industrial arrangements (negotiated between teacher unions and senior bureaucrats in Victoria, for instance) about teacher–student ratios according to 'type' of child and separate courses in teacher training institutions that argue for separate pedagogies for 'disabled' and non-disabled' schoolchildren, provide institutional bases for an educational discourse about disability. We then need to ask whether these institutional bases are so well entrenched that alternative discourses, for instance about inclusive schooling, are, despite their reasonableness, justifiability and democratic nature, nevertheless immediately in a less powerful situation and for this reason unlikely to be accepted, perhaps even *heard*.

Objectives can also be drawn from arenas outside a particular state apparatus, from the wider political context. This is to take the view that 'politics matter'.[12] In Scandinavia, for instance, the strong social democratic political culture and its concern with inequality has provided objectives in a range of state apparatuses: in education this has led to a debate and some practice of comprehensive schooling, a debate which has occurred to a lesser extent in England but almost not at all in Australia. In Australia, democratic socialist politics, though not well established nor extensively articulated,[13] have informed both a concern for reducing inequality in education and suggested an alleged means for achieving this: through what is called participatory decision-making structures: these influences from the wider political context inform both the Victorian Ministerial Papers on Education (1982–84) and the *Integration in Victorian Education* report.

Finally, Hindess's framework held a particular attraction because it is implicitly optimistic about the possibility of political change, of gaining a better deal for schoolchildren called disabled and their teachers. The notion that social actors, not structures or totalizing concepts such as class, make decisions means that there are people with whom we can negotiate, however powerful their institutionalized bases. The idea that social actors make decisions and establish conditions of action for others and that hence they are responsible for their decisions is a key theoretical and political aspect of Hindess's framework. This contrasts with the politics of structuralism: if the structure is all that matters we can retreat to our studies or kitchens, content in the belief that, short of revolution, we can change nothing. This does not mean that the task of tackling the politics in a range of arenas is easy but at least it seems possible.

In sum, the position developed here contrasts with the view that structures are where we should begin our analysis and with the view that institutional procedures are responsible for the outcome of special education practices (Mehan's analysis of Californian schools (1984, etc.) (see chapter 3)). Against structural views, Hindess argues:

> there is no essential structure that determines what politics, and therefore political analysis, must be about. In any given society there are definite connections between its various component parts, but no overall determining structure . What is important as the starting point of analysis depends on its objectives; it is not given in the essential structure of society. In so far as those objectives are political, the way social relations are analysed will be informed by political concerns and objectives (1986:115).

The framework of theorizing and agenda I've argued for helps in explaining why some government-level democratic policy may not be adopted at other levels, and in addressing the book's concerns. It suggests an *agenda*. Thus, given the book's political objectives (how to develop a better deal for schoolchildren called disabled and their teachers) and given the tactical, thus political, nature of discourse, this framework suggests we examine the discourses and objectives people hold about education policy and disability, especially those of the more powerful social actors, and the institutional conditions under which they hold those discourses and in which they and others struggle to achieve their objectives. In this context, democratism and its opponent, professionalism, have been key discourses informing recent Australian policies on special education (Fulcher, 1986b). Democratism is the view that those affected by decisons should take a genuine part in debating the issues and in making these decisions. Democratization is the historical struggle in which democratism has been the key strategy. Professionalism, the view that experts know best, has been the major tactic in professionalization, the historical struggle to gain control of an area of occupational life.

Conclusions

To assess the effects of any policy we must first understand the nature of policy as a general category of action and intervention in social life: we need to conceptualize policy clearly and then theorize it adequately, meaning we need to put it in a wider theory of social relations, rather than treat it as something different from other actions. Only then can we usefully look at its substance and ask why government policy may or may not be adopted as policy at other levels in an educational apparatus.

As I have argued elsewhere (1988b), theorizing is necessary because:

> It is not enough to identify 'good practice' since how this emerges and how it can be maintained needs to be understood. There are parallels here with the need to theorize policy. It's not enough to identify 'good policy' and to blame poor planning or implementation: clearly the Victorian policy would have been described by its proponents at the time as good policy but events since and the theorizing offered here show that social life is inadequately theorized or understood by (moral) reference to good and bad practice. In this context sociological concepts can move from the rhetoric of blame, can clarify what is going on and thus make a highly practical contribution (1988b:42)

The model put forward here is that we need to conceptualize policy broadly: first, as a form of practice, that is, as an instance of the social practices which we carry out all the time and which constitute social life. In each of our social practices we seek to attain our objectives and we deploy discourse, as both our theory of how that bit of the world in which we want to achieve our objective works, and as tactic, that is, as a means of attaining our objective. Second, more specifically, policy is the outcome of political states of play in policy arenas: in the case of education these arenas occur at all levels: they are exemplified by teacher–parent encounters, school meetings, teacher union meetings, bureaucratic arenas and so on, wherever there is debate and decisions are made. Policy is made at all levels; no one level determines another, though it may establish conditions for other levels. One reason government-level policies may fail, then, is that their social theory of how that bit of the world works – the bit which they hope to influence – is wrong: for instance they may fail to allow that policies are made at all levels. Third, it is worth distinguishing between written policy, stated policy and enacted policy, at whatever levels these occur.

This means putting policy in a political framework and locating it in a wider model of social life as consisting of discursive social practices: we act on the basis of our discourse about an aspect of the social world, such as whether we divide schoolchildren into those with disabilities and those without, or whether we see all schoolchildren, firstly, as pupils.

Policy may also be described as the capacity to make decisions and to act on them and this involves, by definition, the exercise of power. Hindess's notion of social actors (individuals and groups that can make decisions) is useful here; this excludes class or capitalism from our conceptual framework, because neither can reach a decision, thus neither are social actors, and because both concepts derive from theoretical frameworks which are reductionist in the sense that they use these concepts to suggest that the only significant struggle is the class struggle, or the only significant 'needs' are those of capitalism. In contrast to this view, the model of policy this chapter argues for, following Culley and Demaine (1983), is that struggles occur over a whole range of objectives which are significant to those engaged in them (they are not a masked manifestation of the class struggle). In this sense, integration struggles *matter* to those involved in them, patently so. And in this context, education matters (Simon, 1985), schools matter (Culley and Demaine, 1983) and clearly and centrally, teachers matter.

Finally, this model provides an agenda which broadly implies tackling the politics of policy practices in a range of arenas at all levels. This may seem a Herculean task, but it is politically more optimistic than the pessimism of structural approaches which in education (Demaine, 1981) have not offered policy makers in Britain, at least, a viable agenda. The politics of negotiation, discourse and their associated strategies derive from the view that policy is made at all levels and responsibility for the decisons made in one arena should be located with the social actors who make them.

This model is used to disentangle the nature and effects of policy practices surrounding integration and mainstreaming in Norway, Denmark, the US, England and Victoria, in chapters 3, 4, 5 and 6. Integration and mainstreaming policies are variously seen as concerned with disability or handicap. Disability and the need to see it as a political construct is the topic of chapter 1.

Notes

1 There are reasons for these formal terms; they are part of the model of policy the chapter puts forward.
2 The evidence for all this is in chapter 6.
3 Lengthy reviews appear in Fulcher (1986a, 1988a).
4 I am grateful to Robin Burns of La Trobe University for pointing this out.
5 As Foucault argues (for example, 1980). See also Codd (1988).
6 Ball points out that 'Foucault puts forward four bases for the isolation and identification of a discursive formation. One, a set of statements which refer to one and the same object. Two, a regular "style" or common way of making statements. Three, a constancy of concepts employed in the making of the statements. Four, a common theme, or 'strategy', or institutional, administrative or political drift or pattern supported by the statements (1988:150).
7 Demaine (1981) uses the notions of arenas and levels and gives examples of level in the English education scene (1981). See also Culley and Demaine (1983).
8 This research was carried out by third-year undergraduates in their course in the sociology of special education at Monash University in 1985.
9 An elusive but necessary term. Wicks is useful: 'It is important to start, however, by raising the question, What is social policy?, not out of academic interest but because it is also a *political* question, as too narrow an answer to it gives a biased view of the Welfare State, and one that fails to confront crucial questions of resource distribution which are essential to an egalitarian strategy. Conversely, a radical view of social policy is necessarily a broad one.
   'According to Marshall, social policy is "the policy of governments with regard to action having a direct impact on the welfare of the citizens by providing them with services or income". Under this definition would be included health, personal social services, education, housing and social security' (1987:187).
10 Offe's term is proletarianization.
11 Much of the Marxist literature and educational literature on policy assumes this.
12 On this see Castles and McKinlay (1979).
13 See, for example, Castles (1985).

References

Ball, S. (1988) 'Comprehensive Schooling, Effectiveness and Control: An Analysis of Educational Discourses' in Slee, R. (Ed) *Discipline and Schools: A Curriculum Perspective*, Macmillan Australia.

Barton, L. (1987) 'Keeping schools in line', in Booth, T., and Coulby, B. (Eds) *Producing and Reducing Disaffection: Curricula for All*, Milton Keynes, Open University Press, pp. 242–7.

Castles, F.G. (1985) *The Working Class and Welfare: Reflections on the Political Development of the Welfare State in Australia and New Zealand, 1890–1980*, New Zealand, Allen and Unwin.

Castles, F.G. and McKinlay, R.D. (1979) 'Public Welfare Provision, Scandinavia and the Sheer Futility of the Sociological Approach to Politics', *British Journal of Political Science*, 9, pp. 157–71.

Codd, J.A. (1988) 'The construction and deconstruction of educational policy documents', *Journal of Education Policy*, 3, 3, pp. 235–47.

Culley, L., and Demaine, J. (1983) 'Social Theory, Social Relations and Education', in Walker, S. and Barton, L. (Eds) *Gender, Class and Education*, Lewes, Falmer Press, pp. 161–72.

Demaine, J. (1981) *Contemporary Theories in the Sociology of Education*, Basingstoke, Macmillan.

Finch, J. (1984) *Education as Social Policy*, London, Longman.

Foucault, M. (1980) in C. Gordon (Ed) *Power/Knowledge: Selected Interviews and Other Writings 1972–77*, Brighton, Harvester Press.

Fulcher, G. (1986a) 'Theorizing Education Policy', paper presented to the Department of Anthropology and Sociology, Monash University, July, unpublished.

Fulcher, G. (1986b) 'Australian Policies on Special Education: towards a sociological account', *Disability, Handicap and Society*, 1, 1, pp. 19–52.

Fulcher, G. (1988a) 'Theorizing Policy: a review of the literature relevant to educational policy', typescript.

Fulcher, G. (1988b) 'Integration: Inclusion or Exclusion' in Slee, R. (Ed) *Discipline and Schools: A Curriculum Perspective*, Macmillan Australia.

Hindess, B. (1986) 'Actors and Social Relations', in Wardell, M.L. and Turner, S.P. (Eds) *Sociological Theory in Transition*, Boston, Allen and Unwin.

Integration in Victorian Education (1984) Report of the Ministerial Review of Educational Services for the Disabled, Melbourne, Government Printer (chair M.K. Collins).

Macdonald, I. (1981) 'Assessment: a social dimension', in Barton, L. and Tomlinson, S. (Eds) *Special Education: policy, practices and social issues*, London, Harper and Row.

Macdonell, D. (1986) *Theories of Discourse: An Introduction*, Oxford, Basil Blackwell.

Mehan, H. (1984) 'Institutional decision-making' in Rogoff, B. and Lave, J. (Eds) *Everyday Cognition: Its Development in Social Context*, Cambridge, Massachusetts, Harvard University Press.

Ministerial Papers on Education, Numbers 1–6, Victoria.

Offe, C. (1984) *Contradictions of the Welfare State*, edited by John Keane, London, Hutchinson.

Quicke, J. (1986) 'Pupil Culture, Peer Tutoring and Special Educational Needs', *Disability, Handicap and Society*, 1, 2, pp. 147–64.

Simon, B. (1985) *Does Education Matter?*, London, Lawrence and Wishart.

Wicks, M. (1987) *A Future for All: Do we Need the Welfare State?*, Harmondsworth, Penguin.

ACTS

England
Education Reform Act, 1988

Part One
Theorizing

Chapter 1

Theorizing disability

The definition of disability, is fundamentally a policy question (Hahn, 1986:134–5).

Disability . . . is a social relationship (Finkelstein, 1980:13).

The presentation of a category or a concept provides a means to find a behaviour to collect under it . . . the category becomes a procedure to search for and locate the behaviour (Mehan *et al.*, 1981:394).

Disability is not about wheelchairs, though judging from what the media present and from the covers of books about disability, this would appear to be the predominant image. Nor is it to be understood as primarily a medical phenomenon: such a perception reflects the authority and influence of the medical profession and the extent to which its ideas penetrate and inform everyday and professional discourses on disability. Rather, disability is a category which is central to how welfare states regulate an increasing proportion of their citizens. In this sense and context, it is a *political and social construct* used to regulate.

There are competing claims about this regulation and its effects. One claim is that the welfare state has been organized to 'provide for the needy', including those with disabilities. In the US, this view is held by Stone (1984) and in Britain, by Blaxter (1976), for example. In this view, disability denotes 'need', help and privilege. In contrast, others argue that disability is a category of oppression. Finkelstein (1980) and Hahn (1985, 1986) in the US, Oliver (1986) and Abberley (1987) in Britain, and Llewellyn (1983) and Meares (1986) in Australia, for example, take this position. These opposing concepts are starting points for opposing theories of disability,[1] though in 1986, Oliver noted there was no 'social theory of disability' (1986). More recently, Abberley has started to develop a social theory of disability based on the concept of oppression (1987). What is the evidence from welfare state and educational practices for theorizing disability as a political construct, which is used to oppress? To examine social practices on disability and to develop Abberley's position we need first, to distinguish impairment from disability and secondly, to look at the place of categories in social relations: why we categorize events and people.

Separating impairment from disability is essential to developing a social theory of disability. Even Abberley's otherwise provocative discussion links disability and impairment. This link derives from medical discourse; I discuss this below but the central point here is that medical discourse on disability connects it to impairment, in its talk, its concepts and practices, despite the fact that this connection is not always there. How does medical discourse achieve this?

The starting point in a medical discourse on disability is a clinical concern with the body, and thus with the individual. The focus is on physical changes and their effects (Stone, 1984). The language in this discourse includes impairment and disability and sometimes handicap. Marles summarizes the meanings which are thought to attach to these terms well:

> Impairment is a medical term for anatomical loss or a loss of bodily function. Disability is the measurable, functional loss resulting from an impairment. Handicap is the social consequence caused by environmental and social conditions which prevent a person achieving the maximum potential a person seeks. Disabilities are what people cannot do . . . (1986:A:2).

There are disputes about the precise meanings of these terms. But the logic and politics of this schema is powerful. The connection it makes between impairment and disability lends a cause-consequence logic to the terms: impairment *therefore* disability, and its theme of loss provides a discourse of deficit in individuals.

To understand how disability as a procedural category works in modern welfare states we need to note that impairment may not always be present when the term disability is used about an individual. This is particularly evident in calling schoolchildren disabled, as the discussion below (and in chapter 5) argues. Whether or not an impairment is present, certain procedural practices occur in relation to disability and it is these that a social theory of disability need to focus on, while simultaneously suspending judgement about the link it sometimes has with impairment. I shall therefore use these terms with specific meanings in order to construct a social political discourse on disability so that we may theorize it more clearly. These meanings are for analytical purposes only, to clarify what is going on; there is no claim that these are what the terms ought to, or really mean, only that they illustrate themes people deploy, which inform what these people do.

Impairment I use to refer to physiological lesions, whether these are genetically- or disease-based or trauma-induced; these are broadly the 'anatomical bases' Marles refers to. Disability I use as a *procedural category*, not as something people cannot do; as a procedural category it is a term used in discursive practices where impairment may or may not be present, but where the presumption is made that it is. We need to suspend presumptions about the presence of impairment when we talk of disability because disability is *relative* to social practices in a number of ways. I shall explain what I mean in a moment.

The social construction of impairment (how social practices contribute to the incidence of impairments) is separate, important, but not where a social theory of disability begins. But it is worth noting what a number of writers say on how social practices produce impairment (Walker, 1980; Borsay, 1986:181; Stewart, 1986; Abberley, 1987). In Britain, Walker notes social class links with impairment at birth and impairments acquired in production processes are related to social class; and Borsay and Abberley describe practices which create impairment. In Australia, Stewart notes the high rate of accidents in industrial production processes, that immigrants are in the highest risk positions in these processes (1986:78) and that there are gender differences (1986:43, 83). There is evidence from a number of countries that democratic styles of supervision produce lower accident rates compared with undemocratic styles of supervision. Impairment is thus socially distributed: social practices produce this distribution. But analytically, the social construction of impairment is separate from a social theory of disability.

Secondly, we need to suspend judgements about the presence of an impairment when we talk of disability because, as noted above, the social construction of disability is *relative* to particular social practices and independent of the presence of impairment. For example, the 'same' impairment does not always lead to an identity of disabled: here disability, in the popular sense of inability to work, may be *relative* to the occupation a person has and to the state of the local labour market; that is, relative to the demand for, and supply of, labour for that occupation. Similarly, social practices may transform someone who has an impairment into someone who has an identity of disability. Oliver calls these social practices the 'disabling effects of economic, social and physical environments' (1986:9). Walker illustrates this point, in part, by noting that not only does the organization of production create impairment amongst certain categories of industrial workers, but that it subsequently denies impaired people 'access to earnings and fringe benefits' (1984:24), thereby transforming injured workers to the category of disabled. Lloyd and Stagoll describe similar practices in Australia where an individual worker who has moderate injuries may be transformed into a chronically incapacitated patient through the adversarial relations which constitute legal and medical arenas in workers' compensation claims (1979). But to say that social practices construct an identity of disability is not a social theory of disability. These comments merely note that there are practices which, in various ways, produce an identity of 'disabled', which put people in that category of persons. A social theory of disability will theorize *how* this occurs and under what conditions. It begins with the point that disability is socially constructed, that is, relative to particular social practices.

To theorize disability I suggested we need, secondly, to look at the place of categories in social relations. As a category, disability occupies, at one level, the same place in social life as other categories. Categories are part of social relations (Hirst and Woolley, 1981:272). Without categorizing people and practices we encounter in our daily lives we could not get through our days (Berger and Luckmann, 1967). There is therefore nothing peculiar about disability as a category except, and in so far as, it is used to exclude rather than to include, and to oppress rather than enable. What sort of category then is disability? or how do discursive practices typically construct its social relations?

First, disability is a *disputed* category: this is clear when we look at welfare state and education practices. Its relevance is disputed: is this, or isn't it, a case of disability? And if so, how much, how disabled? Is this person feigning incapacity? Is this doctor working to lower the company's liability? Or is he/she, the doctor, making an unbiased judgement? The way social institutions should respond (segregate or integrate?) and how (with what resources?): these are all contentious issues. Disability is thus *struggled over* in social practices in a range of arenas; it is a *procedural and political category*. Stone suggests the conflict is about privilege and need (1984), but clearly those who argue for a social theory of disability as oppression do not agree.

Shapiro, who is also interested in a social theory of disability, and who argues for a political concept, suggests that 'If we want to politicize the concept of disability, that is to interrogate the norms for responsibility, authority and power embedded in the discourses that contain it, we must reflect on the ways that disability is constituted in utterances' (1981:86–7). Equally, we should look at who makes these utterances and their power *vis-à-vis* others in encounters where disability is an issue. In this context, educational practices are equally revealing.

Educational practices organized around a notion of disability variously label 20 per cent (the Warnock Committee), or up to 30 per cent of schoolchildren as having 'special educational needs' (Tasmania, 1983:43). In English law (the Education Act, 1981) 'special educational needs' is ultimately defined as disability, and in Tasmania, educational discourse, without the assistance of legislative conditions, has created the same discourse. For the majority of these high proportions of schoolchildren no known impairment is present. But the presumption is made that it is. This is *a highly political act*. An alternative politics would locate deficits in school practices, particularly in curriculum and pedagogical practices.

Secondly, disability is also a feared status. As Oliver comments, disability is mostly seen as personal tragedy (1986:12). This fear and the psychological processes it engenders contribute to the way disability as 'object' is constructed.

Related to this, and thirdly, disability is predominantly seen as a personal trouble, rather than a public issue. As C. Wright Mills (1959) pointed out, nearly thirty years ago, in comparing individualistic and sociological perspecives, which perspective is taken has profound effects for the way a particular phenomenon is understood and acted on: is it regarded as a *personal trouble* or a *public issue*? Commentators argue that currently social practices surrounding disability tend to treat disability as a personal trouble. Thus those who raise its public relevance (Llewellyn, 1983; Hahn, 1985, 1986; Oliver, 1986; Meares, 1986) may well have a different discourse from the individualistic discourse which typically characterizes encounters between professionals (doctors, teachers, etc.) and people called disabled. Welfare state practices while handing out benefits do so in a way which contain the problem as a personal rather than a public issue. Do schools individualize problems surrounding pedagogy and a child called disabled and construct the issues as a personal trouble deriving from that child, or do they see it as a public, curriculum issue?

Thus disability is an 'object' constructed by discourse and, as the Introduction noted, discourses have *uses* rather than inherent meanings (Bowles and Gintis, 1981:23b). The import of this is discussed more fully in the section on educational practices but it is a key point. As Beng Huat Chua states:

> The sociological question . . . [is] how the hegemony of a discourse
> is established as it insinuates itself into the institutional arrangements
> of the social order. It is from these *institutional bases* that the hegemony
> of a discourse realizes itself as a practical system of power and a
> system of social control (1981:22, emphasis added).

This means looking at the institutional bases of different discourses on disability in different countries. This is discussed in later chapters, while the different discourses are described below.

Clearly, disability is an extraordinarily complex phenomenon but this complexity derives, primarily, not from the intricacies of physical lesions but from the social and political use to which the construct of disability is put, independent of the presence, or intricacies, of an impairment.

This claim, that disability is primarily a political construct rather than a medical phenomenon, I shall attempt to sustain in this chapter by looking at how the category of disability is used in a range of social practices. These I shall divide somewhat arbitrarily since they overlap into welfare state practices and educational practices. First, however, the various discourses on disability are described.

Discourses on disability

There are four main discourses on disability. They are a medical, lay, charity and rights discourse. In addition, a fifth discourse, a corporate approach, has begun to emerge: 'managing disability' is one of its themes and its institutional base is emerging among professionals in government welfare agencies and, increasingly, in the private sector in rehabilitation companies.[2] These discourses inform practices in modern welfare states and variously compete or combine to constitute legislative decision, report writing, educational and other practices.

Medical discourse is undoubtedly dominant: it penetrates lay and charity discourse; 'the social world . . . is steeped in the medical model of disability' (Brisenden 1986:174). Medical, lay and charity discourses share a number of themes and have been the traditional discourses. A rights discourse is more recent and challenges the themes in all three traditional discourses. A medical discourse is the source of the dominant and misleading image of disability as physical incapacity. Medicine is the main institutionalized site for its discursive practices and the professions that 'deal' with disability. Social workers, therapists, physiotherapists, nurses, teachers, borrow the logic and politics of a medical discourse on disability and deploy its authority and influence to legitimize their own professional practices. In Britain, Tomlinson has documented the extensive influence of medical practitioners in educational practices on disability (1982) and in America, Stone, for example notes the well established use by the welfare state of medical practitioners to regulate or process who is disabled. This also occurs in Britain and Australia, a use about which some medical practitioners express profound disquiet (Agerholm (1975), for example).

A rights discourse is more recent and its institutional bases more problematic than those of a medical and charity discourse. This issue is taken up in later chapters. A corporate discourse is even more recent, but we need to consider the relative strength of its institutional base in corporations, Parliament and in state apparatuses given that such a discourse now typically informs Western governments' written and stated policy in various areas of public life, including education. This is discussed in chapters 3, 4, 5 and 6.

The various discourses construct disability as follows.

Medical discourse

A medical discourse links impairment and disability. It draws on a natural science discourse and thus on a *correspondence* theory of meaning. This theory assumes objects essentially correspond with the term used to describe them. While this theory may have some relevance in the natural world it misconceives the social world. This point is discussed in the section on educational practices. Here its relevance is that a medical discourse on disability suggests through its correspondence theory of meaning, that disability is an observable or intrinsic, objective *attribute* or characteristic of a person, rather than a social construct.

Through the notion that impairment means loss (see Marles above on how these terms are used), and the assumption that impairment or loss underlies disability, medical discourse on disability has *deficit* individualistic connotations. Further, through its presumed scientific status and neutrality, it *depoliticizes* disability; disability is seen as a technical issue, thus beyond the exercise of power. Medical discourse *individualizes* disability, in the sense that it suggests individuals have diseases or problems or incapacities as attributes. Finally, it *professionalizes* disability: the notion of medical expertise allows the claim that this (technical) and personal trouble is a matter for professional judgment. These aspects of medical discourse are socially powerful: other discourses which are associated with medicine take on these characteristics: this is the case in psychological and educational discourse which, together with medical discourse, have dominated educational practices organized around a notion of disability (Tomlinson, 1982).

A theme of professionalism pervades medical discourse and its associated discourses: psychology, social work, occupational therapy, rehabilitation counselling, physiotherapy and educational discourse. The phrase 'In the best interests' (of the patient, the child, etc.) instances this theme. This is the language of persuasion (Mehan, 1981), which constitutes a discourse of persuasion, this underlies Tomlinson's point that working-class parents find it much harder to negotiate with professionals than middle-class parents.

Thus medical discourse, through its language of body, patient, help, need, cure, rehabilitation, and its politics that the doctor knows best, excludes a consumer discourse or language of rights, wants and integration in mainstream social practices. Policies which attempt to challenge medical dominance and the professional discourses which draw some of their status from aligning with medical discourse have met strong resistance.[3] As Borsay notes, the move from an individualistic help-based model will be met by formidable resistance (1986:102).

Medical discourse on disability excludes the theme of the social construction and distribution of impairment (Walker, 1980; Borsay, 1986). Its theme of epidemological distribution largely obscures this social construction. The individualism of medical concepts provides a context for developing other individualistic concepts relating to disability: accident-prone, compensation neurosis, 'Mediterranean back'.[4] These concepts flourish despite evidence, discussed above, that impairment is socially created and socially distributed. A medical approach encourages a discourse of person blame. Responsibility is assigned to the victim. As the Introduction noted, the assignment of responsibility is politically powerful: in this instance it directs attention to changing an individual's actions, life-style or personality rather than, for instance, changing the social practices of production or in educational apparatuses.

The notion of rehabilitation is a recent theme in medical discourse on disability in welfare states. Medical practitioners have dominated rehabilitation practices, a dominance which is now being questioned (for example, Meares, 1986).

A charity discourse

The charity ethic has sat well with medical discourse and is part of the discourse deployed in corporations which have organized services outside the limited provision the welfare state makes. The charity ethic defines people called disabled as in need of help (Llewellyn, 1983), as an object of pity (Borsay, 1986), as personally tragic (Oliver, 1986), as dependent and eternal children, and, where such institutions hold beauty contests, as low achievers by ideal standards. This discourse has an institutional base in an extensive corporate sector, which has a range of residential, or 'total' institutions in Goffman's sense (1968) and non-residential institutions; its institutions include sheltered workshops and overall it provides extensive employment for a range of professionals and other employees.

In Australia, the Human Rights Commission comments on the origin of a charity discourse. It notes that in Western society in the last century:

> middle class philanthropy was a feature of the Victorian Age. Victorian reformers believed they had a moral duty to give protection and succour to the poor and afflicted ... The repercussions are still felt today. As the [South Australian] Bright report notes 'many of our society's negative attitudes towards handicapped persons, for example that they are objects of pity, a burden of charity and dependent and eternal children, are attributable to the charity model developed in England during this period' (Human Rights Commission 1986:26–7).

In providing the original discourse for some private welfare agencies,[5] a charity discourse contains themes of benevolence and humanitarianism (as Tomlinson has noted for special education, 1982): it expects its clients to be grateful recipients. Because its sources lie in the hierarchical politics of the Victorian era, it excludes the theme of rights which has emerged relatively recently in welfare states. Consistent with these hierarchical politics, it promotes professionalism (the view that 'experts' know best) and deflects attention from the consumer's perceptions and wants.

Lay discourse

Lay perceptions of disability are informed by medical discourse, a charity ethic and fear, prejudice, pity, ignorance, misplaced patronage and even resentment (Marles, 1986:A2). It is these themes which inform social practices which are blatantly discriminatory (Marles, 1986:A2). An American commentator, Hahn suggests that:

> widespread aversion towards disabled individuals may be the product both of an 'aesthetic' anxiety, which narcissistically rejects marked deviations from 'normal' physical appearances and of an 'existential' anxiety, which may find an implicit or projected danger of dehabilitating disability more terrifying than the inevitability of death (Hahn 1983), (Hahn 1986:125).

Hahn notes the 'narcissistic symbols of the dominant institutionalized majority that permeate modern society' (1986:138) and thus points, in part, to the issue of body, control and autonomy in modern society. While lay discourse may not fully articulate these themes, it raises issues central to understanding the construction of disability or what Shapiro calls the 'rules that constitute the meaning of disability' (1981:87).

While control of one's body is central both in interpersonal encounters (Turner, 1984) and to how the welfare state regulates its citizens, it relates, too, to widespread social practice of shunning and devaluing bodies which are not so easily controlled as are the dominant majority's. The issue of less docile bodies is discussed in chapter 2. Moreover, less easily regulated bodies are denied the 'full personal autonomy'[6] expected of those whose bodies are more easily controlled. Less control over one's body means others diminish the personal responsibility of the person called disabled. Hence, widespread practices of paternalism and maternalism which treat those with obvious disabilities as child-like and less than fully responsible.

This theme of (relatively) uncontrolled body, therefore a deviant from the autonomy (albeit constrained) permitted other citizens, is a fundamental theme in lay, medical and charity discourse. As Abberley notes, 'For disabled people the body is the site of oppression, both in form and in what is done to it' (1987:114). The modern preoccupation with the body as image systematically devalues those whose disability is based in a visible (physical) impairment. Hence the unthinking acceptance of physical disability as the stereotype.

A rights discourse

More recently, a discourse on the rights of those called disabled has emerged in some welfare states. Its themes are self-reliance, independence, consumer wants (rather than needs); its concepts are discrimination, exclusion and (in America and Britain) oppression. It is overtly political in contrast to the submerged politics of a professional discourse on disability. Its institutional bases vary: in America there are constitutional and legislative conditions of such rights but, as chapter 4 shows, these are insufficient to guarantee the realization of rights. Elsewhere, where constitutional and legislative conditions for citizens rights are absent, and where other institutional bases for realizing rights are minimal, as they are at a general level in England and Australia, such a discourse constitutes a moral rather than a political stance.[7]

In the US, the conditions for the emergence of the theme of rights to equality for those called disabled emerged in the context of the civil rights movement in the sixties, and from the self-conscious democratism in American political culture (chapter 4). In Britain and Australia, it emerged somewhat later. In Australia, Llewellyn suggests the conditions for the emergence of a rights discourse came from the 'contradictions and inequalities of rehabilitation . . . [which] . . . helped to delineate the independent living movement towards self-care, maintenance, integration, and normalization' (1983:27).

The notion of equality opposes the themes of dependence and 'help' in medical, charity and lay discourse. As Brisenden states, 'the equality we are demanding is rooted in the concept of control; it stems from our desire to be individuals who can choose for themselves' (1986:177). Brisenden's view is that independence means taking control of one's life (1986:178), and the Australian Human Rights Commission notes: 'If one major theme is to be found in recent enquiries into the position of disabled persons in Australia, it is that they are not being given the opportunity to determine their own destinies and that they are no longer willing to let this situation continue' (HRC, 1986a:34).

The independent living movement is based on a radically different view of disability. The problem is not one of individual impairment as the medical model would suggest but rather of dependence on professionals and relatives, of environmental barriers and unprotected rights, all of which limit the choices available to people with disabilities. It thus follows that the solution is not one of more professional intervention but rather initiatives which are geared toward self-help (Human Rights Commission, 1986a:29–30).

The rights discourse is the most recent contender amongst the discourses on disability. It opposes the medical, charity and lay discourses in a number of ways. It presents an overtly political position which contrasts with the covert hierarchical politics of the other three discourses. Its themes are equality of citizenship and its strategy is one of confrontation and demand. The themes underlying medical, charity and lay discourse are those of alleged service and grateful recipient, while the issue of who benefits from these services is rarely made clear: however, this is a question increasingly posed by those concerned about these services: for example, Jamrozik (1987:11), Borsay (1986), Lee and Raban (1988:166).

Finally, the rights discourse is seen as the most progressive and obvious strategy for those excluded from full citizenship in modern welfare states, including those called disabled. This theme underlies much equal opportunity legislation. But given the evidence in later chapters, and that cited above, on the failure of this discourse, two questions arise. Is a discourse on rights the most effective strategy in modern welfare states to achieve full citizenship for those presently excluded from this position? And if it isn't, are there more substantive issues and strategies in, for instance, education which, if pursued, might achieve more equal access than the present claim to rights?

The following two sections briefly examine the extent to which these five discourses on disability inform welfare state practices and educational policy practices. The discussion focuses on Britain and Australia as a basis for looking more closely at the discourses on disability in educational apparatuses in later chapters.

Disability issues in welfare state practices

Evidence from Britain on the place of people with disabilities is remarkably similar to that for Australia. It suggests that a rights discourse which is more recent in Britain and Australia than in America, has had little effect in challenging the hegemony of a professionalized discourse on disability in the institutions of the British and Australian welfare states. This is clear from the *effects* of various institutional practices.

In Britain in 1987, despite legislative conditions such as those following from the Chronically Sick and Disabled Persons Act, and despite a number of surveys of disability and handicap, the plight of those with disabilities is desperate (Wicks, 1987). Borsay documents the poverty and dependence that follow from an individualistic help model and which derive from inadequate benefits. She outlines the dominance of professionals who ally with the welfare state (as employers of professionals) in the inequitable treatment of people with disabilities. She notes how people with disabilities are devalued in the context of competitive values in the capitalist labour market and in the ideals of rehabilitation, and outlines the tension surrounding dependency in capitalist societies. She also notes the selectiveness of the British welfare state's response to those with disabilities, so that some (notably workers and war veterans) are seen as more worthy than others, thereby creating a hierarchy in disability (Borsay, 1986:190–1).

In Australia, analysis of legislative and funding practices reveals disability as a complex procedural status which forces its occupants to live tentative lives of dependence and poverty; therefore as exclusion from mainstream social practices, and thus oppression (Fulcher, 1989). Legislative conditions have encouraged segregated rather than integrated services despite a written policy that services should integrate. For example, former Commonwealth legislation constructed a dilemma for parents of children with severe handicap.

> The Handicapped Child's allowance will be paid to the parents of a handicapped child if they keep the child isolated at home [but] if they try and encourage the child to lead a normal life and integrate the child into its own community by, for example, sending the child to school, then they will probably lose the allowance (HRC, 1986a:69)

Legislative conditions also create funding anomalies which encourage deception (Human Rights Commission, 1986a:45). The fragmentation of services between State portfolios and between the States and Commonwealth, and the bureaucratization of procedures especially notable in education practices, create a procedurally complex existence for those called disabled which is unusually contingent on those who hold power in administrative procedures (Fulcher, 1988). As in Britain, there is a hierarchy of disability, and the welfare state responds selectively in its benefits according to the source of impairment. Impairment deriving from activity in the paid labour force and from war-related impairments have been consistently more highly rewarded than impairments acquired elsewhere (Castles, 1985). The Australian welfare apparatus also responds selectively in disregarding a wide range of occupationally induced diseases (Stewart, 1986).

A medical discourse has informed the most powerful institutional bases for 'dealing' with disabilty, in a variety of Australian state apparatuses,

including education. Quite apart from apparatuses concerned with employment, war veterans, housing, etc., the discourse of various State government written educational policies on disability attest to this (Fulcher, 1989).

The institutional base of a charity discourse has occupied a secure place
in Australian society for some decades and some of its devaluing practices,
such as fund-raising beauty contests, and sheltered workshops practices, have
only recently been challenged by more political individuals and actors.

In Australia, therefore, the institutional base for a rights discourse has
been tenuous. At the federal level, the Human Rights Commission, established
in 1981 for five years, was disbanded at the end of 1986 and combined with
another agency. In one report it documents the extent to which the law has
been unable to protect the rights of disabled people:

> It is clear from the recommendations of the reports outlined in
> Chapter 7, the evidence contained in the submissions and the analysis
> of current, legislative provisions, that disabled people, especially
> pensioners and beneficiaries, cannot adequately seek and attain their
> rights with the law as it stands. All three highlight the continuing
> poverty of disabled people, the gaps and anomalies in income
> maintenance provisions and delivery of services, and the
> fragmentation and confusion in Federal/State funding (HRC,
> 1986a:118).

In the State of Victoria, a rights discourse has an institutional base in the
Equal Opportunity Board (EOB) and in the recently established office of
the Public Advocate. Both are watchdog mechanisms. The EOB is receiving
an increasing number of complaints about education practices surrounding
integration, and its Annual Report for 1986 notes that a resource struggle
dominates in educational arenas and disadvantages students called disabled
(1986:25). The Office of the Public Advocate has recently issued a report
which is highly critical of practices in the criminal justice system which
discriminate against those with intellectual disabilities (Bodna, 1987).

Thus in Australia, legislative conditions and widespread social practices
based on medical, charity and lay discourses on disability have so far
constructed disability as exclusion and therefore oppression. It remains to
be seen whether current federal legislation, the Disability Services Act, 1986,
which purports to tackle unemployment, poverty, dependence and
segregation, can alter this situation. But it is this denial of rights which informs
the theorizing of those who argue that disability is a category of oppression.

The theme of need informs welfare state practices on disability in both
Britain and Australia and is central to professional discourse as is its
educational variant, 'special educational needs'. The introduction of 'need'
as a basis for welfare state practices allegedly aimed at reducing inequalities

has been counterproductive. There are numerous criticisms of how it is those deemed to have needs, its relevance as benevolent tactic must be seriously questioned. Thus Baldwin notes professionals need clients (1986), Blaxter questioned. Thus Baldwin notes professionals need clients (1986), Blaxter that clients' views of needs often differ markedly from those professionals deem them to have (1979), and in the US, Link and Milcarek provide evidence that mental health services are allocated to the most 'desirable' patients rather than those most in need (1980).

In the US, Hahn both documents the centrality of disability as a category in a wide range of policies and contrasts the magnitude of the issue with its relative neglect by policy analysts (1986:122). Stone theorizes disability as the way in which the modern welfare state solves the 'distributive dilemma' and achieves 'distributive justice' (1984). According to Stone, disability is a category of exemption (from work) and privilege (1984). Hahn, in reviewing her book, argues it is a category of exclusion and oppression (1985). As his evidence shows for the US, and as is the case elsewhere, those called disabled have one of the highest rates of unemployment, are most likely to live in poverty and to be placed in a position of dependency on the state. 'America is spending dollars on dependence for every dollar it expends upon programs helping [people with disabilities] to become independent' (Hahn, 1986:124).

Hahn argues that the social environment has failed 'to adjust to the needs and aspirations of citizens with disabilities' (1985:132). These problems he locates in capitalism, in its consumption practices, including its narcissistic symbols. But Hahn's 'socio-political' analysis fails to separate the procedural category of disability from the presumption that impairment is present. It would be interesting to know whether the figure he cites (from Bowe's study) of thirty-six million North Americans as 'disabled', indicates that they have been placed in that procedural category for reasons such as locally high rates of unemployment *or* because they undoubtedly have an impairment. Importantly, however, he notes that law on rehabilitation is circumvented and that policy makers are reluctant to implement (1986:122). This evidence is consistent with the model in the Introduction, that policies are made at all levels.

A rights discourse for those called disabled contains themes of choice, wants and consumer rights. This contrasts with the theme of need in a discourse of professionalism. But discursive practices on disability in Britain, the US and Australia do not construct a position of consumer participation and thus integration in capitalist society for those called disabled.

This brief commentary suggests that Stone's view that the category of disability is contentious, struggled over, because it denotes need and privilege, needs to be re-examined. While much of her discussion is insightful, her general conclusions are not consistent with the effects of welfare state practices in the US, Britain and Australia. The exclusion and oppression which characterize current welfare state practices in Britain and Australia support Abberley's social theory of disability as oppression.

Educational practices and disability

In the British and Australian educational apparatuses, special educational practices have been constituted by discourses on disability and its synonyms, and its traditional connections of deficit and difference.

Medical, psychological and, to a lesser extent, educational discourses, have informed and dominated educational practices surrounding disability in Britain (Tomlinson, 1981, 1982; Ford *et al.*, 1982) and Australia. Each of these discourses is individualistic and clinical in its focus and concepts; each presents issues as though they are technical rather than also moral and political. Professional judgements imply a hierarchy of knowledge and practices based on such judgements are an exercise of power. Thus medical, psychological and educational practices are all moral and political: this is what should and will happen. The notion that all educational practices are political (Apple, 1982; Barton, 1987) can hardly be disputed: this is what, where and how we *will* teach. Relatedly, all educational practices are moral: and this is what, where, how and whom we *ought* to teach.

In educational practices surrounding disability, these clinical individualistic and allegedly technical discourses construct individual deficit as the object of attention and exclude or deflect from consideration of teaching practices. The medical, psychological and educational discourses submerge the tactics they deploy, which are those of professionalization: the struggle to gain control of an area of occupational life. The theme that professionals know best has produced the predominant phrase legitimizing educational practices on disability: 'in the best interests of the child'. This constructs the vocabulary of what Tomlinson calls benevolent humanitarianism (1982) and submerges its politics.

These practices of professionalism include assessing 'deficit' by the numerous sub-categories of disability which have been used in special education (see for example Tomlinson, 1982:61 on British statutory categories from 1886–1981), and which have justified extensive segregation, separate curricula for special students, a separate profession of special teachers, special education training institutions and separate administrative structures within educational apparatuses to regulate this arena. These categories include non-normative categories (Tomlinson, 1982:65) such as learning difficulties. These are categories for which there is no consensus on what constitutes an instance. This is not surprising since, as mentioned earlier in the section on medical discourse, the correspondence theory of meaning misconceives the nature of social life and its practices. A search for common agreement is a positivist endeavour doomed to failure and is a response to bureaucratic regulation of what are complex, social and political constructs; but as chapter 4 shows, for example, there is extensive debate based on these assumptions in the North American educational apparatus.

A sociological critique of categories should dwell not only on the disagreement surrounding non-normative categories (Has this child special educational needs or hasn't he/she?) (Tomlinson, 1982) and their relativity to a particular classroom or schools (Galloway, 1985; Gow and Fulcher, 1986), but also on the practices which construct students' identities as 'disabled' or 'handicapped'. This is discussed more fully in chapter 4 in the context of Mehan's research. Mehan argues labels and identities are a product of routine, institutional practices rather than attributes of students (1981). Thus in Mehan's view, special educational needs reside in interaction processes in school, from practical circumstances in the school district and from conditions created by federal special education law rather than in a student's needs Mehan *et al.*, 1981.

Thus historically, in the British and Australia educational apparatuses, educational practices which construct pejorative categories of student identities, and which are based on a discourse of disability, presume or infer the presence of impairment. These practices are organized around a *political logic* of deficit, loss, difference, marginality, contingent status and thus contingent exclusion and segregation from regular classrooms. The extent to which current practices maintain or undermine these conditions, following recent government-level educational policy on disability, is discussed in later chapters.

Legislative conditions have provided some of the base for these past practices. Legislative conditions in various Australian States illustrate this. The law on disability is often complex (in part because definitions are elusive) and crosses different jurisdictions: for example, the Victorian Minister of Education had powers under the Victorian Mental Health Act, 1959, concerning children with 'intellectual defectiveness'. This situation, and other factors, create complex administrative procedures, and thus a complex *procedural status* for those called disabled in educational apparatuses.

Educational legislation adds to this complexity and regulations. In the Northern Territory, a head teacher may request the Minister to make special educational arrangements for a child if that child appears to him handicapped; if the parent and Minister do not agree on the special educational arrangements the Minister may refer the proposed arrangements to the Supreme Court (Education Act, 1985, Part V, section 38). Thus a parent of a child deemed handicapped in the Northern Territory has a *more highly regulated status* than that of other parents, and has, moreover, a *potentially threatened status*. In Victoria, schoolchildren deemed handicapped have also been more highly regulated (Education Act, 1958, section 64A). In Western Australia, parents of a 'deaf or mute' child, or of a 'blind, cerebrally palsied or mentally deficient child', are also more highly regulated (Education Act 1976, No. 2); an advisory panel (consisting of professionals) may judge a child who has 'a mental or physical disorder or disability of so severe a nature' that his presence in a government school would disrupt the normal operation of that school, and may advise that the child be excluded; however, the parent has recourse to a children's court and the onus is on the Minister to show cause why the order to exclude the child should not be cancelled. Queensland, on the other hand, has repealed both penalty clauses and those sections regulating handicapped children more extensively than others (An Act to amend the Education Act 1964–74, No. 2 of 1984). Thus the legal basis for state intervention varies between Australian States.

But legislative conditions do not determine practices surrounding disability at other levels of Australian educational apparatuses. Political-bureaucratic-administrative procedures may be established, independent of legislative conditions, which construct a special status for those called disabled. In the Victorian educational apparatus, the practice of 'delayed admissions' for those called disabled has been introduced since government-level written policy on integration: this is discussed more fully in chapter 6. Further, while legislative and statutory conditions may legitimate certain categories of disability, such categories are socially constructed and attain a legitimacy outside legislative conditions, on the basis of professionalism. For example, the notion of socio-emotional handicap is widely used in the Victorian education apparatus. This is not a statutory category but it is a powerful discourse.[8] The extent to which the notion of 'special educational needs' retains the political logic of traditional discourses on disability is discussed in later chapters.

Also relevant to the social construction of an identity of disabled, in educational apparatuses, is the issue of who acquires, or who is more likely to acquire such an identity. Tomlinson (1981, 1982), Carrier (1983a, 1983b) and Mehan (1984), Mehan *et al.* (1981) discuss class and ethnic/race links here, and Milofsky (1986) links inner city and suburban school districts with different practices. Discourse-based theorizing can make sense of 'class' effects of special education without resorting to the effects of a 'class structure'. Professionals may have discourses which include themes of class and schooling. Similarly, Tomlinson's point that parents from working-class backgrounds find it more difficult to negotiate with professionals suggests, quite apart from the fact that they are unlikely to have time available to advocate for their rights, that they do not deploy, thus do not have available, a discourse of democratism.

Tomlinson (1982) notes that in Britain, boys are three times more likely to acquire identities of disabled via non-normative categories than are girls (1982) and in Australia a similar ratio applies (Andrews *et al.*, 1979). These differences have yet to be clearly theorized, but if we use Offe's insights, that state policy, including educational policy, aims to control the production of wage labour and must institutionalize the production of non-wage labour, excluding more boys than girls makes sense in light of Tomlinson's view that industrial societies will need a higher proportion of their citizens to be unemployed. Moreover, the control of women as low-paid, part-time or temporary wage labour is already well institutionalized. In this view, boys must be regulated more highly than girls since they, rather than girls, will contend for positions as full-time, full-rate wage labour. Existing constraints, which make it less likely that women will be equal contenders for such positions, regulate women's futures as wage labour and, if one accepts Offe's theorizing, provide the state with means of controlling the production of female wage labour other than through educational policy on disability. But this is to argue a reductionist (the 'state' is organizing this) form of theorizing. Gender links also need theorizing in Hindess-Demaine-Culley's terms: as Culley and Demaine argue, it is politically pessimistic to attribute such practices to an institution called patriarchy (1983).

Summary

In discussing the use of the category and discourse of disability in the British and Australian welfare states, we noted that its practices construct disability as a marginal status of dependence, poverty, unemployment and denial of full rights as a citizen. There was evidence that these practices include regulating those called 'disabled' more highly than others, and constructing these lives as more than usually contingent on those who hold power in administrative procedures, notably medical practitioners and other professionals. These practices construct exclusion rather than inclusion. This exclusion may be physical separation in segregated facilities, or the privatization of the lives of those called disabled through their exclusion from the paid labour force. Whichever form of exclusion applies, it constitutes oppression and supports Abberley's rather than Stone's theory of disability.

The brief survey of the recent history of practices in British and Australian educational apparatuses, shows that a similar fate is the experience of school children called disabled. Educational practices on disability also stigmatize, marginalize, create tentative and complex lives for those deemed disabled and provide segregating 'solutions' to the problems these children are deemed to present to the educational apparatus. In educational apparatuses, the professionals who hold power in administrative procedures are bureaucrats, educational psychologists and teachers. Not all professionals deploy professionalism, however. Other influential actors in certain arenas, at least in Victoria, include teacher unions who provide their members with discourse and 'policy' for making decisions, in, for example, school arenas.

The segregation of students called disabled or by one of its synonyms has been variously theorized. Tomlinson says that exclusion acts as a safety valve for the central educational apparatus, that it benefits professionals rather than students and discriminates especially against parents from working-class backgrounds, and that it provides an underclass of unemployed (through its non-credentialling curriculum), and acts as social control (1981, 1982). Carrier also theorizes this exclusion as class-linked (1983a, 1983b, 1984), though his claim (1984) that students in special education are largely from the lower classes in England and the US, needs substantiating. He also argues that these identities mask socially produced inequalities and performances as 'natural' attributes (1983a). Others also theorize practices of exclusion as social control but without defining what they mean (Ford *et al.*, 1982; Milofsky, 1986).

Class structural accounts of the effects of special education practices have dominated theorizing in this area. The rest of this chapter attempts to theorize disability and its construction as exclusion and oppression in different terms, consistent with the model of policy as practice, and social life as consisting of practical projects, outlined in the Introduction.

Theorizing disability

The analysis of practices surrounding disability in welfare state apparatuses, including educational apparatuses, in Britain and Australia, allows us to conclude that those called disabled are generally an oppressed category of under-citizens.

Abberley theorizes the oppression of those called disabled as benefiting the present social order or, more accurately, capitalism as a particular historical and national form of social order (1987:16). We can develop his ideas as follows. Specifically the social order benefits from the oppression of those called disabled, in its moral aspect and in its institutional order, and those who control production processes also benefit since they can achieve their objectives via these discursive practices which have traditionally surrounded disability.

As Stone points out, the judgement of disability, whether it is apt or not, relates to what she calls the moral economy: what is seen as just exemption from the obligation to work (1984). British and Australian writers make comments about the nature of their welfare states and its selective favouring, both in relation to disability and, more widely, of (male, in Australia) paid workers (Borsay, 1986:188; Castles, 1985:102ff; Jones, 1980:700). From these observations, we can deduce that *paid work is the prime moral category in modern welfare states*. It follows that disability, where it is defined (produced as a consequence of many practices) as an inability to work, together with other categories exempted or excluded from full-time wage labour (those who are old, young or sick), takes on a problematic moral status. This problematic moral status provides a *moral* (though not necessarily defensible) basis for the exclusion and oppression of those called disabled from mainstream social life. It provides an explanation of the low level of benefits and it occurs in a context where values of independence (defined as separation from others), self-reliance, and participation in mainstream political and economic life, constitute a status granted only to some citizens. A theme in this exclusion is that those called disabled are accorded less than the autonomy (albeit constrained) to exercise the personal control and responsibility expected of other citizens.

This claim, that the oppression of those called disabled is consistent with the moral order of late capitalist society, fits with Durkheim's structural theory, that society is morally constructed. But it fits, too, with the discourse-based theorizing in the Introduction. Clearly, discursive themes have moral connotations.

Secondly, a number of writers have noted the connection between production costs and disability (Walker, 1980; Llewellyn, 1983; Borsay, 1986; Brisenden, 1986; Hahn, 1986; Stewart, 1986). Discursive practices on disability in welfare state apparatuses consistently under-conceptualize work-related impairment and disease (Walker, 1980; Stewart, 1986:101–2). Thus by failing to extend the notion of work-related disability to occupationally-induced diseases 'only a portion of the true costs of providing for the diswelfares of production has been allocated to employers'. This reduces production costs (Stewart, 1986:103) and allocates the cost of work-related disability to the private sector (Stewart, 1986:180), where insurance premiums have contributed to the capital accumulation processes. In this context of under-recognition of work-related disability, the social welfare system 'collects instances of this non-recognition' and provides for it, albeit in oppressive ways: this practice is part of the extraction process from wage labour since social welfare is provided for in part by taxes from wage labour. The low rates of pay in sheltered workshops clearly reduce production costs and, as Hirst notes, provides a form of devalued labour (1987).

The connection between production costs and disability can be theorized in a number of ways. A Hindess-based account would suggest that capitalists (as opposed to capitalism) have achieved their objectives by deploying these strategies and that their views have predominated in arenas in which these issues have been debated (such as policy making on occupational health and safety and on work compensation). A Navarro-based account would argue that containing production costs reveals class power on the part of capital (1983); an Offe-based account theorizes the exclusion of 'disabled' persons from wage labour as an instance of the state controlling the production of wage labour; increasingly so, where there are rising rates of unemployment.

The institutional order also benefits from the discourse on disability and the way disability is deployed as a procedural category in welfare state apparatuses. This relates both to those who deploy professionalism and to the main institutional base for professionalism, bureaucracy. Professionalism, as discourse and tactic, was discussed in the Introduction. Where special educational practices are concerned, professionalism has been deployed in both regular and special education practices in the British and Australian educational apparatuses and is an integral part of the bureaucratization of educational practices.

More widely, Borsay notes an 'allegianc between social services personnel and the state [in Britain] which underl es the inequitable treatment of disabled people' (1986:191). Stewart speculates that in work-related disability practices those who benefit from present arrangements are the 'intermediate professionals . . . the lawyers, the doctors, and the investigators, etc.' (1986:112). In educational apparatuses, the equivalent professionals are educational psychologists, bureaucrats, principals, social workers, teachers. Stewart's view is also supported by an analysis of Australian Commonwealth funding, which revealed a proportionally higher rise in public sector jobs concerned with disability compared with the rise in benefits in the same period (Fulcher, 1989). Later chapters discuss whether professionalism has also characterized North American and Scandinavian educational apparatuses. They also discuss whether recent government-level educational policies on disability which deployed professionalism have thereby encouraged bureaucratic regulation of students called disabled, thus increasing a domination by bureaucracy which Weber feared would occur as capitalism developed (1964).

Conclusions

Welfare state practices, including those in educational apparatuses, in Britain and Australia, have traditionally constructed disability as a procedurally complex status, one which is unusually contingent on those who hold power in certain administrative procedures. These are notably professionals. But *not all professionals deploy professionalism*. In these welfare states, those called disabled lead more highly regulated, tentative lives; are more likely to live in poverty and to be dependent on low-level government benefits and to have high rates of unemployment. This exclusion from mainstream social, political and economic life of those who exist in its margins, can justifiably be described as oppression. Practices of exclusion in educational apparatuses organized around a notion of disability are an instance of wider practices in the welfare state. They exemplify oppression rather than democracy.

Such practices support Paul Abberley's social theory of disability as oppression and question Stone's somewhat unexamined stance that the category of disability is about privilege and exemption from work. Insofar as Marx's view was accurate, that men (sic) realize themselves in labour, Stone's analysis may well express the alienation from work produced by the organization of production processes in corporate capitalism.

Stone makes the central point, however, that disability is a category through which those in welfare state apparatuses organize increasing numbers of citizens (Hahn, 1986). Her point about the procedural, thus *practical* nature of disability has been emphasized in the present discussion by dividing the link medical, lay, charity and everyday discourse (and sometimes those who advocate a rights position) make between impairment and disability. Where the category disabilty is used *impairment is presumed to be present*. Apart from the theoretical-political implications which follow from dissolving this connection, the empirical need to do so is clear if we confront the ludicrous claim that 20 per cent of schoolchildren, at some time in their lives, will have special educational needs (ultimately defined as disability, thus deficit). An alternative politics would focus on school practices and suggest that for a large proportion of these children, the deficit lies in failures in pedagogic practices.

Nevertheless, the presumption sustained in disability discourse, that impairment is present, provides a discourse whose themes are deficit, loss, difference, marginality, contingency and exclusion. The exclusion which is the effect of the political logic of a traditional discourse on disability is well exemplified in the extensive segregation of those called disabled from regular schools which has occurred in Western educational apparatuses this century.

Analytical progress can be made if we suspend presumption about the presence of impairment when disability is used. This reveals that disability is essentially a procedural category which has no *necessary* connection with impairment. Sometimes there is an empirical connection, sometimes not. Thus *disability is a political construct whether or not an impairment is present*.

Traditional discourses on disability are deployed as tactic to assert loss, whether this is the case or not, and to individualize 'the problem', depoliticize the social construction of the disabled, and to institute the political logic of difference and exclusion; those who deploy this discursive means benefit from present arrangements rather than those called disabled.

These points are consistent with aspects of Stone's theorizing (that disability is part of the moral order) and with Abberley's (disability is a construction of oppression): we should theorize the oppression which present practices construct around disability in terms of their support for the moral order and for the objectives of capitalists. Presumed inability to work provides a moral (though not necessarily justifiable) rationale for practices of exclusion, from full-rate paid work, from regular classrooms, from decision-making, etc. The lowering of production costs through a range of practices, which include widespread under-recognition of work-related impairment and disease, exclusion of industrial workers with impairments from production and their allocation as individual pensioners of the welfare state, the location of insurance schemes for work-related injury in corporations, all assist the organizers of production processes, capitalists, to achieve their objectives. The extensive and extending employment of professionals to regulate those called disabled in a range of welfare state apparatuses, including educational apparatuses, also benefits professionals, rather than those called disabled. Practices which reinforce professionalism, the master strategy in these practices, are the use of sub-categories of disability and its synonyms. In educational arenas, this includes an extensive range of non-normative categories; it includes the notion of special educational needs.

The extent to which recent government written education policy on disability in Scandinavia, California, Britain and Victoria has sustained or undermined these practices is examined in chapters 3, 4, 5 and 6.

Notes

1 See Fulcher (1989) for a discussion of interpretive and structural accounts of disability.
2 This has given rise, in a multi-ethnic society such as Australia to the extraordinary phenomenon of a young Anglo graduate, newly employed and with a degree in health science, counselling middle-aged non-English-speaking industrial workers on rehabilitation.
3 This occurred in the Victorian Ministerial Review of Educational Services for the Disabled when a proposal was made to use a consumer- or client-based form to establish educational requirements.
4 A term commonly used in Australian medical discourse about ethnic workers.
5 There is of course a high degree of interdependence between the 'private' and 'public' sectors, so that these are more accurately described as the public-privately dependent and private-publicly dependent sectors. On this, see *Integration in Victorian Education*.

6 This is ideological unless we qualify it by saying that such autonomy is constrained by existing power arrangements.
7 In the State of Victoria, the Equal Opportunity Board provides an institutional base for appeals about claims that rights have been discriminated against. In Australia, however, there are no constitutional or federal legislative conditions for realizing rights.
8 This is not to argue for a legislative basis for such categories. The alleged incident of socio-emotional handicap has been the subject of an extensive research project in the Catholic education system.

References

Abberley, P. (1987) 'The Concept of Oppression and the Development of a Social Theory of Disability', *Disability, Handicap and Society*, 2, 1, pp. 5–20.

Agerholm, M. (1975) 'The Identification and Evaluation of Long-Term Handicap', paper delivered to the Medico-Legal Society on April 10.

Agerholm, M. (1978) 'The Classification of Personal Handicap', paper given at the 1978 meeting of the Medical Commission of Rehabilitation International, September.

Andrews, R.J., Elkins, J., Berry, P.B., and Burge, J. (1979) (Schonell Report) *A Survey of Special Education in Australia: Provisions, Needs and Priorities in the Education of Children with Handicaps and Learning Difficulties*, Fred and Eleanor Schonnell Educational Research Centre, Department of Education, University of Queensland, July.

Apple, M.W. (1982) *Education and Power*, Boston, Ark Paperbacks (1985 edition).

Baldwin, S. (1986) 'Problems with Needs – where theory meets practice', *Disability, Handicap and Society*, 1, 2, pp. 139–45.

Barton, L. (1986) 'The Politics of Special Educational Needs', *Disability, Handicap and Society*, 1, 3, pp. 273–90.

Barton, L. (1987) 'Keeping schools in line', in Booth, T., and Coulby, B. (Eds) *Producing and Reducing Disaffection: Curricula for All*, Milton Keynes, Open University Press, pp. 242–7.

Berger, P.L., and Luckmann, T. (1967) *The Social Construction of Reality*, London, Allen Lane.

Blaxter, M. (1976) *The Meaning of Disability: A Sociological Study of Impairment*, London, Heinemann.

Bodna, B. (1987) *Finding the Way: The Criminal Justice System and the Person with Intellectual Disability*, Melbourne, Government Printer.

Borsay, A. (1986) 'Personal Trouble or Public Issue? Towards a model of policy for people with physical and mental disabilities', *Disability, Handicap and Society*, 1, 2, pp. 179–95.

Bowles, S. and Gintis, H. (1981) 'Education as a Site of Contradictions in the Reproduction of the Capital-Labour Relationship: Second thoughts on the "Correspondence Principle"', *Economic and Industrial Democracy*, 2, pp. 223–42.

Brisenden, S. (1986) 'Independent Living and the Medical Model of Disability', *Disability, Handicap and Society*, 1, 1, pp. 173–8.

Carney, T. (1982) 'Civil and Social Guardianship for intellectually handicapped People', *Monash Law Review*, 8, 3, March, pp. 199–232.

Carrier, J. (1983a) 'Masking the social in educational knowledge: the case of learning disability theory', *American Journal of Sociology*, 8, 5, pp. 948–74.

Carrier, J.G. (1983b) 'Explaining Educability: An investigation of political support for the Children with Learning Disabilities Act of 1969', *British Journal of Sociology of Education*, 4, 2, pp. 125–40.

Carrier, J.G. (1984) 'Comparative Special Education: Ideology, Differentiation and Allocation in England and the United States', in Barton, L., and Tomlinson, S. (Eds) *Special Education and Social Interests*, London, Croom Helm.

Castles, F.G. (1985) *The Working Class and Welfare: Reflections on the Political Development of the Welfare State in Australia and New Zealand, 1890*–1980, New Zealand, Allen and Unwin.

Chua, Beng Huat (1981) 'Genealogy as Sociology: An Introduction to Michel Foucault', *Catalyst*, 14, pp. 1–22.

Culley, L., and Demaine, J. (1983) 'Social Theory, Social Relations and Education', in Walker, S., and Barton, L. (Eds) *Gender, Class and Education*, Lewes, Falmer Press, pp. 161–72.

Finkelstein, V. (1980) *Attitudes and Disabled People – Some Issues for Discussion*, New York, World Rehabilitation Fund.

Ford, J., Mongon, B., and Whelan, M. (1982) *Special Education and Social Control: Invisible Disasters*, London, Routledge and Kegan Paul.

Fulcher, G. (1986a) 'Australian Policies on Special Education: towards a sociological account, *Disability, Handicap and Society*, 1, 1, pp. 19–52.

Fulcher, G. (1988) 'Integration: inclusion or exclusion?', in Slee, R. (Ed) *Discipline and Schools: A Curriculum Perspective*, Macmillan Australia.

Fulcher, G. (1989) 'Disability: a social construction', in Lupton, G., and Najman, J. (Eds) *Sociology of Health and Illness: Australian Readings*, Macmillan.

Galloway, D. (1985) *Schools, Pupils and Special Educational Needs*, London Croom Helm.

Goffman, C. (1968) *Asylums*, Harmondsworth, Penguin.

Gow, L., and Fulcher, G. (1986) Report to the Commonwealth Schools Commission on Integration in Australia, Part 2, *Towards a Policy Direction on Integration*, prepared as a discussion paper for the Commonwealth Schools Commission, June 24.

Hahn, H. (1985) 'The disabled state', *Public Administration Review*, 45, pp. 878–9.

Hahn, H. (1986) 'Public Support for Rehabilitation Programs: the analysis of US disability policy', *Disability, Handicap and Society*, 1, 2, pp. 121–37.

Hindess, B. (1986) 'Actors and Social Relations', Wardell, M. L., and Turner, S.P. (Eds) *Sociological Theory in Transition*, Boston, Allen and Unwin, pp. 114–26.

Hirst, M. (1987) 'Careers of Young People with disabilities between Ages 15–21 years', *Disability, Handicap and Society*, 2, 1, pp. 61–74.

Hirst, P., and Woolley, P. (1982) *Social Relations and Human Attributes*, London, Tavistock Publications.

Human Rights Commission (1986a) *The Treatment of Disabled Persons in Social Security and Taxation Law*, Occasional Paper No. 11, Camberra, Australian Government Publishing Service.

Human Rights Commission (1986b) *Ethical and Legal Issues in the Guardianship Options for Intellectually Disadvantaged People*, Human Rights Commission Monograph Series No. 2, Canberra, Australian Government Publishing Service.

Integration in Victorian Education (1984) Report of the Ministerial Review of Educational

Services for the Disabled, Melbourne, Government Printer.

Jamrozik, A. (1987) 'Evaluation of Research in Social Policy/Social Welfare: Is It Needed? Is It Feasible?', paper presented at the Sixth National Conference of The Australian Evaluation Society, Canberra, 29–31 July.

Jones, M.A. (1980) *The Australian Welfare State*, Sydney, George Allen and Unwin.

Lee, P., and Raban, C. (1988) *Welfare Theory and Social Policy: Reform or Revolution?*, London, Sage Publications.

Link, B., and Milcarek, B. (1980) 'Selection Factors in the Dispensation of Therapy: The Matthew Effect in the Allocation of Mental Health Resources', *Journal of Health and Social Behaviour*, 21, pp. 279–90.

Llewellyn, R. (1983) 'Future health services – a challenge for disabled people', *Australian Rehabilitation Review*, 7, 4, pp. 24–31.

Lloyd, J., and Stagoll, B. (1979) 'The accident victim syndrome – compensation neurosis or iatrogenesis: a social system perspective', *New Doctor*, 13, pp. 29–34.

Marles, F. (1986) 'Methods of Policy Development and Information Dissemination designed to improve understanding between Organizations of People with Disabilities, Government Authorities and the Public', paper presented by Commissioner for Equal Opportunity Victoria, to the International Expert Meeting on Legislation on Equalisation of Opportunities for People with Disabilities, Vienna, 2–6 June, 1986 organized by Rehabilitation International in Equal Opportunity Board Ninth Annual Report (1986), Melbourne, Government Printer, Appendix 2.

Meares, L. (1986) 'What progress for disabled people?', *ASW Impact*, December, pp. 6–8.

Mehan, H. (1984) 'Institutional Decision-Making', in Rogoff, B., and Lave, J. (Eds) *Everyday Cognition: Its development in Social Context*, Cambridge, Massachusetts, Harvard University Press.

Mehan, H., Meihls, J.L., Hertweck, A., and Crowdes, M.S. (1981) 'Identifying handicapped students', in Bacharach, S.B. (Ed) *Organization Behaviour in Schools and School Districts*, New York, Praeger, pp. 381–422.

Mehan, H., Hertweck, A.C., and Meihls, J.L. (1985) *Handicapping the Handicapped*, Stanford, Stanford University Press.

Milofsky, C.D. (1986) 'Special Education and Social Control', in Richardson J.G. (Ed) *Handbook of Theory and Research for the Sociology of Education*, New York, Government Press, pp. 173–202.

Navarro, V. (1983) 'The Determinants of Social Policy, a Case Study: Regulating Health and Safety at the Workplace in Sweden', *International Journal of Health Services*, 13, 4, pp. 517–61.

Oliver, M. (1984) 'The politics of disability', *Critical Social Policy*, 11, pp. 21–32.

Oliver, M. (1986) 'Social Policy and Disability: some theoretical issues', *Disability, Handicap and Society*, 1, 1, pp. 5–17.

Shapiro, M.J. (1981) 'Disability and The Politics of Constitutive Rules', in Albrecht, G.L. (Ed) *Cross-National Rehabilitation Policies*, Beverly Hills, California, Sage Publications, pp. 84–96.

Special Educational Needs (1978) Report of the Committee of Enquiry into the Education of Handicapped Children and Young People, London, HMSO (Warnock Report).

Stewart D. (1986) *Workers' Compensation and Social Security: An Overview*, SWRC Reports and Proceedings No. 63, November.

Stone, D. (1984) *The Disabled State*, Basingstoke, Macmillan.

Strategies and Initiatives for Special Education in New South Wales (1982) A Report of the Working Party Plan for Special Education in NSW, Government Printer, NSW, May.

Tasmania, Education Department (1983) *A Review of Special Education*, Government Printer, Tasmania, April.

Tomlinson, S. (1981) *Educational Subnormality: A study in decision-making*, London, Routledge and Kegan Paul.

Tomlinson, S. (1982) *A Sociology of Special Education*, London Routledge and Kegan Paul.

Turner, B.S. (1984) *The Body and Society*, Oxord, Basil Blackwell.

Victoria Commissioner for Equal Opportunity, (1986) Ninth Annual Report, Melbourne, Government Printer.

Walker, A. (1980) 'The Social Origins of Impairment, Disability, and Handicap', *Medicine in Society*, 6, 2, and 3, pp. 18–26.

Weber, M. (1964) *The Theory of Social and Economic Organization*, New York, The Free Press.

Wicks, M. (1987) *A Future for All: Do We Need the Welfare State?*, Harmondsworth, Penguin.

Wright Mills, C. (1970) *The Sociological Imagination*, Harmondsworth, Penguin.

ACTS

Britain
Education Act, 1981
The Chronically Sick and Disabled Persons Act

Australia
Disability Services Act, 1986

Northern Territory
Education Act, 1985

Victoria
Education Act, 1958
Mental Health Act, 1959

Western Australia
Education Act, 1976, No. 2

Queensland
An Act to amend the Education Act 1964–74, No. 2 of 1984

Chapter 2

Theorizing integration and mainstreaming

'The . . . highly political question of integration' (Warnock, 1982:56).

Governments in Scandinavia, England and Australia have presented their recent education policy on disability as integration policy and, in America, as mainstreaming.[1] Tomlinson notes that English integration policy is presented as benevolent humanitarianism and that, somewhat curiously, segregated education has also been justified this century in the same terms, as in 'the child's best interests' (1982). How can two allegedly opposing policies have the same rationale? Are the 'new' policies so different from past practice? Or, is the rationale mistaken? Does the discourse of professionalism on integration which pervades the English and Victorian educational apparatuses, through its themes of benevolent motives, of knowing what is best for the child who is 'different', obscure rather than clarify what is going on? Is this what Barton and Tomlinson mean when they say integration is ideology (1984)?

In this chapter, I shall focus briefly on integration discourse in government written policy in the English and Victorian educational apparatuses, in order to theorize integration as a particular kind of policy struggle. Themes in these policies are examined more fully in chapters 5 and 6. First, however, I shall argue that the discourse on handicap in US federal law PL 94–142, *The Education for All Handicapped Children,* 1975, does not warrant separate discussion here.

PL 94–142 is generally seen as mainstreaming law, though it does not mention the terms, and handicap is a central theme. Despite the differences in the terms integration and mainstreaming and disability and handicap, the discourse in these respective government policies share a political logic and discourse about difference. As chapter 1 argues, this contains a political logic of difference, loss or deficit, marginal and contingent presence in regular classrooms; therefore, under certain conditions, exclusion. Definitions of handicap can be found which oppose this theme, but this does not undermine the claim. What matters in discourse is how terms are used; the fact that different definitions exist is irrelevant. As chapter 4 shows, the discourse on handicap in PL 94–142 has loss and difference as central themes.

Beyond this thematic similarity, the *discursive means* deployed in the US and English policies differ. US policy is much less informed by professionalism than is its English counterpart. A legal discourse with themes of procedural safeguards informs US federal policy; the notion of an Individualized Education Program has a central place in US policy and was included in the legislation as a discursive means to be deployed to ensure a 'free appropriate education': there is no equivalent theme in English policy. Moreover the policies have different objectives: chapters 4 and 5 discuss these more fully. While the *institutional conditions* in North America and England, into which these policies are inserted, differ both at other levels of their respective educational apparatuses and more widely, none of this detracts from the point that the two policies share themes of difference, loss, and marginality, despite the use of different terms: disability in English policy and handicap in the US policy:

Integration discourses

Integration discourses are complex and contain a variety of objectives. Hence they are the subject of intense struggles. These struggles relate to integration's connection with disability, a connection I shall argue later is not necessary but which is presently dominant in discursive practices surrounding integration. Following Paul Abberley's social theory of disability as oppression, chapter 1 suggested we should look more specifically at what aspects of the present social order are sustained by, and which social actors are able to realize their objectives via, dominant discursive practices organized around a notion of disability. It was also argued that disability is a political construct which has no necessary connection with impairment despite the assumption that when disability is used an impairment is presumed to be present.

Integration as political

Integration is often presented as a technical matter and thus a professional concern which belongs primarily to teachers and special educators; as already and undeniably happening in schools or as not happening because there are too few resources; as relating to individual children who have disabilities or handicaps or 'special educational needs'; and (and this is the dominant view) as being about getting students from segregated educational locations into regular schools (Quicke, 1981). Each of these messages or themes may be deployed in encounters between teachers and parents who seek to enrol their child called disabled in a regular school. Each, as Quicke points out in relation to the dominant view, misconstrues the nature of integration practices and submerges the politics of the underlying issues.

To clarify the politics of integration we need to examine the nature of the discourses which inform a particular integration policy, whether written, stated or enacted (Introduction). Is a divisive or an inclusive discourse deployed? That is, is there a focus on disability or is there a concern with pedagogy? The differences between these was discussed in the Introduction. As Ball points out, objects in discourse exclude consideration of other 'objects': they construct the problem in a certain way (1988). Educational policy on disability needs to be read, listened to, or looked at, for whether it constructs the theme of *disability* rather than that of teaching strategies. Since policy is tactic and has objectives, it needs to be read, listened to, or looked at, for the main discursive means it deploys to achieve its objective(s): In what sense is 'integration' being used? As Beilharz urges, 'the object is to seek to understand policy better than its authors, to locate and identify the meanings in the text, in its language or perspective' (1987:393).[2]

Thus the theme of integrating children with disabilities constructs a particular discourse. The political logic of this discourse and focus was spelt out in chapter 1. This logic and discourse applies in English policy at government written level in the Warnock Report, *Special Educational Needs* and in the Education Act, 1981, and in some Australian State written policies (Fulcher, 1986). In the English and Victorian government-level written policies,[3] *integration is presented as being about children with disabilities.* Thus integration policies need to be read, listened to, or looked at, for their central themes: are these disability and handicap or teaching practices and curriculum?

The Introduction suggested professionalism and democratism are discursive means deployed in the opposing historical struggles of professionalization and democratization to control various areas of public life. These discourses distinguish 'integration' policies. Australian policies vary here (Fulcher, 1986), as do Scandinavian and English policies (chapters 3 and 5). The democratism in US federal law PL 94–142 finds a place in American political discourse and educational apparatuses which, in their institutional conditions, vary significantly from those in England and Victoria, and which shape the US struggles against democratism somewhat differently.

Deciding whether an integration policy deploys professionalism or democratism means looking at other themes in a policy. These may include rights, resources, accountability and equality (Gow and Fulcher, 1986:40). How policies vary on these themes reveal their objectives. An *unconditional commitment to integration*, an anti-segregationist stance, is based firmly in principles of, and a concern for, equality and parity of treatment for all students in educational apparatuses (Gow and Fulcher, 1986:40). Its view is that the vast resources in segregated educational locations should be redeployed in regular schools.

A second objective is contained in defining integration as a process of *increasing the participation of all students in the social and educational life of regular classrooms*. This is consistent with Tony Booth's position (for example, 1983) and the Victorian report's definition of integration: both refer to processes and are associated in the case of Victoria, with a theme about rights, and for Booth, with a theme of comprehensive education. These themes are different routes to the same objective, that is, of integration as a process of increasing the participation of all children, but it is important to note the difference in themes and their institutional conditions. In Australia, there is a debate on a Bill of Rights but so far no legislative or constitutional conditions beyond some State legislation (such as the Equal Opportunity Act in Victoria) for realizing such rights. In England, there has been a more clearly articulated discourse on comprehensive education, and more of a struggle to make educational practices comprehensive (for example, Fish, 1985; Gordon, 1986) than has occurred in Australia. But it is clear that a comprehensive school policy has had a weak institutional base in the English educational apparatus (Ball, 1988).

A third objective in a debate about integration can be described as a *qualified approach to integration* (Gow and Fulcher, 1986:40). This provides no new direction for moving from segregation to integration: that is, from exclusion to inclusion. It is consistent with past practices; thus, with extensive segregation or exclusion of various kinds. Clues which reveal whether integration policy has this objective can be found in the position taken on resources: 'A hard-line position on resources is incompatible with the spirit of an objective of integration, as increasing participation' (Gow and Fulcher, 1986:40). A discourse on resources is part of professionalism since expertise implies additional costs. Consistent with these themes, policies with this objective may also be revealed by talk of extending professional expertise in this area as opposed to changing regular teaching practices to include a wider range of students. Principles of equality may be gestured at in this discourse but will be submerged by talk of resources and expanding expertise.

While policies which take this third, qualified objective may talk of rights, this may occur in a context where few, if any, institutional bases are available to enact those rights. In both the English and Australian context, there is no constitutional or federal legislative basis for enacting rights and where there are no strategies proposed to overcome this the policy may be seen as merely gesturing at rights.[4] This contrasts with institutional conditions in North America. As Beilharz and Watts and Hindess (1987) have pointed out, the *institutional conditions* of these written policies are crucial: 'the problems of "radical" policy development lie mainly *outside* policy, in the institutions (and their traditions) into which policy will, it is imagined, be inserted' (Beilharz and Watts, 1986a, cited by Beilharz, 1987:404). Thus, as noted earlier, the *institutional conditions* of policies need examining.

Despite institutional conditions unfavourable to a policy's objective, such as the lack of constitutional conditions in Australia for a policy theme of rights, there are written policies which have a more or less serious intent to grapple with rights: this was the case in Victoria. But the lack of favourable wider institutional conditions may significantly affect policy practices at other levels. In England, however, written government policy shows little evidence of a serious intent to enact rights. In contrast, the Victorian government written policy included recommendations on participatory decision-making structures at various levels which were seen as a democratic strategy or conditions of such (putative) rights. An energetic struggle occurred around rights in and outside Review meetings, between those who engaged in professionalization and those in democratization (chapter 6). Hence the conflicting recommendations on the membership of decision-making structures. These were informed by professionalism, whereas Extension Note 2, inserted at the last minute, dissents from these recommendations and is informed by, and deploys, democratism. Despite wider institutional conditions of policy which may not favour democratism, this does not discount the *content* of policy documents, since the nature of government-level discourse and strategies for what it sees as implementation may have significant influences on debate at other levels.

Where an objective for integration is of the very qualified kind, integration would seem to be *a new name for special education* rather than a new policy (Tomlinson, 1982). The second objective reveals an intent to shift from past practices of extensive segregation. The differences between objectives mean that policy practice, whether written, stated on enacted, must be examined not only for its discourse, themes, objectives, and tactics (professionalism or democratism, for instance) but also for their effects: have such policies meant more or less inclusion for schoolchildren described as disabled?

In sum, since policy is struggle, integration is political. It is a term which covers a range of objectives, an issue people take sides on and in which they will deploy tactics, including a particular discourse. As noted above, all education practices are political (Apple, 1982; Barton, 1987): they sustain or undermine particular educational and social practices. Thus technical issues of how to teach are not separate from political issues: this is what, how, whom and where we will teach. As Warnock noted (1982:56), integration is an intensely political issue and practice: thus its technical or pedagogic practices should be located in their political context.

Integration and control

Further, integration relates to practices of social control in education. A number of writers have claimed that special education works as social control (Ford *et al.*, 1982; Tomlinson, 1982; Carrier, 1984; Milofsky, 1986) but they generally fail to define what they mean by this somewhat flabby concept. Is the notion of social control sociology's conceptual escape from the political nature of social practices so that sociologists can talk instead, somewhat elliptically, about practices exerting social control because they reproduce say, class or gender relations? Others use the term to encompass socialization practices, the eliciting of compliance and the containment of dissent: these are all practices by which social order is constructed. In this sense, *social control consists of practices which construct patterns of social relations.*

Clearly a discourse on disability, or its synonyms, has provided powerful categories, discursive means, which have been deployed to construct patterns of social relations in Western educational apparatuses. A discourse on disability distinguishes 'normal' and 'special' students. Its political logic and its themes of deficit, loss, difference, marginality, and contingent presence, together with the other institutional bases of segregation (separate schools, separate classes, separate and particular professions, etc.) are central in constituting segregating practices. Categories which epitomize these themes include learning difficulties, hearing impaired, disruptive, and socio-emotionally handicapped.

Beyond this level of analysis, that integration constructs patterns of social relations in classrooms and in the wider educational apparatus, integration touches on more specific control practices in educational apparatuses: these are knowledge control via the curriculum, and discipline, understood as meaning the maintenance of particular standards and types of social order or relations in classrooms (Wolpe, 1985). But as Wolpe notes, both the literature and practice, as this is generally understood, fail to connect these two forms of control. She argues, following Foucault's discussion of forms of surveillance, that discipline, as the production of docile bodies, is the pre-condition for the exercise of knowledge control via the curriculum. Classroom order requires docile bodies. This regulation of the body in classrooms, instances welfare state practices which rigorously regulate how bodies are deployed, what is done with them and where we take them (Turner, 1984). Herein lies some of the resistance to integrating those with less docile bodies: toiletting, larking about, dribbling, wandering, absence, verbal abuse, etc., all instance the failure to subordinate bodies to the requirements of classroom docility. The control responses to these forms of disruption include categorizing students, suspension and other sanctioning practices, including exclusion from regular classrooms for long or short periods.

While discipline, as the production of docile bodies, is seen as a precondition for the exercise of control via the curriculum, as Slee and others note, curriculum relates to discipline (Slee, 1986; Booth and Coulby, 1987).

What to teach and the creation of conditions of receptiveness and cooperation, so that it can be taught, are the two great control issues in educational practices. Both these practices of control have moral and political dimensions. Discipline is political where it is imposed but also moral in what kind of discipline is exerted: is this an imposed conformity or a self-regulating desire to learn?[5] It is political-moral too in its objective: docility in order to teach *this*. Furthermore, curriculum is a practice of knowledge control and content, a moral and substantive matter (this is what we should teach), and a political (we *will* teach this) and technical or pedagogic (in *this* way) practice (Fulcher, 1988).

Hence integration, where it is a policy enacted in classrooms, and in which I've argued curriculum is one of two central issues, is a practice of control, morality, substance, politics and technique. It is never merely a technical issue though, as noted above, this is often the way it is presented. From this stance, *integration is basically about discipline and knowledge control: it is not about disability* (Fulcher, 1988). It is this submerged politics which underlies the highly contested nature of integration policy practices.

Since integration is about discipline and control rather than disability, it is at the centre rather than the periphery of educational practices. It may therefore be argued that *it is the educational apparatus's failure to provide an inclusive curriculum,* a curriculum which includes all (Fish, 1985; Booth, Potts and Swann, 1987), rather than the problems specific disabilities pose, *which constructs the 'problems' and politics of integration.* Integration practices then raise the question of what is, or what should be, the nature of schooling? In Britain, Barton, Booth, Fish, Hegarty and others represent those who locate integration practices with debate about comprehensive education. It is here that a discourse on integration belongs. The extent to which integration discourse is located in this wider debate in the Scandinavian, English, and Victorian educational apparatuses and how this affects integration discourse and practices at various levels is examined in later chapters.

Conclusions

While integration is often presented as a technical matter, it is more accurately, as Warnock suggests (1982) a highly political question. Integration has a range of meanings, thus an array of practices and objectives traditionally organized around the notion of disability. It raises political questions: Are more children to be integrated in regular schools or are more to be segregated as has occurred in the past? It also raises pedagogical questions of what to teach and how. It thus refers both to what are generally seen as 'matters of policy' and to teaching programs or curriculum. But following the model in the Introduction, both are policy practices and as such are political and moral and may involve technical aspects.

The debate it raises and the range of practices integration covers and its political, moral and pedagogic dimensions make integration discourse mystifying.[6] This mystification derives also from the tactics of those who deploy professionalism, a discourse which is clearly not available to all participants in educational arenas, including some parents, and which, to put it differently, may not be read or heard for what it is. Here, themes such as 'in the best interests of the child', or techniques of linguistic persuasion (Mehan, 1983), are deployed at other levels in educational apparatuses despite government-level written policy. Thus US federal policy refers to rights of parents and students and attempts to institute those rights in 'procedural safeguards' (chapter 4), and Victorian government written policy also refers to rights of parents and students and attempted to institute these via democratic participatory decision-making structures. But, for example, in Californian schools, professionals may deploy linguistic techniques of persuasion which deny these rights and in Victoria, 'failures' of democratic decision-making structures are reported.

The mystifying nature of integration discourse also derives in part from a failure to theorize policy as made at all levels of state apparatuses. Once we articulate policy in this way, we should expect diversity in policy practices at other levels. Integration struggles will be replayed in a variety of arenas and at a number of levels in an educational apparatus.

Part of the mystification also derives from the dominant discourse traditionally informing debate on integration as about disability. Medical discourse, which presumes impairment is present when the notion of disability is used, through its hegemony, obscures the ludicrous nature of the claim that one in five children will, at some time, have special educational needs. A political logic thus characterizes educational discourse on disability. Given the range of meanings of integration, which in some instances are consistent with past practices of extensive segregation of children deemed different (this co-exists with the presence of some children also deemed 'different' in regular classrooms), integration discourse is in many arenas merely a new name for special education. Thus it raises the question of whether such policies contain a real intent to change from past practices. This is discussed in chapters 3, 4, 5 and 6.

As political practice, and with whatever meaning, integration is more accurately seen as a struggle which occurs at all levels in educational apparatuses. In this context, it is part of policy shifts (of control, Cohen suggests (1979)) in other state apparatuses, in the health and judicial apparatuses. Given that disability is generally a central theme in integration discourse (as handicap is in mainstreaming discourse), and given that disability is an increasingly important procedural category by which welfare states regulate increasing numbers of their citizens (Stone, 1984; Hahn, 1986), we need to examine whether integration policies regulate an increasing proportion of schoolchildren. A number of British writers say this is occurring (Swann, 1985; Tomlinson, 1985) and this is clearly the case in Victoria (Fulcher, 1988). The evidence is examined more fully in later chapters.

This chapter has argued that *integration is basically about discipline and knowledge control: it is not about disability*. It thus raises the central issue of the nature of schooling and its real place, as discourse and practice, is in a discourse on comprehensive education. It is the achievement of an integration discourse, where the central 'object' or theme is disability, to have distracted attention from the pedagogical issues of curriculum and to describe disruption, whether 'it is based on handicap, impairment, behaviour or performance' (Oliver, 1985:53), as a disability a student has. Thus it was also argued that *it is the educational apparatus's failure to provide an inclusive curriculum* rather than the problems specific disabilities pose, *which constructs the 'problems' and politics of integration*.

An integration discourse which focuses on pedagogical practice raises questions of the kind Biklen (1985) puts: What can this student do? How does he/she learn? What does he/she want and need to learn so as to be as fully a participating member of mainstream society as possible? This kind of question contrasts with questions which arise in integration discourse where the central object is disability. A focus on disability leads teachers to ask: How are we meant to teach children with that sort of disability, when we haven't the training? This kind of question emerges from a (sometimes unacknowledged) discourse of professionalism, which is institutionalized both in regular and special teacher training institutions and more widely in educational apparatuses in, for instance, England and Victoria. The present practice in teacher training institutions is to separate 'special' education courses from other education courses; such practices institutionalize, and produce teachers with, that discourse. 'How can we teach children with that sort of disability, when we don't have the training?' may be a relevant question and rationale where a student has an especially severe impairment, but it may not. This would apply justifiably to a very small percentage of the total school-aged population. It is much more likely to be a question raised and a tactic deployed to construct an identity of disabled for a wide range of students whom teachers find difficult to teach in regular classrooms: for many of those described as having a 'learning difficulty', or as disruptive or socio-emotionally handicapped, an impairment cannot be presumed to be present. In such instances, the notion of disability is revealed for the political construct it is.

It is in the extraordinary political use of disability and its synonyms, as relevant to one in five (Warnock) or 30 per cent (Tasmanian, 1983:43) of the school population, that the control and political aspects of 'integration' discourse become obvious. I have argued that this occurs at least in part because *disability* is the object of concern rather than curriculum. In the chapters on local practices the nature and effects of policy discourses on integration will be examined and the US federal law PL 94–142, with its potentially different discourse, which includes individualized programs as a central concern, will also be discussed.

Notes

1 Brief reference is made in this chapter to what documents and/or legislation constitute these government policies. For further details, see chapters 4, 5 and 6 and Fulcher (1986) on Australian State policies.
2 Bellharz refers to written policy only. Nevertheless his comments also apply to stated or enacted policy (chapter 1), since he includes the notion of perspective.
3 The main Victorian policy document on *Integration in Victorian Education* (1984) but see also chapter 6.
4 Australian State policies, with the exception of the Victorian report, have failed to propose strategies which might grapple with these institutional conditions (see Fulcher, 1986).
5 See Knight (1988) on this.
6 See Booth (1981) on demystifying integration.

References

Abberley, P. (1987) 'The Concept of Oppression and the Development of a Social Theory of Disability', *Disability, Handicap and Society*, 2, 1, pp. 5–20.
Apple, M.W. (1982) *Education and Power*, Boston, Ark Paperbacks (1985 edition).
Ball, S. (1988) 'Comprehensive Schooling, Effectiveness and Control: an analysis of educational discourses', in Slee, R. (Ed) *Discipline and Schools: a Curriculum Perspective*, Macmillan Australia, pp. 132–52.

Barton, L. (1987) 'Keeping schools in line', in Booth, T., and Coulby, B. (Eds) *Producing and Reducing Disaffection: Curricula for All,* Milton Keynes, Open University Press, pp. 242–7.

Barton, L., and Tomlinson, S. (Eds) (1984) *Special Education and Social Interests,* London, Croom Helm.

Beilharz, P. (1987) 'Reading Politics: Social Theory and Social Policy', *Australian and New Zealand Journal of Sociology,* 22, 3, pp. 388–406.

Biklen, D. (1985) *Achieving the Complete School: Strategies for Effective Mainstreaming,* Teachers College, Columbia University.

Booth, T. (1981) 'Demystifying Integration' in Swann, W. (Ed) *The Practice of Special Education,* Basil Blackwell for the Open University, pp. 288–313.

Booth, T. (1983) 'Policies Towards the Integration of Mentally Handicapped Children in Education', *Oxford Review of Education,* 9, 3, pp. 255–68.

Booth, T., and Coulby, D. (Eds) (1987) *Producing and Reducing Disaffection: Curricula for All,* Milton Keynes, Open University Press.

Booth, T., Potts, P., and Swann, W. (Eds) (1987) *Preventing Difficulties in Learning: Curricula for All,* Oxford, Basil Blackwell in association with Open University Press.

Carrier, J.G. (1984) 'Comparative Special Education: Ideology, Differentiation and Allocation in England and the United States', in Barton, L. and Tomlinson, S. (Eds) *Special Education and Social Interests,* London, Croom Helm.

Cohen, P. (1979) 'The punitive city: notes on the dispersal of social control', *Contemporary Crises,* 3, pp. 339–63.

Fish, J. (1985) *Special Education: The Way Ahead,* Milton Keynes, Open University Press.

Ford, J., Mongon, B., and Whelan, M. (1982) *Special Education and Social Control: Invisible Disasters,* London, Routledge and Kegan Paul.

Fulcher, G. (1986) 'Australian Policies on Special Education: towards a sociological account', *Disability, Handicap and Society,* 1, 1, pp. 19–52.

Fulcher, G. (1988) 'Integration: inclusion or exclusion?', in Slee, R. (Ed) *Discipline and Schools: A Curriculum Perspective,* Macmillan Australia, pp. 28–47.

Gordon, T. (1986) *Democracy in One School: Progressive Education and Restructuring,* Lewes, Falmer Press.

Gow, L., and Fulcher, G. (1986) Part 2 *Towards a Policy Direction on Integration,* Discussion Paper prepared for the Commonwealth Schools Commission, June 26.

Hahn, H. (1986) 'Public Support for Rehabilitation Programs: the analysis of US disability policy', *Disability, Handicap and Society,* 1, 2, pp. 121–37.

Hegarty, S. (1982) 'Integration and the "Comprehensive" School', *Educational Review,* 34, 2, pp. 99–105.

Hindess, B. (1987) *Freedom, Equality and the Market: Arguments on Social Policy,* London, Tavistock Publications.

Integration in Victorian Education (1984) Report of the Ministerial Review of Educational Services for the Disabled, Melbourne, Government Printer, (Chair: M.K. Collins).

Knight, T. (1988) 'Student Discipline as a Curriculum Concern', in Slee, R. (Ed) *Discipline and Schools: A Curriculum Perspective,* Macmillan Australia, pp. 321–40.

Macdonell, D. (1986) *Theories of Discourse: an introduction,* Oxford, Basil Blackwell.

Mehan, H. (1983) 'The role of language and the language of role', *Language in Society,* 12, pp. 187–211.

Milofsky, C.D. (1986) 'Special Education and Social Control', in Richardson, J.G. (Ed) *Handbook of Theory and Research for the Sociology of Education,* New York, Government Press, pp. 173–202.

Oliver, M. (1985) 'The Integration – Segregation Debate: Some sociological considerations', *British Journal of Sociology of Education,* 6, 1, pp. 75–92.

Quicke, J.C. (1981) 'Special Educational Needs and the Comprehensive Principle', *Remedial Education,* 16, 2, pp. 161–7.

Slee, R. (1986) 'Integration, the Disruptive Student and Suspension', *The Urban Review,* November.

Special Educational Needs (1978) Report of the Committee of Enquiry into the Education of Handicapped Children and Young People (Warnock Report), London, HMSO.

Stone, D. (1984) *The Disabled State,* Basingstoke, Macmillan.

Swann, W. (1985) 'Is the integration of children with special needs happening?: an analysis of recent statistics of pupils in special schools', *Oxford Review of Education,* 11, 1, pp. 3–18.

Tasmania, Education Department (1983) *A Review of Special Education,* Government Printer, Tasmania, April.

Tomlinson, S. (1982) *A Sociology of Special Education,* London, Routledge and Kegan Paul.

Tomlinson, S. (1985) 'The Expansion of Special Education', *Oxford Review of Education,* 11, 2, pp. 157–65.

Turner, B.S. (1984) *The Body and Society,* Oxford, Basil Blackwell.

Warnock, M. (1982) 'Children with Special Needs in Ordinary Schools: Integration Revisited', *Education Today,* 32, 3, pp. 56–62.

Wolpe, A.M. (1985) 'Schools, Discipline and Social Control', in L. Barton and S. Walker (Eds) *Education and Social Change,* London, Croom Helm, pp. 152–72.

ACTS

England
Education Act, 1981

US
Federal law PL 94–142, The Education for All Handicapped Children Act, 1975

Victoria
Equal Opportunity Act, 1977
Equal Opportunity Act, 1984

Part Two
Local practices

Chapter 3

Scandinavian policy practices

Introduction

While other chapters focus on practices in particular countries or states in them, this chapter discusses the Scandinavian countries of Denmark and Norway.[1] Thus it is somewhat more general and inconsistent with the attempt in other chapters to examine, in more detail and more closely, the relationship between government-level written educational policy on handicap[2] and school practices. There are two reasons for this. First, the literature tends to treat Denmark, Norway and Sweden as sharing a number of characteristics which distinguish them from, for instance, other Western European countries. Secondly, not being able to read any of the Scandinavian languages, and not having visited Scandinavia, are significant drawbacks to the research. For one thing, what non-Scandinavian language readers can read and thus 'discover' about practices in these educational apparatuses is limited. It may well be that what is written in English is what Scandinavians want to be known. Nevertheless, a general discussion on these countries may, within the limits mentioned, provide both some insights into their practices and some useful comparisons for understanding practices elsewhere. Despite the limits to the research, it is important to attempt to look at Scandinavian practices, given general views of these countries as model welfare states and as humane towards those called handicapped.

Scandinavia and the wider institutional context of educational practices

Particularly high levels of public welfare provision characterize the Scandinavian countries (Castles and McKinlay, 1979:157). In a careful examination of both the data and competing explanations of variations in public welfare provision, Castles and McKinlay reject the then prevailing sociological orthodoxy that high levels of welfare spending derive from high levels of economic development. They demonstrate that the Scandinavian levels of welfare spending have their source in the 'dominant role of the social democratic parties in Denmark, Sweden and Norway over the last half century' (p. 160), and specifically, in the party's ideals about equality. Castles and McKinlay thus defend their position that 'politics matters', a view argued for in the Introduction, which challenges orthodox sociological theorizing that economics and class power, in the last analysis, matter. As Castles and McKinlay show, the impact of politics and party ideology in particular, is of vital importance in policy outcomes (p. 171) where *levels* of welfare spending are concerned.

The dominance of social democratic parties in the Scandinavian countries derives from historical and structural factors and the mechanisms 'by which the solidarity of the labour movement in Scandinavia operates to maximize welfare outcomes'. The Scandinavian labour movement achieved a unity and integration through 'an absence of major impediments to working–class industrial and political organization, by the timing and context of organizational growth, and by the nature of the strategic choices faced by the various movements at different times. Each of these factors is interrelated to the anomalous development of the Right in Scandinavia' (1979:170). Castles and McKinlay thus argue that a *small* party of the right is a necessary, but not sufficient, condition for high levels of welfare spending. In the Scandinavian countries, this occurred through:

> a large class of independent peasantry, which, in varying degrees, opposed the prerogatives of the established political élite. The Liberal movement, with roots amongst the independent peasantry, pressed for the widening of the franchise; supported by the nascent Social Democratic party it secured political citizenship for the masses. In the years of the Great Depression, the labour movement achieved a *modus vivendi* with agrarian parties to preserve industrial employment and provide agricultural subsidies. This was the historical springboard from which the Scandinavian social democratic parties were able to achieve their dominance from the 1930s onwards (1979:170).

The social democratic parties retained their dominance at least until the 1960s, by collaborating in 'increasing productivity and minimizing labour disputes'. In return they gained 'full employment, increasing living standards and welfare provision'. Thus '[in] Scandinavia, there was a "politics of virtuous circles" by which the social democrats gained or maintained support by protecting working-class interests, and the working class gained in so far as they supported the social democratic labour movement' (Castles and McKinlay 1979:170).

Despite these favourable conditions, the social democratic parties have by no means achieved classless societies in Denmark, Norway or Sweden. As the then leader of the Swedish Social Democratic party stated in 1968, '"We're far ahead compared to what Sweden looked like thirty or forty years ago. But we have *not* gone very far if you want your dream of a classless society to come true. In that case, most of the work remains to be done"' (cited by Castles and McKinlay, 1979:160). Nevertheless the effect has been to foster greater levels of equality than in other countries. Castles and McKinlay note that while:

> the development of public welfare has neither radically affected the reward structure of capitalism nor brought about any major vertical redistribution of wealth . . . it is absurd to pretend that no progress towards equality has been made. Public welfare provisions do foster equality and the greatest steps toward equality have come from the democratic socialist parties of Scandinavia (Castles and McKinlay 1979:171).

Thus a wider discourse in which equality was a central and serious political theme, and relatively high levels of public welfare spending compared with North America, Britain and Australia, have constituted significant *political and economic conditions* of educational policies in Scandinavia. The election in the eighties of non-socialist parties to coalition governments in both Denmark and Norway and the effect of this on educational practices is discussed below.

Denmark

In Denmark education is high on the political agenda: in 1983, 12 per cent of overall State and Municipal budgets were spent on education, making it the second highest (tied with pensions and services) after 'other income transfers' and ahead of expenditure on health services (10 per cent) and social security (11 per cent) (figures from J. Hansen (1984) whose source was the Budget 1983, Ministry of Finance). Given that education may be *seen*, as social policy, as a means to more equality, its high position in welfare outlays may be taken as an indicator of the commitment to equality in the Danish political system. These conditions of educational practices surrounding handicap in Denmark differ considerably from the political and economic conditions of North American, British and Victorian practices. The election in 1982, and again in 1987, of a conservative party to government appears not to have had a direct effect on the educational apparatus. Not only does 'conservative' have less right-wing connotations in Denmark but educational policy is an issue on which parties generally agree.[3]

The general development of special education practices in Denmark is depicted in Figure 3.1, drawn from Jorgen Hansen's work (1984).

Thus special education practices became a formal, State-level responsibility only in the 1950s. However, special classes for pupils with learning difficulties were first established in primary and lower secondary schools in 1903, in a few municipal areas, a development which was gradually followed in other areas. These derived from 'real pragmatic, local responsibility', not from 'central political or administrative forces' (J. Hansen, 1984:5). When these local practices showed that this development was possible and appropriate, *legislation followed.* Hansen notes this sequence as a *key characteristic* in Danish policy making: 'We can't change the world by laws but law based upon good practice is a profitable tool' (1984). In the Danish context, legislative conditions are deployed to maintain improvements

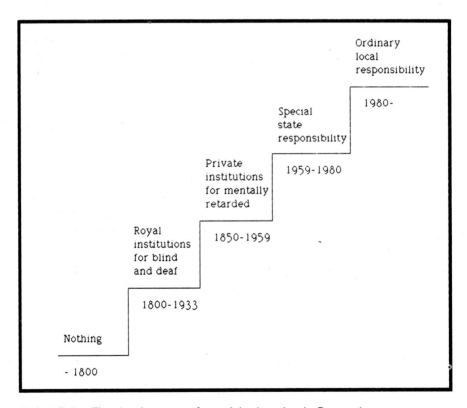

Figure 3.1: The development of special education in Denmark
Source: Hansen (1984)

and to encourage further improvement. Statuary statements thus describe what have been a possibility for some as a right for everyone (J. Hansen, 1984:5).

The more recent events leading to legislative decisions began in the 1950s when the idea that some children were ineducable was still part of pedagogic and legal discourse and part of actual practice. Official statistics suggest that in 1955, about 2500, and in the early sixties, about 2000 children with severe handicap were considered ineducable (Pedersen, B.). This practice opposed Section 76 of The Constitution of the Kingdom of Denmark (1953), which states that 'Every child at the compulsory school age has a right to receive free teaching in a primary school . . .' (cited by Pedersen, A:2). Thus the *constitutional conditions* of educational practices surrounding handicap are limited in their effect and constitute only an important statement of principle.

Public debate in the 1960s, which was due largely to parents who sought a regular education for their children (J. Hansen), questioned the notion of ineducability. This debate and struggle were part of a wider, significant discourse on normalization of services. Commissions and committees of enquiry were first established in 1964 with the brief to investigate ways of achieving normalization. This was to 'comprise . . . a thorough revision of the overall social security system with substantial consequences in the social, health and educational sectors' (Ministry of Education, 1986:9). A number of Parliamentary Resolutions and *legislative decisions* affecting educational practices followed. These are seen as *guidelines* only and not as directly controlling local authorities' practices. Some of the legislative conditions altered the political-administrative control of education via decentralization.[4]

The Parliamentary Resolution of 30 May 1969 on Reform of Fundamental Schooling contained the principle that 'Teaching of handicapped pupils should be expanded in such a way that the children can be taught in an ordinary school system' (cited in Pedersen A:2) Pedersen comments that this resolution implicates four main principles which are guidelines to local authorities. They are:

(1) *The principle of proximity:* assistance to a handicapped child must be offered as close to the child's home and school as possible.

(2) *The principle of minimum intereference:* a child should not receive any more help than is necessary in order to overcome his or her handicap or its consequence.

(3) *The principle of efficiency:* the situations prepared for the child must be worked out in such a way that the handicap can be surmounted and/or its consequences can be eliminated.

(4) *The principle of integration:* the entire developmental process which can be followed historically and was adopted in the Parliamentary Resolution of 1969 (Pedersen A:3).

In the 1980s, judging from the literature surveyed (which is admittedly small), these principles are still widely discussed. This suggests that pedagogical integration is unevenly developed in Denmark's fourteen counties and 125 municipalities, a view for which there is further evidence discussed below.

Significant *legislative conditions* emerged in 1975 in The Primary Act on the Folkeskole (the Danish primary and lower secondary school) (since amended), which 'in principle, established a comprehensive basic school from the 1st to the 10th forms' (Ministry of Education, 1986:1). This Act included a number of principles for guiding the integration of children with handicap into regular schools. It emphasized the importance of cooperation between parents and teachers, that schools are more than conveyers of knowledge and that the Folkeskole, in addition to supporting and stimulating the intellectual development of the individual child, should 'also take responsibility for the upbringing of the child' (Pedersen, A:3).

Also significant is the Administrative Reform of 1 January 1980. Jorgen Hansen (1984) notes this Act abolished, changed or adapted more than twenty other laws and contained two principles which affected educational practices, including those surrounding handicap, in a number of ways. These were *administrative decentralization* and *legal normalization.* The first meant that responsibility for services, including education, was transferred from state level to county and local government level. Educational decentralization was part of the wider 'political/administrative development which took place in Denmark in all fields', where the aim was 'to establish a local grass-roots democracy' by joining small local districts so that they were 'sufficiently large to ensure the citizens a satisfactory level of service' but not too big to exclude local democracy (Ministry of Education, post 1981:2). Hansen depicts this decentralization in Figure 3.2.

The political-administrative decentralization of schooling means that the 'same politicians, the same authorities, the same school director are asked to provide resources and facilities' across the range of programs, including, for instance, those for very gifted children and those with profound intellectual problems (J. Hansen, 1984:7). Thus *legislative conditions* in Denmark have instituted the local level as the central arena in decisions on public services. Local arenas are thus *political-administrative* arenas. But this local control operates (or is said to operate) within legislative and statutory rules or guidelines on standards and quality of services. For instance, legislative conditions allow streaming only in the 8th and 9th grades (Pedersen, A). Thus legislative conditions both institute local control and seek to ensure

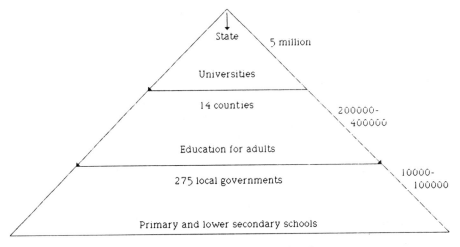

Figure 3.2: Decentralization in the Danish educational apparatus
Source: Hansen (1984)

that certain standards are maintained. The diversity of local practices within these legislative and constitutional conditions is discussed below, as are the economic conditions of educational practices.

The second principle that guided the 1980 Administrative Reform, that of *legal normalization,* refers to 'all the efforts towards putting the handicapped citizen on an equal footing with all other citizens in the society *vis-à-vis* laws, administrations and political authorities (normalization is thus a challenge to society and not a wish or a demand for adapting the individual to make him normal)' (J. Hansen 1984:6).

The principle of legal normalization had a number of effects on educational practices. In abolishing special laws it transferred the responsibility for children formerly classed as 'patients', from the Ministry of Social Affairs to the Ministry of Education. These children became pupils at county and municipal schools. Local authorities thus took on the daily responsibility of providing educational services for all children and for 'realising . . . children's right to sufficient and relevant education'. Under the 1980 Act all children between the ages of seven to sixteen are entitled to 'a given row of subjects, a given amount of weekly education (but certainly with different content)' (J. Hansen 1984:7).

The combined effects of administrative decentralization and legal normalization mean, as Pedersen notes, that 'the process of integration is locally determined, there is no law on integration, only guidelines' (A:4). Thus it is openly recognized in the Danish educational apparatus that *schools make their own policy practices* and that, as Hindess argues (1986), legislative decisions are only one site of decision-making. This contrasts with commonly held views on the role of law in the North American educational apparatus (chapter 4).

The notion of a comprehensive school open to all children has been a central theme in education discourse in Scandinavia for some decades. But as a form of organization it has clearly developed unevenly in the Scandinavian countries. The relevance of comprehensive schools – those that seek to integrate all students – to a policy of integrating those with handicap, was discussed in the Introduction. But as Booth notes, comprehensive schooling provides only the *potential* for integrating schoolchildren (1982). As a former Swedish Minister of Education comments:

> In spite of 10 years of nationwide experiments with the comprehensive school, after the parliamentary decision of 1972, the *grundskola* was still a school which had to be created. Pedagogical ideas were to be put into practice, principles and guidelines were to be embodied. But how? Only those – or primarily those – who worked in the classroom or close to it would know (1984:242).

Rodhe's later comments reinforce this: 'Teachers in their practical classroom situation reported their great difficulties in fulfilling the objectives of the new *grundskola,* as they tried to use the traditional teaching methods' (1984:247).

In 1980 the Decision of the Nordic Council of Ministers promoted the idea of a 'school for everyone'.

> The idea of a school where any child – even severely handicapped – can have her/his education underlies this decision. From this idea can be deduced that we no longer ought to use the term 'integration', which originally (in the 70s) meant a transfer of handicapped children into normal classes. Now integration has become a process, a way of working, with the intention of avoiding segregation (Pedersen, A:4).

Thus stated and written policy at government level supports an objective of integration.

Aside from the legislative conditions it constructed, the 1980 Act, in creating an identity of student for children formerly classed as patients, also marked a shift from medical to a *pedagogical discourse.* This is consistent with more recent statements from the Ministry of Education. These state that children do not fall into two groups, those who are handicapped and those who aren't, and that a connection between 'diagnosis' and placement cannot be sustained (J. Hansen, 1982:156–7; O. Hansen, B:4): 'categorization is false and artifical and very often not only meaningless but a real dangerous trap in which children for years or maybe for all their lives can be caught by a totally wrong and misleading assessment' (J. Hansen, 1984:10). The Ministry's written policy emphasizes that all children are pupils and that functional descriptions should replace categorization (O. Hansen, 1981; A; B). *This written policy suggests a pedagogical discourse on special education practices has an institutional base in the Ministry.*

However, official statistics on *current practice* (1981/82) describe the proportion of children receiving special education both by forms of assistance and by school psychological statements (by category ?) (Tables 3.1 and 3.2). But it needs noting that statements about school psychological assessment have, as a central theme, the idea that all children are pupils (see, for example, O. Hansen, 1981; A; B). The pedagogical themes which thus characterize written statements by the Danish School Psychology Advisory Service contrast with the clinical deficit view which elsewhere typically constitutes psychological discourse and practice (chapter 1).

Table 3.3 suggests that overall almost 13 per cent of students aged 7 to 16 were assessed for extra services, while those in forms three to seven (aged 9 to 13) were more likely that those in other forms to be assessed. The proportion of special educational assistance to regular programs for those assessed is discussed below.

Table 3.4 provides official data on the location of special education services and numbers of pupils in them. This suggests that about one-quarter of students receiving additional assistance do so in a regular class.

Table 3.5 presents official data on these numbers as a percentage of all students.

Economic conditions of educational practices derive, firstly, from local taxes, then from state grants, and these reflect wider economic conditions. State

Table 3.1   Denmark: Students assessed to special education in the different forms of assistance 1981/82

Form of assistance	Pupils Total	% of the total number of handicapped	% of the total number of students
No reported	17,836		
Normal class	9,865	12.0	1.6
Special class Special school	15,137	18.3	2.4
Special group	12,667	15.4	2.0
Clinic	33,125	40.1	5.3
One person in charge of teaching	8,329	10.1	1.3
Other forms	3,390	4.1	0.5
Total	100,359	100.0	13.1

Source: J. Hansen (1984)

Table 3.2   Denmark: Pupils who were given special education on the basis of school psychological statements in the scholastic year 1981/82 (all pupils 0–18 years of age)

Handicap/ category	Total number	Percentage of all pupils in special education	Percentage of all pupils 0–18 years
Unexplained	3,048	3.0	0.4
Speech and language disabilities	18,586	18.0	2.4
Hearing handicaps	2,275	2.2	0.3
Visual handicaps	336	0.3	0.04
Motor handicaps	861	0.9	0.1
Reading and spelling disabilities	47,195	47.7	6.2
General learning disabilities (mentally handicapped)	13,587	13.5	1.8
Behavioural and emotional problems	9,540	9.4	1.3
Other disabilities	8,702	8.6	1.1
Total	104,166	100.36	13.64

Source: Pedersen, B.

Table 3.3   Denmark: Students receiving special pedagogical assistance in primary and lower secondary school 1981/82 compared with the total number of students

Form	Assessed to special education	Total number of pupils in Folkeskolen	%
10	4,743	45,519	10.4
9	7,113	79,597	9.0
8	9,025	75,265	12.0
7	11,205	70,105	16.0
6	11,887	67,787	17.5
5	11,818	67,763	17.4
4	12,390	70,761	17.5
3	11,072	70,906	15.6
2	7,700	67,605	11.4
1	4,939	67,305	7.3
Bornehavekl	4,435	62,775	7.1
Total	96,327	745,377	12.9

Source: Hansen, J. (1984)

Table 3.4   Denmark: Location of special education services and number of pupils

Year	School structure	Special school		Special class in a normal school		Normal class	
		Number of pupils	%	Number of pupils	%	Number pupils	%
1981		3,159	50	1,528	24	1,634	26
1983		3,046	50	1,574	26	1,503	24

Source: Pedersen, B: 3

Table 3.5   Denmark: Structural organization of the special education imparted (1981/82)

Structure	Number of pupils	Percentage of all pupils in public schools
Special support in a normal class or in connection with a normal class	22,214	2.9
Group lessons (particularly in Danish and mathematics) in a special classroom–but generally only for a few hours per week	55,918	7.3
Special classes	18,384	2.4
Other types of segregated special education	3,830	0.5
Total	100,359	13.1

Source: Pedersen, B: 2

taxes are delivered to local goernment as block grants; there are no ear-marked funds (J. Hansen, 1984:8). However, economic conditions of integration have changed. The Ministry of Education's booklet describes economic conditions as more difficult than formerly:

> The will to fulfil all handicapped persons' right to a permanent education in harmony with the ordinary society is unmistakably present with the authorities, the politicians and the engaged staff, but the economic situation of the society does not favour these efforts. Whereas the social reform in Denmark was initiated and prepared in a period of prosperity and unlimited resources, it is now to be implemented in times of depression and economic decline (1986:16).

This reveals that government written statements on integration are only one level of decision-making; funding practices at different levels constitute significant economic conditions of educational practices.

In so far as economic decisions are made at the local level, *economic conditions* intersect with *political-administrative* and with *legislative* conditions.

The principles of decentralization and normalization in the 1980 Act, together with the 1975 Act's in principle establishment of a comprehensive school for students aged 7 to 16, both instituted local arenas as a key level of decision-making and sought to provide political–administrative conditions which aimed to facilitate integration. The Ministry of Education's information booklet describes:

> *Integration* [as] a far more complicated and binding concept in relation to the prevailing administrative principles of normalization and decentralization, [which] . . . can hardly be promoted *directly* through legislation; on the other hand, it may be impeded or prevented *directly* or *indirectly* by the manner in which the legislation and the public administration of a nation are built up. Therefore, the three basic principles of the social reform constitute a necessary whole, where the two first principles have been embodied in laws which in the long run are to prepare the way for the last one (1986:10).

> The [sic] integration has not been directly legalised – which could hardly have been desirable or expedient either – and the only political decision on school integration is still a parliamentary resolution from 1969 to the effect: 'that the primary and lower secondary school should be expanded so as to provide for the teaching of handicapped pupils, to the greatest possible extent, in an ordinary school environment' (1986:11).

This use of the legal process contrasts sharply with the legal strategies pursued by advocates of special education reform in the US (chapter 4) and with the legislative decisions deployed in Britain (chapter 5).

That local administrative conditions are also political, is acknowledged by the use of the term political–administrative (a concept which follows, too, from a model in the Introduction) and in an especially noteworthy reference to the political decisions surrounding counselling:

> In the geographical area [under study] . . . three relatively small communities (the municipalities of Hadsten, Hinnerup and Rosenholm) situated near Aarthus, Jutland, run a School Psychological Counselling in common. The School Psychological Counselling is central for the assessment procedures of special educational support and for the administration of the political decisions on the special educational aims (Pedersen A:4).

Elsewhere, in Victoria for instance, counselling decisions are most frequently presented or deployed as technical, apolitical therapeutic matters.

In discussing the *political-administrative practices* for deciding the nature of special education assistance a child may require, the Ministry emphasizes the importance of collaboration between the teacher, the child's parents and the pedagogical psychologist (1986:19). This collaboration, the Ministry notes, contrasts with many countries where the responsibility for such decisions is given to psychologists. However, without research on this 'collaboration', such as Mehan's on Eligibility Placement Committees in California (1984) (chapter 4), we cannot assume that Danish practices concerning collaboration necessarily differ from those in California where professionals use processes of linguistic persuasion to ratify prejudged decisions, thus departing from the intent of the US federal law.

The Ministry's view is that intake practices should be guided by five principles (1986:20). These are *proximity, minimal intervention, integration, efficiency* and *motivation* (integration should be guided by 'what the teachers involved and the parents think is suitable for this particular child' (1986:20)). It also acknowledges that those involved may have different objectives and will be influenced by their attitudes and motives (p. 20). Thus the Ministry acknowledges the *struggle* between contestants over educational practices surrounding handicap. This limited reference to the politics of integration invites further research.

While students ordinarily have a right to, and must go to, school for nine years, those with severe handicap:

> have a special right to eleven years of schooling in the Danish primary and secondary school. The purpose of this provision is to give some of these students a greater chance of acquiring the qualifications necessary for passing the final examinations in the lower-secondary school, or, if this is not possible, to offer an instruction which may strengthen these students as much as possible in their transition to adult life (Ministry of Education, 1986:14).

In this context, the Ministry's written policy, with its emphasis on qualifications, cannot easily be subsumed by Tomlinson's argument that the extension of special education practices, in so far as they are non-credentialling, meets the needs of industrial societies for greater numbers of unemployed people (1985).

In a survey of *current practice*, the Ministry noted:

> great differences from one district to another concerning the number of children referred to special education (from five to thirty per cent of the total number of students), and also that the rich municipalities, as a rule, referred more children to special pedagogical assistance than the relatively poor municipalities (Ministry of Education 1986:21).

Disabling Policies?

Eighty per cent of the students who received special education assistance in 1981/82, did so for less than five hours a week: thus 'special education only made up a small proportion of their total education' (1986:21). This last statistic suggests that the official written policy on integration, as a process of avoiding segregation, is enacted in schools, despite considerable variations between schools and districts.

Summary

In sum, Danish educational policy practices surrounding handicap vary. They also occur within institutional conditions of some flexibility, in which local arenas and actors (municipal committees and school-related arenas and teachers) appear to be of considerable importance in decision making.

At government written level there seems a high degree of consensus on the desirability of integration, as a process of avoiding segregation, as a matter to be controlled by local authorities, and as a pedagogical rather than medical issue and one which requires flexible primary and secondary schools. These written statements suggest the politics of exclusion which begin with a discourse on disability, handicap and difference, appear to be well understood at government written level (see, for example, Ministry of Education, 1986; Jorgen Hansen, 1985; and Pedersen; A, a consultant to the Ministry).

There is also a concerted effort by the Ministry to research the bases of integration, and to publicize the results of this research. Government educational discourse on handicap and integration is part of a wider policy of social reform aimed at normalizing the situation of people hitherto called handicapped, and a discourse on normalization and pedagogy, rather than disability and difference, appears to find institutional bases both in wider social democratic discourse, with its theme of equality, and in the Ministry of Education, including its School Psychology Advisory Service.

At the local level, in county and municipal schools, practices vary. Schools and local districts vary in the proportion of students deemed to require special educational assistance and the Ministry's written policy of integration, as avoiding segregation, is not always school practice. An official reason for this is the decline in economic conditions, but the Ministry acknowledges that those involved may have competing objectives, thus that struggles surround integration in Denmark. Nevertheless, in so far as the majority (80 per cent of students receiving special education in 1981/82) receive pedagogical assistance for less than five hours a week, integration, as a process of avoiding segregation, appears to dominate segregating practices. The finding that rich municipalities make more use of special pedagogical assistance suggests some similarities with Milofsky's finding that, in North America, suburban schools in middle-class areas used special educational assistance more frequently and more often that did 'administratively disrupted' schools in poorer, inner suburban areas (chapter 4).

In general, the institutional conditions for integration, as a process of avoiding segregation, appear favourable in Denmark. The wider social democratic discourse on equality and the local control, deriving from legislative conditions, favour local democratic practice within a municipality. However, the inequalities between well resourced and poorly resourced municipalities, hinted at in the Ministry of Education's booklet (1986), suggest that there are inequities between schools, so that overall practices may not be democratic in the sense of equal changes regardless of which municipality a child happens to live in. There is an apparent *lack* of reliance on formal bureaucratic *procedures* as an attempt to direct local practices by central regulation. This contrasts strongly with the statementing procedures in Britain, with procedures instituted in the US following PL 94–142, and with the proliferation of political-bureaucratic-administrative practices in Victoria, following the 1984 integration report (chapters 4, 5 and 6). The Danish use of legislative conditions, as an attempt by government to *encourage* rather than *direct* local practices, also contrasts with the US and with Britain. The consultative process, which was deployed as a political process and which began some eleven years before even the first legislative reform, also contrasts with the expedient use of consulting constituencies in Victoria.[5]

Whilst most of this interpretation is based on a survey of official views, despite the limits inherent in this, there are certain aspects of Danish educational practices surrounding handicap which are worth noting and which appear to be *enacted* practice rather than rhetoric or merely written practice, and which contrast with practices in other countries.

The available statistics (Tables 3.1, 3.2 and 3.3) suggest that 13 per cent of students are assessed as requiring special pedagogical assistance, and additional evidence suggests that for 80 per cent this was for less than five hours a week. This suggests that integration, as a process of avoiding segregation, is occurring in Denmark. Second, there is an absence of professionalism as a discourse for controlling special education practices: thus issues are not presented as merely technical. On the contrary, the *political* nature of administrative practices is acknowledged: this is especially noteworthy in a reference to counselling services. This relates, thirdly, to a particular use of the political process. Local consultation preceded, by some years, legislative decisions. Fourth, the use of legislative decisions to encourage the spread of good practice contrasts with the use elsewhere of legislative decisions to *regulate* teachers, administrators and students. Fifth, the apparent absence of bureaucratization in connection with a 'national policy' of integration, is consistent with the equally apparent lack of professionalism as a discourse to control practices. This contrasts with bureaucratization in North America, Britain and Victoria (chapters 4, 5 and 6). This absence cannot be attributed to a relatively small population in Denmark, which is just over five million. In Victoria, with a population a little over four and a quarter million in 1988, educational practices are considerably bureaucratized. The lack of bureaucracy in Denmark is conducive to (a necessary condition for) democratic practice: this is discussed more fully in chapter 6. Sixth, the themes in the Ministry's written discourse are predominantly pedagogical rather than medical. Finally, this discourse in Denmark is reinforced by the Ministry establishing research programs on the bases of integration and by its disseminating the knowledge gained. This contrasts with the lack of such research in, for example, Victoria (chapter 6). These practices occur in legislative, political and political-administrative conditions which differ considerably from conditions in North America, Britain and Victoria.

Norway

In a recent, comprehensive review for UNESCO on educational practices surrounding handicap, on which this discussion draws extensively,[6] Vislie *et al.* note that Norway has a population of just over four million; less than half live in urban areas and natural features (a large country, 60 per cent of it above the timber line, much of it islands and deep fjords) are a major influence on economic and social life. More than 90 per cent of the population are members of the Norwegian Evangelical Lutheran Church which is State-maintained (Ministry of Church and Education, A:8) and the main portfolio on education is a combined Ministry of Church and Education (MCE). Vislie *et al.* claim that culturally and socially the people are and always have been fairly homogeneous (1987:2); however, there are two official languages: country Norwegian and a Norwegianized version of Danish and 'local education authorities decide by ballot, which language is to be used as the language of instruction at the schools concerned' (MCE 1987:9).

Economic conditions, in the view Vislie *et al*'s, are 'generally good', though currently somewhat difficult given the recent fall in oil prices (1987:2); others note that while 'Norway has become an oil producing country, budgets for public expenditure remain stagnant' (Kyvik, 1983:29). Education has risen on the political agenda since World War II. Expenditure on education in 1947 was 2.2 per cent of the gross national product and in 1979, 7.1 per cent (MCE, 1982:7). Unemployment is less than 1.3 per cent and the administrative and service sectors, both public and private, are providing an increasing proportion of the population with paid work. This suggests bureacracy is increasing, as does the figure that in a population of just over four million approximately 90,000 work in the education sector. This interpretation is reinforced by Haywood's noting that a key agency in the post-war reconstruction of the Norwegian educational apparatus, the National Centre for Innovation in Education (NCIE), was 'regarded as a bureaucratic organization of "desk-bound pedagogues" intent on doing things *to* teachers, rather than *for* or *with* teachers' (1986:192).

Where *political conditions* are concerned, Vislie *et al.* describe:

> Norwegian society [as] generally characterized by an egalitarian profile with an apparent lack of class distinction. There are historical reasons for this situation, but there are also some important political factors involved, which should be noticed here: During the economic expansion which has taken place in this century, the egalitarian profile has been kept up by a highly developed system of social security, combined with an extensive and highly selected use of economic transfers from the more prosperous sectors and geographic areas to the less prosperous ones. The *welfare state* has become a fairly generally accepted political objective (Vislie *et al.*, 1987:2).

But there is evidence, discussed below, that Norwegian society and the educational apparatus have been more divided and divisive than this. The emergence in the sixties of 'problems of the handicapped' shows that egalitarianism was far from present. As Vislie *et al.* note, 'When the problems of the handicapped in society came to the forefront in Norwegian politics, in the sixties, the fundamental problems were recognized as being largely the same, – that of diversities and divisions and the resulting injustice and conflicts about power' (1987:5). But according to Vislie and her colleagues, the politics of handicap in the sixties led to 'a breakthrough of public policy and responsibility in 1966–67' which 'replaced private charity and casual and very limited public provisions of support' (Vislie *et al.*, 1987:5). The aim of these reforms was to normalize the environment for those with handicap, an objective which has been 'repeated in later policy documents to Parliament' (Vislie *et al.*, 1987:5). These wider social objectives constitute part of the *legislative* and *political conditions* of educational practices surrounding handicap but it needs noting that these are written claims about written policy, and do not indicate or determine the nature of practices at other levels in the educational apparatus.

More recently, the election of a non-socialist government in Norway in 1981 has substantially altered the *political conditions* of educational practices (Haywood, 1986). 'Major educational policy decisions are increasingly being determined by fiscal considerations and budget technicians whose only reference points in education are to the "bottom-line" of the accountability sheet and to the contribution of education as a service agency to other national institutions' (Haywood, 1986:191). Again, the extent to which corporate themes have affected school practices cannot be deduced from such statements but Vislie's lack of comment on the change in political climate is surprising, given the frequent acknowledgment in official and academic statements of the close links between politics, meaning the party in power, and educational policy (MCE, A; Haywood, 1986; Vislie *et al.*, 1987).[7]

Educational practices and more specific conditions

The literature on educational practices in Norway contrasts with that on Denmark. Norwegian policy practices appear to be more complex, more overtly politically-related (see, for example, MCE, 1982:13; Vislie *et al.*, 1987) and more bureaucratic than those in Denmark. These claims are examined below in the context of a discussion of handicap and the compulsory years of schooling. The MCE is the central portfolio for education and the one relevant to compulsory education: children in Norway must attend school from the age of seven to sixteen.

As is common elsewhere, *legislative* and *political-administrative conditions* of educational policy practices in Norway are complex and intersect but the divisions between levels and sectors of education, and between portfolios[8] suggest a fairly high degree of both politicization and bureaucratization, despite the relatively small population of just over four million.

Since the Second World War, legislative and political conditions of educational policy have been influenced by the government's objective to reform the educational system. There 'was a conscious and positive attempt to define and to develop centrally a national philosophy, plan and policy for educational reform' (Haywood, 1986:187).[9] As part of this post-war reconstruction of education, a National Council for Innovation in Education (NCIE) was established by an Act of the National Assembly in 1954 (the Research and Development Act). This body was seen as central to establishing comprehensive schools for all and it is relevant here to discuss this objective since it underlies the postwar reform.

There are claims that comprehensive schools, with a common curriculum and without streaming practices, were established in the 1920s in Norway (Vislie *et al.*, 1987) but it seems clear that such schools were not widespread until the 1950s. Moreover, as noted above, such schools provide only the *potential* for integrating all students (Booth, 1982). Swedish experience is also relevant: a former Minister of Education, Birgit Rodhe, notes that ten years after the Swedish Parliament passed a bill on a nine year comprehensive school (the *grundskola*) and despite 'ten years of nationwide experiments . . .

the *grundskola* was still a school which had to be created' (1984:241–2).

Despite the struggle to establish comprehensive schools and despite the extensive segregation which characterized special educational practices in Norway from the early 1800s to at least the 1950s, there are claims that for the past century, and especially since the Second World War, educational practices in Norway have been organized around egalitarian themes of providing *equal educational opportunity for all* (Vislie *et al.*, 1987:3; MCE, 1982:13). The Ministry suggest 'the realisation of [these] principles has been a leading democratic issue for a series of governments'. However, inequalities in educational practices have clearly existed: for example, there are insufficient places available in post-compulsory schooling (MCE, A:6); upper secondary education was divided into types of schools, and students entered high schools as recently as 1978. An Act establishing in principle comprehensive secondary schools was not approved by the Storting until 1974 (an Act concerning the Upper Secondary School); it 'took effect' on 1 January 1976 (MCE, 1982:19). Moreover, as Booth notes, while '[i]n Norway integration is seen explicitly as an extension and development of the comprehensive school; and while mixed ability classes have been an official practice in these schools since the 1920s, *how* those mixed ability classes are taught matters. Booth noted differences *between* comprehensive schools:

> teachers in many schools in Norway still instruct their mixed ability groups, chalk in hand, from the blackboard without any concession to variations in pace or content of learning. Integration requires the creation of an opportunity for the handicapped to participate in ordinary schools but it also requires people to act on that opportunity. Integration in its broadest sense is about all children participating in their schools. We still have a long way to go before all comprehensive schools offer curricula which cater for the needs and interests of the vast majority of their pupils (1982:24).

Thus, despite themes of comprehensive schools and integration in wider educational discourse, Norwegian schools clearly vary in the extent to which teachers integrate their students.

Vislie *et al.* acknowledge the discrepancies between objectives of comprehensive schooling in Ministry written statements and legislative decisions, and school practices. She notes that ability groupings are now permitted legally, and that legislative conditions followed from experience which showed that the problems of inequality are complex, that 'a *school for all* has to accept inequality', and that a principle of *positive discrimination* should guide educational practices. Legislative decisions were made concerning compulsory and upper secondary education consistent with this experience. Thus since 1974/75, 'all children and young people have the right to an education in accordance with their own needs, interests and capabilities' (Vislie *et al.*, 1987:3). Schools may now group students but the Ministry reports 'not much use is made of such organizational differentiation . . . possibly . . . because it seems to conflict with egalitarian values stressed in Norwegian culture' (MCE, A:59). The theme of need in educational discourse applies to all school children and thus subsumes those who may, additionally, be called handicapped.

Levels and arenas in educational policy practices are depicted in Figure 3.3. While this suggests political-adminstrative practices are decentralized,

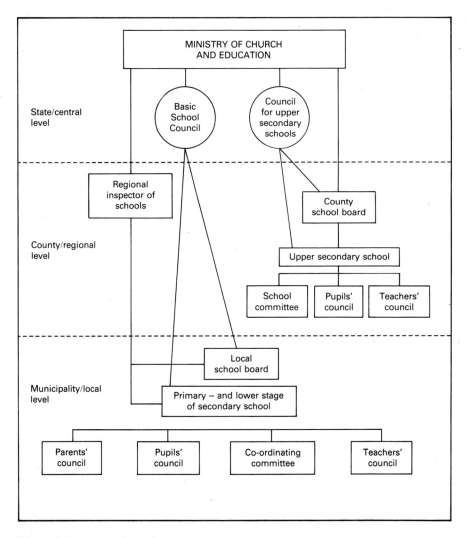

Figure 3.3: Norway: Educational administration on central, regional and local level Source: Vislie et al. 1987:39

it seems more appropriate, given the ambiguities of 'decentralization', to see the relations between levels as political, thus as struggle. There is evidence for this: for instance, Haywood's account of the recent demise of the NCIE, following the election of the non-socialist coalition government in 1981, attests to the struggle which occurred in various educational arenas concerning the NCIE, a struggle which included unions and issues surrounding curriculum objectives (1986:192). Similarly, Booth notes 'the dependence of a supposedly centralised and uniform education system on the goodwill of local teachers and administrators before integration was encouraged in local schools' 1982:21). Thus local decisions are not controlled by central legislative or political-administrative conditions: Norwegian schools make their own policy practices.

Prior to postwar objectives for education, educational practices on handicap had been characterized by exclusion of two sorts. Children called handicapped either had no education or were segregated in special schools. Figure 3.4 provides an overview of provision from the 1860s to 1951.

This shows that for about a century and a half children called handicapped were excluded from regular schools. There was 'a vast growth of segregated education for the handicapped . . . partly due to the fact that more children were considered educable' (Dahl *et al.*, 1982:75). Most of this expansion occurred in the State special system where, between 1962 and 1975, the costs of these schools rose by a factor of six, where the increase in number of pupils occurred early in this period and the number of employees in State special schools rose by 140 per cent. Thus 'relatively few pupils (2600 in 1975) were getting intensive special education and other treatment' (Dahl *et al.*, 1982:75). 'Outside this provision, the number of children in *social and medical institutions* rose from 3000 to 12,000 between 1956–7 and 1972–3' (Dahl *et al.*, 1982:75–6). In the *basic school* the number of students receiving special education almost doubled between 1962–3 and 1972–3, rising from 23,000 to 42,000. Thus the main development to 1975 was a *binary system* of special education with, on the one hand, relatively few children receiving intensive and expensive services in State special schools, and, on the other, a much larger number of pupils receiving much less intensive services in basic school (Dahl *et al.*, 1982:77).

Changes in the *legislative conditions* of education practices surrounding handicap began to occur in the context of the wider educational reform. An Act Concerning Special Education was passed in 1951. Its *legislative conditions* contrasted with the objectives for comprehensive schooling. They extended the designated categories of handicap to include 'pupils with auditory problems, learning difficulties, language problems and emotional behavioural problems' (Vislie *et al.*, 1987:7). Following the 1951 Act, the State gradually took over private institutions and established schools, 'at least

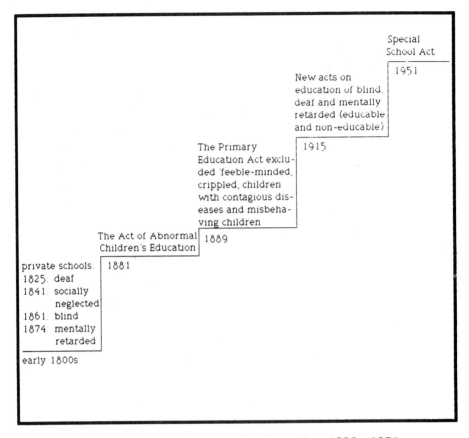

Figure 3.4: Norway: segregated educational provision, 1800s–1951
Adapted from Vislie et al. (1987:6)

one for each category of handicap' (Vislie *et al.*, 1987:8). The expansion of segregated provision in the fifties was seen as part of the post-war expansion of education in general (Vislie *et al.*, 1987:8). Increasing segregation clearly opposed the principles of a comprehensive educational policy which also informed the post-war reorganization of education. Thus, as the Ministry acknowledges, there has been a struggle in the Norwegian educational apparatus between those seeking integration and those whose objective was segregation.

While the 1951 Act gave responsibility to the State to provide special education services and local authorities were not required to provide special programs in regular schools, a number of schools began to establish special classes (Vislie *et al.*, 1987:8). Consequently

> In 1955 local school authorities were for the first time legally instructed to provide special education for pupils who could not

otherwise profit from teaching in ordinary schools. As a consequence a differentiated system of special classes and other more flexible arrangements for special education provisions grew up on a local basis (Vislie, 1987:8).

From 1955 then, either the State or local municipalities had *political-administrative* responsibility for providing special education. According to Vislie *et al.* this marked 'the beginning of a new policy in this field, the main impetus for which came from wider educational reform' (1987:8).

In 1963 a Special School Council was established and a new postgraduate teacher training programme for special education began in 1961 (Vislie *et al.*, 1987:7). Thus in the 1950s educational segregation had an institutional base in legislative conditions, in the sixties additional institutional bases appeared in a discourse of difference, in a separate teacher training course, and in separate pedagogy (see Vislie, 1987:8). Further, despite the normalizing intent of the 1975 amendment, at least two institutional bases for a discourse of difference remain: a separate teacher training course and thus a separate pedagogy. This implies, thirdly, that a discourse on difference for a population termed 'handicapped' remains and that the *politics of exclusion have secure institutional bases* in Norwegian educational practices.

Significant *legislative conditions* emerged in the 1969 Act concerning the Basic School. This established nine years of compulsory schooling for those aged 7 to 16 (it was previously 7 to 14) but did not revoke the 1951 Act Concerning Special Education. The 1951 Act required the State to provide 'special education' and the municipalities provided 'remedial reading'. Debate during the sixties suggested existing provision for special education was inadequate, and there were views that students who required special education should go to their local, regular schools.

> It then seemed natural to give the greatest possible responsibility to the authority responsible for basic education: the local municipalities (MCE, A:60). A commission was appointed and new legislative conditions, consisting of an amendment in June 1975 to the Act Concerning the Basic School, came into effect from 1 January 1976. This annulled the 1951 Act and emphasize[d] ... the responsibility of each municipality to ensure that all children are given a suitable education (MCE, A:61).

The 1975 legislative decisions thus changed the *political-administrative conditions* of special education practices, in so far as responsibility for the schooling of all children was removed from the central level of the State to the local level of the municipalities. Thus it was not until 1975 that legislative conditions of educational practices surrounding handicap became consistent with the objectives spelt out in the fifties for comprehensive schooling and with the 1969 Act's principle of decentralizing political–administrative conditions of social policy.

The 1975 amendment to the 1969 Act contains a number of competing discourses. It seeks to move from a discourse of difference: thus it does not distinguish 'normal' and 'special' students. But the amendment also states that special education must be provided 'whenever necessary' (MCE, 1982:4) and these programs are linked *not* to categories of handicap but to 'need': thus it reinstates a discourse of difference. And it distinguishes education (Section 7) and special education (Section 8). Section 3 requires local authorities to provide appropriate education for all children (Dahl *et al.*, 1982:30). The notion of appropriate education implies someone has the expertise to make such a judgement: as a theme it belongs to professionalism and is part of the strategy deployed in professionalism to control educational practices, both generally and those surrounding handicap or disability. That professionalism informs the amendment's statements is clear in that 'special education shall be offered to those who according to expert judgement need it' (MCE, A:61). The 1975 amendment also provides for:

> special social-pedagogical advisory bodies whose task it is to decide whether pupils need special education. They are also to help schoolchildren solve personal and social problems, advise them on their choice of subjects and future career, and act as contacts with parents and bodies outside the school (MCE, 1982:17).

Moreover, 'most of these duties are carried out by teachers – often specially trained for the purpose – whose teaching load is reduced. Staff specially qualified in psychology, medicine or social work are also associated with the advisory bodies' (Ministry of Church and Education, 1982:17). Thus the 1975 amendment creates *professionalized political-administrative conditions* of educational practices surrounding handicap.

The opposing discourses which characterize the 1975 amendment reveal the struggle between competing objectives. Underlying this struggle is the inconsistency between the discourses of normalizing and professionalism. That political struggles continued after the 1975 amendment, between for instance, the Storting and the Ministry, is clear in the account of Dahl *et al.* (1982:41f1). As they note, 'the law itself was broadly formulated and opened for different interpretations and development along different lines' (p. 41). While authoritative statements were made that a *gradual policy of integration* was to be adopted struggles ensued about the rate this implied.

Economic conditions also derive from the 1975 amendment. Schools are obliged to use 10 per cent of their total teaching resources for special education purposes (Dahl *et al.*, 1982:32). School staff decide which children should go into these programs, whether they need the help of the pedagogical-psychological services and what the programs will cover. 'In most cases . . . these programs are directed towards children with the least severe difficulties and learning problems' and schools are required to 'inform' parents and guardians in advance (Dahl *et al.*, 1982:33).

Other special education programs are funded through extra resources. For these programs, formal admission procedures are to occur, including assessment by the staff of the pedagogic-psychological service, written consent by the parents and 'application for extra resources for a local programme or for placement of the child in a special school or institution' (Dahl *et al.*, 1982:33).

The postwar reform has improved the level of resources in schools. Dahl *et al.* note that, correcting for inflation, the costs of schools increased by 95 per cent between 1969 and 1978 (1982:56). Though this covers higher wages for teachers who were more highly trained, they conclude that the level of resources has meant that the basic school is better prepared to integrate handicapped children (p. 56). However, State expenditure on schools has been reduced since 1978 and the 'commune economy' has lately become more difficult. But since the State no longer pays for special schools there is no economic advantage to communes in sending children to such schools (p. 57). State and commune expenditures on special education in the basic school between 1975 and 1981 are shown in Table 3.6.

This shows increases in resources for both 'integration' (items 1 and 2) and segregation (items 3, 4 and 5).

Extra special education funds, known as 'B'-funds, are available to communes, practices for obtaining these funds vary between counties but at least some depend on 'a professional evaluation of the child's needs and a formal administrative procedure, which means that the child is clearly defined as a "special" child' (Dahl *et al.*, 1982:63).

Despite the statements of Dahl *et al.* that the level of resources in basic schools now favours integration, it is clear from other statements that there is a resource struggle surrounding handicap (1982:63H). Teachers are reported as stating that if 'the provision of resources continues to lag behind the actual integration of pupils . . . [they] anticipated a situation in which they could no longer take responsibility for the education of "integrated" pupils' (p. 68). Thus despite themes in wider educational discourse of comprehensive schools and integration, as well as wider political themes concerning equality, it is clear, as Dahl *et al.* note, that teachers and local school authorities have not fully accepted responsibility for integrating students called handicapped into their schools.

The connections between professionalism and resource arguments and economic conditions emerge in the following extract Dahl *et al.* cite:

Disabling Policies?

Table 3.6 Expenditures on special education in the basic school in the years
1975, 1977, 1979, 1981

	1975	1977	1979	(N kr 1000) 1981
A. State expenditures				
1. Special education within the teaching hour resources allocated to the ordinary schools	106,396	143,358	167,790	192,054
2. Integration efforts ('B-funds)*	27,478	59,583	107,500	149,529
3. Social and medical institutions*	41,327	84,000	99,200	99,899
4. Special schools/classes run by the communes*	18,516	74,585	95,400	98,536
5. State special schools	121,424	122,897	150,200	171,438
6. Efforts at the pre-school level*	–	12,244	28,400	31,703
Total State expenditures	315,141	496,667	647,490	743,159
B. Commune/county expenditures	83,804	166,910	256,263	280,000
Total expenditures for special education	398,945	663,577	903,753	1,023,159

*Figures for 1981 are estimates.
Source: Dahl *et al.* 1982:58

Finally, the gradual building up of extensive resources in terms of teachers qualified in special education, other experts specializing in dealing with such problems, and institutions prepared to cater for children with special problems, lead to an increased tendency to define children as being in need of such services. This is specifically the case in a system which, like the Norwegian, largely puts the responsibility for needs assessment on institutions and individuals at the local level, while the resulting additional expenditures are charged to central government funds. In all likelihood, the Norwegian system of special education facilities has a built in tendency for expansion, irrespective of the object situation of its clients (cited by Dahl *et al.*, 1982:64).

Teachers are paid according to qualification and Dahl *et al.* estimate that more than half of teachers have higher qualifications which may include additional training in special education (p. 65) and 'that Norway has given *high priority to the training of special teachers* . . . much more than [to] curriculum guidelines, teaching materials and accessibility to school buildings' (p. 67). *There thus appears to be a well established institutional base in Norwegian teachers' training colleges for a divisive discourse on a pedagogy based on 'difference'.*

Central decisions bureaucratize local *political-administrative conditions*. The Ministry appoints a director of schools in each region whose duties are advisory and supervisory. The local council, which is popularly elected and is 'the supreme authority in local administration', appoints a school board with between seven and thirty-five members who include representatives of the political parties proportional to the parties' representation on local council.

The exercise of bureaucratic decision-making at local levels is also revealed in Booth's observation:

> The Norwegians, as much as ourselves, are beset by bureaucratic absurdities over money. In their special schools an average of more than one teacher is allocated to a teaching group of four pupils. But it is often impossible to release the money spent on education in a special school to assist the integration of the same pupils in an ordinary school. A child in a special school receives funding whilst s/he continues to attend schools but the applications for funding have to be justified each year for the same pupil in an ordinary school (1982:24).

Unfortunately, Booth does not say who, or what level, is responsible for such decisions. But given that responsibility for economic decisions for educational practices in general lies at local level, it seems plausible that it is in local arenas that decisions are made not to shift resources from special to regular schools. The key point is that decisions *in* educational apparatuses to maintain funding segregated practices are independent of wider political economic conditions such as an international economic recession which has been said to occur in the eighties. The relevance of this point for a critique of Marxist theorizing which suggests educational practices and equality and democracy (and thus integration) depend on global capitalism, is discussed more fully in chapter 6. In the model outlined in the Introduction, *who* makes such decisions is politically and theoretically crucial. As Booth also points out, educational programs surrounding handicap are seen as competing with other educational practices for scarce resources. But this is, in part, to adopt a resource argument that integration requires extra resources. However, this is a significant discourse on integration in Norway, the US, Britain (Booth, 1982:24) and Victoria (chapter 6).

In sum, Norwegian educational practices have been characterized by a struggle between integration and segregation, a struggle which is wider than practices surrounding handicap. It is relevant then to ask: Does integration, in the sense of avoiding segregation, characterize *current practices* surrounding handicap? There are claims that integration is well advanced in Norway. Vislie *et al.* note, 'integration is and has for a long time been a vital issue in education politics in this country' (1987:4) and a 1984 OECD review of Norwegian educational policies noted that integration policy has been 'implemented' in many areas of Norwegian education (cited by Vislie *et al.*). But we need to look more closely at the conditions of these policy practices and at the evidence from research.

Political conditions of educational practices have changed recently (Haywood, 1986; Dahl *et al.*, 1982). There are views that 'the new Government may be interested in slowing down the process of integration' (Dahl *et al.*, 1982:44). *Legislative conditions* in Norway promote an objective of integration: the 1969 Act Concerning the Basic School, the 1975 amendment revoking the 1951 Act Concerning Special Education, the Upper Secondary Act, 1974, The Kindergarten Act, 1975, and the Adult Education Act, 1976, were based on principles of comprehensive schooling and education (Vislie *et al.*, 1987:12), yet we have already noted struggles in the 1975 amendments: for example, between a discourse of difference, professionalism and 'need' and a discourse which seeks to dissolve distinctions between those called handicapped and those not. Further, while the 1975 Act stresses that as many children as possible should be 'educationally provided for at the local school or as near home as possible', it is also the case that 'special education schools will continue to exist as an offer to pupils whose especially great needs cannot be met by the local school'. This statement indicates the *struggle* between integration and segregation which, as the Ministry notes, are the two competing processes underlying the development of the comprehensive school in Norway (1982:13). *Political-administrative conditions* reveal some bureaucratization and a discourse of professionalism characterizes practices surrounding handicap.

Schools differ on a range of educational practices: in their content and activities, forms of organization and number of teaching periods stipulated (Vislie *et al.*, 1987:17). Clearly, *schools, comprehensive schools included, make their own policy practices* within the non–determining limits of legislative conditions and political-administrative conditions. In this context, schools will vary in the extent to which they integrate students. Teachers teach mixed ability groups differently: some well and some not, as Booth noted. Since special educational practices are flexible, there are difficulties in gathering precise data but Vislie *et al.* suggest that 'About twelve per cent of the compulsory school population receive some kind of special education/support' and that for the great majority this support occurs as *'pupils in ordinary classes'*. The extent of special education provided outside the ordinary school classes in 1981/82 and in 1984/85 is shown in Table 3.7. This suggests that the

Table 3.7   Norway: special education at the compulsory stage by different types of organizational arrangements 1981/82 and 1984/85

| | 1981/82 | | 1984/85 | |
	N	%	N	%
Population aged 7–15 in compulsory education	578,413	100.00	547,936	100.00
In special schools/classes	3,199	0.57	2,610	0.47
In social & med. inst.	2,041	0.40	1,006	0.18
Educated outside the ordinary school classes	5,230	0.97	3,616	0.66

Source: Vislie et al. (1987:19)

'percentage of all children aged 7–15 who [were] educated in special schools/classes or in social and medical institutions was less than one per cent . . .' in 1981/82; in 1984/85 this percentage was 0.66 per cent.

From these figures on compulsory schooling, integration in the sense of avoiding a process of segregation outside regular classrooms, appears to be occurring. This is reinforced by Vislie *et al.* who note that the State still provides 'a few central schools and institutions for handicapped pupils', that few pupils are enrolled and the numbers are declining, that future plans are to keep a few of these schools only for 'sensoric-motor disabilities' and that the remainder 'will probably become resource-centres for the local/regional schools' (1987:20). But what appears to be missing from Norwegian practices, in contrast to Denmark, if the literature is an adequate guide, is an emphasis on pedagogy and that all children are firstly pupils. Dahl *et al.* note that there has been a focus on special teacher training (thus a divisive pedagogy and professionalism?) rather than curriculum.

In upper secondary education, special educational practices have expanded in the last decaade (Vislie *et al.*, 1987:32). Table 3.8 shows that in 1978, 35 per cent of students receiving special education did so in special classes and groups, while 65 per cent received individual assistance in ordinary

Table 3.8   Norway: Special education in upper secondary education by different types of organizational arrangements (1978–1982)

	Total	No. of students in spec. classes/groups		Extra support to stud. in ord. classes	
1978	4,330	1,479	35%	2,815	65%
1979	4,306	1,573	33%	3,233	67%
1980	4,400	1,743	40%	3,222	60%
1981	4,412	1,848	42%	2,654	58%
1982	4,648	2,047	45%	2,551	55%

Source: Vislie et al. (1987:32)

classes. In 1982, these proportions were 45 per cent and 55 per cent respectively: this suggests that within the proportion of students receiving additional assistance a *process of segregation* rather than integration has occurred in upper secondary education in Norway in the five years from 1978 to 1982. But this statistic is problematic, given the absence of adequate data overall on any increase or decrease in the proportion enrolled by special education (see Vislie *et al.*, 1987:33 for problems in gathering statistics here) in upper secondary education and the number of students enrolled in special and ordinary classes. Vislie *et al.* discuss aspects of this and suggest that possibly half of those students admitted to upper secondary education through:

> special entrance arrangements are enrolled in special classes, half in regular classes and that overall these students constitute five per cent of the total enrolment in upper secondary education. Given the recent changes in post-compulsory education in Norway, including changing quotas for special entrance it is clearly difficult to obtain an overall statistical picture (Vislie *et al.*, 1987:33).

Other conditions of current practices concern the power relationship between parents and professionals. The account of Vislie *et al.* of the procedures for obtaining extra assistance for a child suggests that professionals from the Pedagogical Psychological Service, and teachers, make this assessment, that parents are not necessarily members of these arenas but that they have the 'right' to say no to a recommendation that their child be transferred to a special school. Their written permission is to be obtained before a child is transferred out of regular schools. Given the lack of available research findings on these processes, it cannot be assumed that these practices avoid the control processes reported elsewhere: for example, in California by Mehan, in Britain by Tomlinson and in Victoria by Fulcher. However, Booth comments that 'I was struck by the way families of handicapped children have made their presence and wishes felt. If the family of a handicapped child insist that she/he is educated in their local school the administration can do little to stop them and has to arrange for the appropriate support' (1982:25). However, these rights are not always realized, as one father's comments illustrate: 'We would like to see them given the right to schooling in their community, the right to three years of post-compulsory schooling, the right to work training, the right to *real* work and the right to live independently from their families' (cited by Booth, 1982:225). Parent 'rights' are thus struggled over in the Norwegian educational apparatus.

Particular problems surround integration in Norway in remote districts. As Vislie *et al.* note, very small schools are unlikely to be able to arrange for extra assistance on a regular basis and where a child requires a range of additional services on a daily basis and where these are, as is frequently the case, 'nowhere up to a sufficient or acceptable level', parents may decide against their child attending a regular school (p. 47). These comments suggest a complex range of factors may be relevant to decisions about some children: this undermines any single connection, in the case of Norway, between, say, professionalism and the degree of integration, a link which might justifiably be made where these factors are less relevant and the overall organization of educational practices surrounding handicap are more clearcut. Moreover, it reinforces the claim of Vislie *et al.* that geographical features influence educational and social policy practices.

Nevertheless, some statistics suggest clear connections between certain factors and integration or segregation. Local school authorities in *more urbanized areas* segregate more frequently than those in rural areas: in 1979, in Oslo, 1.8 per cent of the school population were educated outside regular schools (in special schools, medical and social institutions) compared with 1.06 per cent for the country as a whole. Similarly, 'the figures on special classes were relatively much higher for Oslo than for the country as a whole' (Vislie *et al.*, 1987:49). But Vislie *et al.* suggest local school authorities in rural areas make *less* use of segregated facilities than opportunity offers (p. 49).

In considering factors which promote integration, Vislie *et al.* note a study in 1981 by the Council for Compulsory Education which shows that *co-teaching*, meaning cooperation between a regular teacher and a special teacher 'seems to have been gaining ground over the past few years' (p. 51). They suggest that 'flexibility and continuity in roles and functions between teachers and special education teachers are probably a prerequisite to integration' and note that a study by Dalen in 1982 suggested that teachers, classroom observers and students in general, particularly the 'more able' 'seem to react positively to the co-teaching lessons' (p. 52). Schools mostly, and at least initially, place students with special needs in regular classrooms and spend 83 per cent of special education resources, according to the Council for Compulsory Education study in 1981, on teaching the two core subjects of Norwegian and mathematics (p. 54). At upper secondary level there is a 'general lack of appropriate teaching materials/aids for special education' (p. 58).

Summary

In Norway education practices surrounding handicap are diverse. This derives from factors such as remoteness, urban–rural differences, as well as the variation we might expect if we adopt a model of policy practice made at all levels (Introduction). It also derives from an uneven development of comprehensive schools, different teaching practices within comprehensive schools, and despite a widespread discourse on comprehensive schools for everyone, a *struggle* between objectives to integrate or segregate which has historically and currently characterizes the Norwegian educational apparatus. It seems educational practices surrounding handicap are more bureaucratized and professionalized than in Denmark. Statements at government level reveal struggles between a discourse on difference and 'need' and professionalism, and a discourse on equality. Government written policy lacks a pedagogical model of integration which, in contrast, informs government-level written policy in Denmark. In the eighties, Ministry-funded school-oriented research has been substantially reduced (Dahl *et al.*, 1982:69).

Statistics for Norway, however, suggest that, at least in compulsory schooling, integration in the sense of avoiding segregation may be occurring: most students who receive additional pedagogical assistance do so for a small proportion of their week in school and this is typically in the regular classrooms; but, at best, these figures indicate only *locational* integration. Moreover, these statistics do not sit easily with Booth's comments that in some comprehensive schools styles of teaching in mixed ability classrooms in Norway did not work towards integrating students; nor with the lack of a pedagogical discourse in government written policy, an omission Dahl *et al.* note in commenting on the absence of a focus on curriculum development. As noted in chapter 2, curriculum is at the centre of meaningful integration practice.

Conclusions

There are claims that in Scandinavia the integration of pupils with handicaps is relatively advanced and that this derives from 'a political consensus . . . that a segregated school and educational system does not fit the type of society' the 'equality-oriented Scandinavian welfare societies' are working towards (Andersen and Holstein, 1981:482–3). Similarly, there are claims that the development of comprehensive schools has been central to the progress of integration. While it is clear that a social democratic discourse on equality has influenced welfare provision in the Scandinavian countries to expenditure levels higher than elsewhere (Castles and McKinlay, 1979), and while a discourse on *comprehensive schooling* is more dominant than it has been in Britain (a discourse which is notable for its absence in North America and Victoria), these generalizations about Scandinavian integration and about the effects of comprehensive schooling objectives need qualifying.

First, the Scandinavian countries are not as homogeneous, socially and economically, as these statements imply (Plunkett, 1982:45). There have been differences between these countries, in their social policy development and in the political conditions in which this has occurred. Denmark has been ahead on a number of indicators: union membership was substantially organized in Denmark by 1905, ahead of Sweden (and the UK) and Norway, where it was not until 1908 that 30 per cent of workers became organized (Therborn *et al.*, 1978:43). Free compulsory primary education was legislated in 1814 in Denmark, and not until 1842 in Sweden (1870 in Britain), although real moves towards making primary education widely available did not occur until 1903 in Denmark, 1920 in Norway and 1928 in Sweden (Therborn *et al.*, 1978:45). Denmark and Norway were among the first countries to pass social security laws and 'by the beginning of the social democratic period in 1932 Sweden was still lagging behind Denmark ... [but] ahead of Norway' (Therborn *et al.*, 1978:47). Where social service expenditure as a percentage of GNP is concerned, Denmark has been consistently ahead of Norway on the data Therborn *et al.* produce for the years 1949 to 1970, but not on other measures such as the coverage of the population by these measures nor on an egalitarian distribution of income (1978:48–57). However, Therborn *et al.* note the severe limitations of their overview (1978:53). A further indicator lies in Denmark's and Sweden's approaches to policies to reduce the risk young, unqualified people have of being unemployed: in this context, Swedish and Danish reform of their educational system has been in advance of other Western European societies but 'there is clearly a much more urgent and comprehensive concern in the Danish case' (Plunkett, 1982:45). Historically and currently, then, Denmark has been ahead of Norway (and of Sweden) on a range of indicators of social democratic policy.

Secondly, while both countries have elected coalition conservative governments in the eighties, 'conservative' it should be noted which is less right-wing than its counterparts in other Western countries, the Danish government appears not to have moved against comprehensive schooling in the way that the government in Norway has, through its closure of the National Council for Innovation in Education, a body which was seen as central to the postwar reorganization of Norwegian education and to the objective of comprehensive schooling. Haywood notes that the NCIE was seen as part 'of the centralized process of educational reform' (1986:185) and its closure as an end 'to monocratic centralized development' (p. 188). Given that, in Norway, as in the other Scandinavian countries, educational reform is 'part of a larger policy for the transformation of society as a whole' (p. 185), the closure of the NCIE by the non-socialist government poses questions about the extent to which a theme of equal educational opportunity currently informs the Norwegian National Assembly's objectives for and via education.

Haywood's view is that the 'production-ideology' of the Norwegian non-socialist government means that 'major educational policy' decisions are increasingly being determined by fiscal considerations and budget technicians whose only reference points in education are to the 'bottom line' of the accountability sheet and to the contribution of education as a service agency to other national institutions (1986:191). Overall, Haywood's view is that the closure of the NCIE exhibits conditions of 'strong central resolve' in the Norwegian educational apparatus in the eighties. Moreover, the NCIE was seen as central to the development of comprehensive schooling and education generally. Both the wider political conditions surrounding the closure of the NCIE, and the effect of its closure in the educational apparatus, constitute *changed political-economic conditions* of educational practices in Norway. There appears to have been a shift from a concern with comprehensive schooling and therefore from integration.

Thirdly, and quite apart from the fact that comprehensive schools are unevenly developed in both countries, as Booth notes, a school organized along comprehensive ideals merely provides the *potential* for integrated classroom practices rather than their realization (1982); moreover, as a former Swedish Minister of Education stated recently, there is much still to be learned about a comprehensive pedagogy (1984). Thus, as noted above, comprehensive schooling as a theme in educational discourse, does not of itself tell teachers how to integrate their students. *Integrating classroom practices* are a practical project for teachers: they do not follow merely from the use of terms such as 'comprehensive schooling'. Part of the mystification which attaches to such themes in national written policies is to generalize such statements to classroom and pedagogical activities as though they had an unequivocal meaning or clear implications for how to teach. The evidence for comparing Danish and Norwegian classroom practices is slight. Booth has noted the differences between teachers in Norwegian 'comprehensive' schools and we would expect such differences to characterize Danish teaching practices. However, Danish official literature presents integration as primarily a pedagogical issue and students, whether called handicapped or not, as first and foremost pupils.

Fourth, in both countries, schools vary in how far teachers' practices encourage integration, and schools vary in the number they ask for special assistance for and in the number they refer to segregated settings. Statistics on the progress of integration are similar for both countries, suggesting that a process of integration is occurring in both. But there are a number of other indicators which suggest integration in Denmark is more advanced that in Norway. Danish practices appear to be less bureaucratized and less politicized. These are significant absences: their presence in other educational apparatuses is discussed more fully in chapters 4, 5 and 6.

Fifth, in Denmark, a pedagogic discourse informs Ministry written policy and the Ministry funds research into pedagogic issues surrounding integration and actively disseminates this information. This contrasts with the apparent absence of such a discourse and such research in Norway. Given the pedagogical themes in the Danish Ministry of Education's written policy and its enacted practice of funding research into the pedagogical bases of integration, it seems reasonable to suggest that classroom practices on meaningful integration in Denmark are generally ahead of those in Norway.

Finally, this chapter is tied to available literature and the comparisons between Denmark and Norway should be treated with some caution.

Notes

1 For reasons of length, Sweden is not discussed.
2 Handicap, rather than disability, is the term used in Scandinavia. While there is an extensive debate on what these terms really mean, what matters is the *discourse* within which these terms appear. Thus, for example, 'integration' has no unequivocal meaning. What matters in integration discourse are the objectives surrounding the use of the term.
3 Verbal information from a spokesperson for the Royal Danish Consulate (8 February 1988).
4 But see, for example, Haywood (1986) on the complexities and implications of 'decentralization' and Lane and Murray (1985) on its ambiguities. In Victoria, statements about decentralization may be made when other practices denote increasing central control.
5 This is based on the author's experience as main policy analyst/researcher for the Victorian Ministerial Review of Educational Services for the Disabled.
6 The sources for Vislie *et al.*'s review include public documents, White Papers, recommendations, reports, most of which are not in English, and Dahl, M., Tangerud, H. and Vislie, L. *Integration of Handicapped Pupils in Compulsory Education in Norway,* 1982 (Universitetsforlaget, Oslo) and Vislie, L. *Handicapped Students in Upper Secondary Education in Norway* (under preparation for the Ministry of Education/OECD).
7 The present author uses politics in a wider sense: see the Introduction.
8 The MCE 'exerts government authority as far as compulsory, post-compulsory and adult education is concerned (the Ministry of Consumer Affairs as far as pre-school education is concerned, and the Ministry of Cultural and Scientific Affairs as far as higher education is concerned)' (Vislie *et al.*, 1987:36).
9 While Haywood's discussion is useful, it is also confusing and potentially confused: this appears to derive from Haywood's lack of a conceptual framework concerning levels and arenas of decision-making and by his failure to define bureaucracy.

References

General
Andersen, S.E., and Holstein, B.E. (1981) 'Integration of blind children into schools in Denmark', *Prospects,* XI, 4, pp. 482–9.

Disabling Policies?

Castles, F.G., and McKinlay, R.D. (1979) 'Public Welfare Provision, Scandinavia, and the Sheer Futility of the Sociological Approach to Politics', *British Journal of Political Science,* 9, pp. 157–71.

Lane, J., and Murray, M. (1985) 'The Significance of Decentralization in Swedish Education', *European Journal of Education,* 20, 2–3, pp. 163–70.

Plunkett, D. (1982) 'The Risk Group: education and training policies for disadvantaged young people in Sweden and Denmark', *Comparative Education,* 18, 1, pp. 39–46.

Rodhe, B. (1984) 'Development and Research – Foundations for Policy-making in Education: Some Personal Experiences', in Husen, T. and Kogan, M. (Eds) *Educational research and policy: how do they relate?,* Oxford, Pergamon Press.

Therborn, G., Kjellberg, A., Marklund, S., and Ohlund, U. (1978) 'Sweden Before and After Social Democracy: A First Overview', *Acta Sociologica,*pp. 37–58.

Denmark

Booth, T. (1982) 'Working Towards Integration', *Where,* No. 178, pp. 21–5.

Hansen, J. (1982) 'Educational Integration of Handicapped Children', *Child Health,* 1, pp. 156–61.

Hansen, J. (1984) 'Handicap and Education: the Danish Experience', an Elwyn Morey memorial lecture, Monash University, Melbourne, Australia.

Hansen, O. (1981) *A Research Prospect in the Municipal School: Integration of Mentally Retarded,* School Psychology Advisory Service, Hinnerup.

Hansen, O. (no date:A) 'The Knowledge Seeking Pupil: A model to trade describe "Special Instruction"', School Psychology Advisory Service, Hinnerup, typescript.

Hansen, O. (no date:B) 'A model of Guidance – Declaration of Special Education', School Psychology Advisory Service, Hinnerup, typescript.

Hindess, B. (1986) 'Actors and Social Relations' in Wardell, M.L. and Turner, S.P. (Eds) *Sociological Theory in Transition,* Boston, Allen and Unwin, pp. 113–26.

Mehan, H. (1984) 'Institutional decision-making', in Rogoff, B. and Lave, J. (Eds) *Everyday Cognition: Its Development in Social Context,* Cambridge, Massachusetts, Harvard University Press.

Ministry of Education (no date) *Education in Denmark: Educational Normalization for Handicapped Persons 1st January 1980,* Special Education Section, Copenhagen.

Ministry of Education (1986) *Handicapped Students in the Danish Educational System,* A survey prepared for the IX international school psychology colloquium, Copenhagen, Ministry of Education, Special Education Section, August.

Pedersen, E.M. (no date:A) 'Integration of Retarded Children in Theory and Practice', typescript.

Pedersen, E. (post 1982:B) 'Some statistics on special education', typescript (Consultant to the Ministry of Education).

Tomlinson, S. (1985) 'The expansion of Special Education', *Oxford Review of Education,* 11, 2, pp. 157–65.

Norway

Booth, T. (1982) 'Working Towards Integration', *Where,* No. 178, pp. 21–5.

Dahl, M., Tangerud, H., and Vislie, L. (1982) *Integration of Handicapped Pupils in Compulsory Education in Norway,* Position Paper to OECD/CERI, Universitetsforlaget, Oslo.

Haywood, R. (1986) 'The life and death of two national agencies: implications for curriculum support strategies', *Journal Curriculum Studies,* 18, 2, pp. 185–96.

98

Kyvik, S. (1983) 'Decentralization of Higher Education and Research in Norway', *Comparative Education*, 19, 1, pp. 21–9.

Ministry of Church and Education (no date:A) *Innovation in Education: The National Council for Innovation in Education – Its Structure and Work,* Oslo.

Ministry of Church and Education (1982) *Education in Norway,* Oslo.

Vislie, L., Kierulf, C.B., and Pukstad, P. (1987) *Review of the Current Status: Case Study: Norway,* made for UNESCO by The Institute of Educational Research of Oslo, typescript, June.

Chapter 4

Californian policy practices

Conditions of policy practices concerning minority groups in the United States vary significantly from those surrounding similar policies in Britain or Australia. The American constitution empowers the federal legislature to pass laws which aim to protect the rights of minority groups; a tradition has evolved of using both law and litigation (court procedures) to pursue these rights; politically, the self-conscious democratism of American political discourse contains an 'ethic of participatory democracy and self help [which] . . . facilitates the activities of consumer groups and other grass roots organizations' (May and Hughes, 1987:215). Historically, the civil rights movements of the 60s helped construct a political culture which transformed debate on minority groups to a focus on rights rather than need, and thus on the organization of services and social responses rather than an individual's alleged characteristics (May and Hughes, 1987). However, the notion of needy (Stone, 1984) is a significant sub-theme in welfare provision, while the coexistence of these opposing themes attests to the struggle between them as competing strategies. Moreover, professionalism, as discourse and tactic in defining need, is readily available in some arenas, including schools.

Despite these struggles, the civil rights movement has encouraged minority groups, including those with 'handicaps' or 'disabilities', to pursue their 'rights'. Debate on minority groups, including those called handicapped, has thus become overtly political, in at least some arenas, such as the courts. These general conditions are part of the wider conditions of struggles in the United States to reform educational policy on disability or handicap, an objective Hargrove *et al.* suggest dates back to at least the 1950s (1983:1).

In the struggles surrounding this objective, education and judicial apparatuses in a variety of North American States have been politically significant arenas. This includes the State of California which Forness suggests provides 'a unique opportunity to study public policy in special education' (1985:56). California's educational practices are relatively well researched, as are related policies (see, for example, Milofsky, 1974, 1976, 1986; Shapiro,

1980; Mehan *et al.*, 1981; Mehan, 1983, 1984; Forness, 1985; Cicourel and Mehan, 1985; Mehan *et al.*, 1985; Ferguson, 1985; Benveniste, 1986; Cummins, 1986; Jensen and Griffin, 1986; Swidler, 1986; May and Hughes, 1987; Guthrie and Koppich, 1987).

In this chapter, within the limits of the available literature, I shall therefore focus on practices in California in attempting to assess how federal legislation, the 1975 Education for All Handicapped Children Act (PL 94–142), relates to school practices surrounding handicap and to practices at other levels in the educational apparatuses. This focus is pragmatic and the discussion includes practices elsewhere: notwithstanding Forness's view, other States have played a significant part in struggles to reform schooling practices for those called handicapped. Some key legal decisions have been brought down in other States but California is interesting: the number of children receiving special education is high and lawsuits in California have been amongst those which have created nationally significant legal decisions and influenced reform.

In 1985, there were 356,000 children receiving special education in California; this was a third more than any other State. This number represented 9 per cent of the entire special education school population in the United States and 8 or 9 per cent of the Californian public school enrolment, which was slightly below the national average of 10.5 per cent (Forness, 1985:36–7). Where lawsuits are concerned, Forness provides a brief historical overview:

> Special classes for the mentally retarded were mandated in California in the late 1940s and continued as the primary placement for mentally retarded school children until the early 1970s. At this time, burgeoning evidence on efficacy of special classes (Klaufman and Alberto, 1976) and a number of class action lawsuits against various California school districts (*Arreola*, 1968; *Covarrubias*, 1971; *Diana*, 1970; *Larry, P.*, 1972) led to major changes in policy on segregated special classes. A major study in the Riverside (California) public schools on mislabeling of minority students in EMR classes (Mercer and Lewis, 1973) also led to policy changes. The net effect was a change in California law that resulted in (a) massive retesting of EMR students, (b) eventual decertification of an estimated 18,000 children in EMR classes, and (c) a limited two-year provision for transition assistance for these students upon their return to regular classrooms (Macmillan, 1972; Yoshida, Macmillan, and Meyers, 1976). (1985:37)

The Californian educational apparatus has thus been a central arena in struggles to reform special education practices in the United States. Its State-level written policy consists of three documents: these are the Californian

Master Plan for Special Education (Californian State Department of Education 1974), which preceded the enactment of the 1975 PL 94–142, and two principal enactments of the Californian Code: Senate Bill No. 1870 (effective 12 July 1980) and Senate Bill No. 760 (effective 30 September 1981). In addition, a 1982 amendment (Title 5, Education, effective 7 July 1982) is also relevant. Forness suggests the first three documents are 'considered the major enactment provisions of Public Law 94–142 at the state level' in California (1985:37). But this view derives from a top-down model of government policy being translated into 'practice' and it contrasts with the model in the Introduction: more accurately, and as the evidence below confirms, these documents are State-level written policy practice and thus only one level and one type of policy practice concerning 'handicap' in the Californian educational apparatus.

Background to The Education for All Handicapped Children Act, 1975 (Public Law 94–142)

The struggle to reform educational policy on handicap was a struggle to remove the inequities of special education provision. The inequities lay 'in a tradition of exclusionary practices in public schools, second-class citizenship, stigmatization through labelling and inadequate funding' (Chambers and Hartman, 1983:3). Some of these practices were referred to in PL 94–142's statements of findings:

(1) there are more than eight million handicapped children in the United States today

(2) the special educational needs of such children are not being fully met

(3) more than half of the handicapped children in the United States do not receive appropriate educational services which would enable them to have full equality of opportunity

(4) one million of the handicapped children in the United States are excluded entirely from the public school system and will not go through the educational process with their peers

(5) there are many handicapped children throughout the United States participating in regular school programs whose handicaps prevent them from having a successful educational experience because their handicaps are undetected (20 USC 1401 note).

Other studies had revealed that minority group children were over-represented in special education classes: according to Shapiro, California State Department of Education figures showed Spanish surnamed children comprised 13 per cent of the total school population but 26 per cent of those in classes for the 'educable retarded' (1980:212). Equality of access to public educational institutions, culturally and linguistically unbiased testing and avoiding labelling children were thus all key issues in the struggle to reform educational practices surrounding 'handicap'.

Key policy actors or advocates of this reform deliberately used litigation (Tweedie, 1983) to emphasize these inequities and to assert the notion of rights to equal educational opportunity, despite the fact which Kirp and Jensen note, that this notion had not always been part of 'educators' lexicon' (1986:36) or discourse. This strategy of litigation created an institutional base in the courts and judiciary for deploying a discourse on rights of education. The court cases included *Brown* vs the *Board of Education* 1954 (347 vs 483), *Hobson* vs *Hansen* 1967 in Columbia (348F. Supp. 886, D.D.C. 1972), *Larry P.* 1972 in California, *Pennsylvania Association for Retarded Children* vs *Pennsylvania* 1972 (343F. Supp. 279), *Mills* vs *Board of Education* (348F. Supp. 866, D.D.C. 1972). The legislative decisions made in these lawsuits provided precedents and strategies for legislative reform at a federal level.

The 1954 decision of the Supreme Court in *Brown* vs the *Board of Education* provided some of the legal justification for PL 94–142. As Hargrove *et al.* note:

> The issue in *Brown* – the ending of racial segregation through integration of schools and classrooms – is a cornerstone decision in the education for the handicapped although it may at first appear only tangentially related. Both the legal questions upon which *Brown* was decided and the policy developments that came from it laid foundation for the judicial role in special education reform. It established the applicability of constitutional protections to public education, bringing educational issues within the realm of civil rights. In addition, it legitimized subsequent antidiscrimination legislation, and provided an entry for the federal government into education policy. Finally, the plaintiffs' argument in *Brown* relied on both the stigma and detrimental educational consequences of segregation. These precedents established by the *Brown* decison were successfully applied by advocates for the handicapped in later cases (Hargrove *et al.*, 1983:5).

In *Hobson* vs *Hansen*, Judge Wright's decision regarding tracking (streaming) in the District of Columbia schools 'confirmed a lower court decision that abolished tracks because they discriminated against racially and/or economically disadvantaged students' (Hargrove *et al.*, 1983:2). But, as shown below, this decision has not abolished streaming: its effect has been limited. The decision also supported a 1968 critique of special education programs for those called mildly retarded by a leading special educator, Lloyd Dunn, who concluded that 'regular education programs were better able to serve the needs of special education students' (Hargrove *et al.*, 1983:2–3). Dunn's critique preceded a spate of similar critiques by special education classes appeared not to enhance learning outcomes for mildly handicapped students, services should support these students in regular classrooms, and thus possibly reduce negative labelling and exclusionary effects (Hargrove *et al.*, 1983:4).

Tweedie notes that in *Pennsylvania Association for Retarded Children* [PARC] vs *Pennsylvania*, PARC 'rejected co-operative strategies': their strategy included extensive professional testimony that education benefits all handicapped children. Those experts insisted that education be seen as 'individuals learning to cope and function within their environment' (1983:53). The PARC case led to Pennsylvania education officials making statements agreeing 'to identify handicapped children, provide them with a suitable education, integrate them with normal children where possible, and provide due process hearings to resolve parental complaints' (1983:53).

As Chambers and Hartman note (1983:3) and Tweedie's chapter in their book describes, these cases were part of the confrontational strategy adopted by the principal policy actors associated with PL 94–142. Their choice of tactics was based in:

> the belief that school officials were reluctant to include all handicapped children in their programs, were unlikely to initiate program reforms to develop and provide appropriate educational programs and services, and were unable or unwilling to demand additional resources sufficient to find the needed expansion of special education (Chambers and Hartman, 1983:3–4).

In response to these confrontational tactics 'school officials lobbied the congress for financial assistance to help support the new responsibilities and activities to which they had acquiesced' (Chambers and Hartman, 1983:4).

Thus a legal strategy was deployed which used litigation and adversarial hearings, rather than political cooperation, in the attempt to gain congressional reforms; moreover, legal strategy was then 'incorporated . . . into the reform in order to retain effective leverage' (1983:50–51) via the procedural safeguards in PL 94–142. As Kirp points out, lobbyists for the education of the handicapped:

> borrowed many of [their] tactics from the civil rights movement . . . [and] convert[ed] the issues surrounding the education of the

handicapped into questions of civil rights. [Thus i]solating the mildly retarded from normal school life and depriving the seriously handicapped of any schooling were both depicted as inequitable. Arguments over policy were turned into constitutionally rooted claims of unequal educational opportunity (1983:99).

The politics of legalization were thus a key strategy in struggles to reform educational practices of children called handicapped in the United States.

In this context, a discourse on rights, due process, least restrictive environment and appropriate education emerged. This discourse combined themes from American political culture with terms from the vocabulary of professional educators, including free appropriate education. Given the professionalism inherent in phrases such as 'appropriate education', which imply someone has the expertise to provide a 'technical' allegedly apolitical judgment, the discourse contains and reveals a struggle between constitutionally based, allegedly guaranteed rights and professional judgment. The opposition here lies in the antinomy between equal rights as a 'citizen' and difference, as judged by a professional.

Once the lawsuits had established both a discourse on rights and decisions which ruled against the inequities of special education practices, advocates believed that legislative reform rather than more litigation was a better strategy: it was 'broader in scope and backed by substantial resources. [And t]he congressional commitment could be safeguarded [it was thought] by a bureaucracy already in place' (Kirp and Jensen, 1986:370). As has been the case elsewhere, Congressional decisions were thus deployed where litigation and practice were inadequate. These events and strategies culminated in the passing of PL 94–142 in 1975. The first full school year in which this Act was seen as applying was 1981–82.

The passage of PL 94–142 in 1975 was thus part of the gradual legalization of the educational apparatus which began in the early 1950s. This legalization reflected and encouraged other developments. As Kirp and Jensen comment (1986:1), legalization at federal level challenged the tradition of local control of education as a State and local school district responsibility; it encouraged central control and the development of bureaucracies at both federal and state levels to regulate the new practices envisaged in law. Whereas, in 1965, there were twelve pages of federal regulations governing education there were some 1000 pages in 1977. Legislation, regulation and bureaucratization were also part of an increasing politicization of educational practices. Presenting educational issues as a matter of rights encouraged politicization: 'The history of America generally and of the public schools in particular may be told as a tale of progressive inclusion in the policy, and in that telling, the forms and values of law have a central place' (Kirp and Jensen, 1986:6).

In sum, the passage of PL 94–142 occurred at a time when educational apparatuses throughout the United States were becoming increasingly regulated centrally, increasingly bureaucratized and politicized. Advocates of a legal strategy appear not to have considered its potential disadvantages.

The Education for All Handicapped Children Act, 1975 (PL 94–142)

The Education for All Handicapped Children Act, 1975 (PL 94–142) and its 'implementing' regulation (34 C.F.R. 300-EHA Regulation) sought a legislative solution to educational inequities: it was designed to redress the '*de facto* denial of the *rights to education* of the handicapped' (Yanok, 1986:49). The Act is voluminous and complex, not only in content but in its relationship to the constitution and to other federal laws which seek to regulate education practices; moreover, it constructs a complex division of power and responsibilities between State education agencies (SEA), local education agencies (LEA) and parents.

The key provision in PL 94–142 was the requirement that 'public schools throughout the United States provide free appropriate public education for every handicapped child irrespective of the nature of his or her disability' (Yanok, 1986).

> (c) It is the purpose of this Act to assure that all handicapped children have available to them, within the time periods specified in section 612(2) (B), a free appropriate public education which emphasizes special education and related services designed to meet their unique needs, to assure that the rights of handicapped children and their parents or guardians are protected, to assist States and localities to provide for the education of all handicapped children, and to assess and assure the effectiveness of efforts to educate handicapped children (PL 94–142 89 STAT. 775).

Thus the Act is informed by competing theories: by a medical model, by the covert politics of the theme of needs, by a submerged theme of professionalism and by the overt politics of a discourse on rights. The antinomies between these themes reveal the struggle between these discourses as competing strategies to control educational practices surrounding handicap. Professionalism, the notion of need, and a medical discourse each provide a discourse on difference, while a claim to rights leads into a discourse on equality as a citizen in a democratic state.

Mehan *et al.* also note that a medical model provides significant themes in the Act:

In the medical model, the organism is the focus of assessment and pathology is perceived as a condition in the person, an attribute of the organism. Thus, we say a person *is* tubercular, or *has* scarlet fever (Mercer, 1979, p. 95).

The Education For All Handicapped Children law has specific provisions for answering questions about the *physical* state of the organism, for example, measures of 'health, vision, hearing . . . and motor activities [Federal Register 121a532[3]F'.[1] However, the underlying assumptions of the medical model have been extended beyond the physical aspects of students considered for special education, such that 'intelligence', 'aptitude', 'potential', or 'mental ability' are also treated as internal states, attributes, or personal possessions of the individual (Mehan *et al.*, 1982:301).

Incorporating these educational 'attributes' within a medical framework implies some loss in these 'attributes', some personal deficit.

The notion of free appropriate public education, which is central to the 1975 Act, has become a key issue in struggles surrounding handicap. As Yanok points out, the Act defines *free appropriate public education* in terms of special education services:

Special education and related services [are those] which (A) have been provided at public expense, under public supervision and direction, and without change, (B) meet the standards of the State educational agency, (C) include an appropriate preschool, elementary, or secondary school education in the State involved, and (D) are provided in conformity with the individualized education program required under section 1414(a)(5) of this title (Education for All Handicapped Children Act, section 1401[18], 1975).

The term *special education* means specially designed instruction, at no cost to parents or guardians, to meet the unique needs of a handicapped child, including classroom instruction, instruction in physical education, home instruction, and instruction in hospitals and institutions. (section 1401[16]) . . . The term *related services* means transportation, and such developmental, corrective, and other supportive services (including speech pathology and audiology, psychological services, physical and occupational therapy, recreation, and medical and counselling services, except that such medical services shall be for diagnostic and evaluation purposes only) as may be required to assist a handicapped child to benefit from special education, and includes the early identification and assessment of handicapping conditions in children (section 1401[17]) (Yanok, 1986:49–56).

There are mechanisms in PL 94–142 which aim to ensure that all children receive a 'free appropriate education'. These consist of a number of legal and administrative demands placed on State education agencies (SEA) and local education agencies (LEA). The legislation thus requires SEAs

(a) to develop a state plan (policy) 'that assures all handicapped children the right to a free appropriate public education' which contains '(i) a goal of providing full educational opportunity to all handicapped children, (ii) a detailed timetable for accomplishing such a goal, and (iii) a description of the kind and number of such facilities, personnel and services necessary throughout the State to meet such a goal' (Section 20 USC 1412);
(b) an individualized education program (IEP) for each child to provide a free appropriate education which was to be developed by a team of people, including parents, and
(c) procedural safeguards (20 USC 1415) to be established by SEAs, LEAs and any other educational units needing federal assistance in order to safeguard the provision of free public appropriate education.

The development of an IEP by a team of people was seen as the key process for ensuring that a child receives a free appropriate education. The process is meant to constitute an operational standard to guaranteee a free appropriate education.

But quite what a free appropriate education means is debatable. Not surprisingly, appeals to this principle, in constructing a case at law, have failed to clarify a meaning which can be widely applied and Yanok notes two Supreme Court decisons have merely established the principle of a 'basic floor of opportunity' (Yanok, 1986). However, Noel *et al.* believe that progress towards a definition is occurring:

> the definition of services as well as questions regarding what constitutes 'appropriate' education remain to be clarified within the structure of special education policy. This clarification is occurring through a complex interaction involving the state and federal courts, the Congress, state legislatures, and the Executive Branch of government. Throughout the process, the scope of some concepts has been expanded, such as the right to an extended year program, and others proscribed (e.g., Hendrick Hudson District Board of Education v. Rowley decision that appropriate education could not be defined in terms of 'maximizing' the potential of the student). In addition to the court decisions, administrative proposals for regulatory changes have been made that would have substantially

altered the implementation of PL 84–142. Thus, special education policy cannot be seen as an alternative set of laws, or blueprints, but rather is best described in terms of a set of guidelines which are continually being changed by those who must put them into practice (Poister, 1978) (Noel *et al.*, 1985:13).

Elsewhere, Noel and Fuller note that despite the highly prescriptive nature of PL 94–142,

> states and local schools were nonetheless required to assume primary policy-making and financial responsibilities for the education of handicapped students. The initial responses to the mandates were to develop sets of regulations, procedures, and standards that established special education's position within the educational bureaucracy (1985:27).

According to Gerry, a Washington lawyer prominent in struggles to reform special education, PL 94–142 differs significantly from several other civil right laws because it:

> creat[es] a direct and active role for both states and parents in defining what equal educational opportunity (i.e. a free appropriate public education in the least restrictive environment) is. State standards are an essential ingredient in determining the substance of a free appropriate public education and parental involvement is a crucial ingredient in the process of creating the individualized education program which contains the practical definition of appropriate education and a description of how it is to be provided (Gerry, 1985:14).

Gerry also sees the 'rights' achieved in 94–142 as different from those in other federal laws: PL 94–142

> establishes an individual, enforceable right to all needed special education and related services for every school age handicapped child. Not only is this right universal, but unlike the limited scope of other federal education programs, in this instance the right to education is comprehensive and unconstrained by the services actually supported by federal funds. PL 94–142, thus, represents a unique hybrid of two different federal statutory traditions (Gerry, 1985:14).

This somewhat positive or determinist view of the conditions legislative decisions create is discussed below. But Gerry usefully depicts the complex relationship between PL 94–142 and the constitutional and statutory background of federal and state education laws:

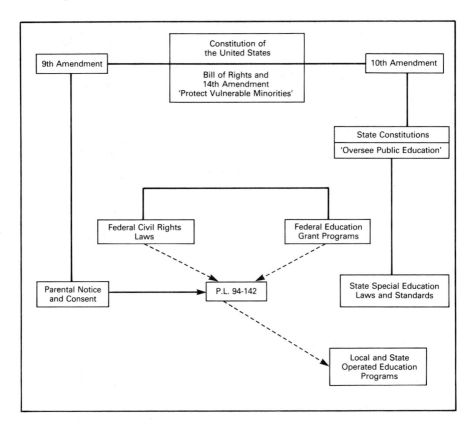

Figure 4.1: Overview of the Constitutional and statutory background of federal and state special education laws
Source: Gerry (1985:11)

Gerry suggests that there are four discrete sets of legal or administrative demands placed on SEAs or LEAs:

(1) requirements governing the submission of SEAs to the state plan,
(2) requirements governing the submissions of local applications to SEAs,
(3) the practical demands for standards against which an SEA can measure LEA actions and the related use of procedural safeguards and
(4) the avoidance of litigation.

The extensive bureaucratization in these practices is summarized in Tables 4.1 and 4.2, drawn from Gerry (p. 11).

PL 94–142 is thus an ambitious law. It establishes a broad bureaucratic, legal and political structure. From a sociological stance, we would expect legislative decisions, especially of this intended scope, to be only one site of decision-making and to allow policy to be remade at various levels in

Table 4.1   Areas To Be Addressed in Submission of SEA Policies and Procedures

Policy Areas	Regulatory Requirements (34 C.F.R. 300)
Right to free appropriate public education within age ranges and time frames	300.121
Full implementation of PL 92–142 requirements	300.122
Full education opportunity goal	300.123
Identification, location, and evaluation of handicapped children	300.128
Confidentially of personally identifiable information	300.129 & 300.561
IEP development, implementation, review, and revision	300.130(b)
Placement of handicapped children in least restrictive educational environment*	300.132
Protection in evaulation practices*	300.133
Use of funds available under other federal programs*	300.138
Provision of services to students enrolled in private schools	300.140
Recovery of funds for misclassified children	300.141
Conduct of hearings on local applications*	300.144
Annual evaluation of programs*	300.146
Proper expenditure of Part B funds	300.148
Consolidation Application for Part B funds	300.192
Ages at which free appropriate public education must be provided	300.300
Conduct of 'due process' hearings**	300.506(b)
Selection of surrogate parents**	300.514(c)
Children's right of privacy	300.574
Enforcement of SEA policies and procedures	300.575

*   The Regulation requires only procedures.
** The Regulation implies the policy developed responsibility.
   Source: Gerry (1985:11)

Table 4.2   Areas To Be Addressed in Submission of LEA Policies and Procedures

Policy Areas	Regulatory Requirements (34 C.F.R. 300)
Confidentially of personally identifiable information	300.221
Implementation and use of the comprehensive system of personnel development	300.334
Participation and consultation of parents in meeting full educational opportunity goal	300.226
Participation of handicapped children in regular educational program	300.227
Implementation of individualized education program requirements	300.235
Implementation of procedural safeguard requirements*	300.237
Continuum of alternative placement**	300.531

*   The Regulation requires 'assurance to the state educational agency'.
** The Regulation implies the policy development responsibility.
   Source: Gerry (1985:11)

state educational agencies, whether such practices are legal, administrative or more technically educational. As we shall see, and as Noel and Fuller note (1985), this is what occurs. But various critics of PL 94–142 appear to assume that, tidied up or tightened, the law would better achieve its aims. These views are discussed below.

Institutional conditions of PL 94–142

The institutional conditions of PL 94–142 are complex. I shall discuss them initially in terms of intersecting constitutional, legislative, economic and political-bureaucratic-administrative practices.

Constitutional conditions of education policy in general are both extensive and yet limited. On one hand, as Secretary Bell stated in 1982, while on testimony before the Subcommittee on Federal Education of the Committee of Education and Labour of the US House of Representatives:

> 'all major and minor educational policy issues can be interpreted, i.e. supported or opposed by claims and reference to the Constitution. School uniform, the job rights of radical, ex-Vietnam teachers, the control of school textbooks, have all at various times been debated (and sometimes judged legally) within the frame of appeals to principles held to be present in the Constitution' (cited by Gerry, 1985:13).

On the other hand, as Secretary Bell also said:

> 'the statement establishing the US Department of Education contains very strong language prohibiting the Secretary and his staff from exercising control over American education. We want our schools controlled from the grass roots where decisions are close to the home and communities. The locally elected school board is a rich and necessary tradition in our total system of governance in education. 'How do we protect this great tradition and – at the same time – protect the rights of handicapped children? How do we respect the state legislators and the laws they have enacted and live up to the great ideals of equality and opportunity?' (p. 6) (cited by Gerry, 1985:13).

Limited federal control of state education practices accords with the tradition of local control but it conflicts with the federal legislation's aims to protect the right of students called handicapped and with the extensive legalisation of practices which follow from the legislation (Table 4.1 and 4.2 above).

Constitutional conditions and the federal legislative decisions in PL 94–142 intersect with *legislative conditions* deriving from state laws. These are diverse. As Gerry notes:

> There are 50 states with 50 different sets of state laws. It is hard to write a rule or draft statutory language on the Federal level that respects all state laws. Federal education legislation and Federal regulations laid down on this very large and complex universe of 16,000 school districts working within the framework of 50 different sets of laws enacted by the state legislators and affecting 4,000,000 children must, to the extent that it is feasible, be general in nature. As we strive to assure equal educational opportunity on the Federal level, we must remember that the entire responsibility for education was left to the states when our Federal system was established (1985:13).

This means that state and LEA policy practices are diverse and inconsistent:

> Each of the 50 states has a set of laws, rules, guidelines, and regulations for the provision of education. There is nothing that says that these must be consistent across states. And, decisions are made at the local school district level. Sometimes local districts comply with state requirements; sometimes they do not (Ysseldyke, 1986:13).

This locally diverse context also characterizes special education practices so that PL 94–142 seeks to regulate state arenas where:

> Special education is a state rather than a federal responsibility. Yet, there is a federal law mandating that states are to provide special education services to all handicapped youngsters. This law, the Education for All Handicapped Children Act (Public Law 94–142), was passed in 1975. There is nothing that says that states must comply with this federal law; yet, any state that does not comply with federal law stands to lose considerable money in the form of federal support for special education (Ysseldyke, 1986:13).

Economic conditions, in the form of sanctions, are thus a key mechanism for regulating PL 94–142, but compliance with legal requirements does not mean that the substantive aims of the legislation (a free appropriate education as a matter of right, however this is defined) are attained. Thus constitutional, legislative and economic conditions intersect and increasingly regulate practices concerning handicap at various levels of educational apparatuses but *not* in the sense of determining or achieving key, substantive practices and aims of the legislation. Constitutional and federal legislative conditions are somewhat anomalous, given the tradition of local, state and local school district control of education practices. Legislative conditions at state level are also diverse.

Further economic conditions of PL 94–142 derive from the fact that funding is by 'category of handicap' and that:

> In some states funding is differential. That is, school districts receive more money for the education of certain kinds of students than for others. For example, in some states a district might receive 1.4 times the amount of money ordinarily allocated for the purpose of educating a learning disabled student but only 1.2 times that amount of money for the education of a mentally retarded student. The differential funding rate creates a differential incentive for identifying a student as evidencing a particular handicap (Ysseldyke, 1986:13).

Economic conditions may also encourage segregating practices. As Cicourel and Mehan note:

> School districts are provided funds from state and federal sources for each student in regular classrooms, and a greater amount of money for students in special education programs. They will receive more money for students in 'pullout' special education programs, and still more money for students in 'whole day' programs on a sliding scale. This additional source of revenue also serves as an incentive to search for students to place in special education. Just as there are incentives to locate and place students in special education in order to receive the maximum state and federal support, so too, there are disincentives to find too many students. Funds for special education are not unlimited. A funding ceiling is reached when a certain number of students are placed in one Educationally Handicapped classroom, in one Learning Disability program, etc. No additional money is provided if more students than the quota are assigned to particular programs. These financial and legal considerations constrain placement decisions, and often override judgements based on students' talent, ability, or social class (1985:17).

Economic conditions rather than a student's 'needs' thus influence or construct a particular handicap identity. Further sources of constructing identities for students independent of their educational performance or 'needs' are discussed below.

Economic conditions also underlie differences between SEA practices and, in turn, reflect a state's wealth, its commitment to those called handicapped, and available resources (Noel *et al.*, 1985:27). Moreover states have provided more money per capita than federal sources: in 1979–80 states provided an average of $855 per pupil (a total of *c.*$3.4 billion) while federal sources provided $218 per pupil (Noel *et al.*, 1985:27). States' 'contributions to local programs ranged from 98 per cent to 17 per cent with the remaining money coming from local sources' (Moore, Walker and Holland, 1982) (cited in Noel *et al.*, 1985:27). A further condition, or effect, of PL 94–142 is that according to state reports 'some agencies that once met some major program needs now leave all services to the educational system' (Noel *et al.*, 1985:27).

Further economic conditions derive from the way a state chooses to determine per pupil costs of special education services (Noel *et al.*, 1985:29). States vary here: 'Some . . . provide a fixed amount for every handicapped child, regardless of handicap, while others provide allowances based on numbers of teachers or classes. Each of these models can have different influences on the quality of services provided (Noel, *et al.*, 1985:29).

Changes in *economic and political conditions* in recent years under the Reagan Administration have also affected special education policies (1985:32).

> The political climate which supported growth of strong federal programs for the handicapped changed drastically with the Reagan Administration. Essentially this administration believes that the federal government has taken on responsibilities in education, as well as health and social services, that are not its constitutional responsibilities. This administration also believes that states and locales are capable of providing these necessary services more efficiently and economically than the federal government. Furthermore, while states may need additional revenues to meet their responsibilities, the funds should come with a minimum of regulation and control (Noel *et al.*, 1985:32).

Reduced federal funding, both for education in general and special education programs in particular, are a further economic condition affecting all state educational apparatuses, including California (Forness, 1985:41). Forness's view is that this creates conditions where students may be sent to the cheapest special education programs (those for the 'learning disabled') and that this explains in part what he clearly regards as misclassification and misdiagnosis of Californian schoolchildren with 'mental retardation' or 'emotional disturbance' (1985).

State *political-bureaucratic-administrative* practices are highly diverse. Forness attributes the diversity of practices in Californian schools to the number and geographical 'spread' of children;

> With such a large and scattered population [356,000 children receiving special education services], with more than 1000 different school districts, and with more than two dozen colleges or universities with special education departments, it is understandably

> difficult for the California State Department of Education to exercise
> a central or focused influence on public policy . . . California schools
> have thus found themselves relatively free to exercise a wide range
> of approaches to such special education issues as identification,
> assessment, eligibility, labelling, mainstreaming, and classroom
> practice (Forness, 1985:36).

Clearly *policy is remade* at different levels of the California educational
apparatus.

Constitutional, legislative, economic and political-bureaucratic-
administrative conditions thus intersect and constitute different aspects of
the same practices. PL 94–142 appears to be an instance of 'social policy
[in the United States] becom[ing] excessively legalistic' (Berman, 1986:47).
Under these complex conditions, and quite apart from Offe's views on the
role of state policy, a general law like PL 94–142 clearly initiates conflict
at other levels of the educational apparatus and sets only broad limits to
practices at these other levels. This is certainly the case for other federal
educational legislation. As Berman comments:

> Despite some success, the following frustrating cycle of
> implementation often has unfolded: legislation, regulations or court
> decisions are met at the local level by confusion, resistance, or
> painfully slow and half-hearted compliance; judges, agencies, and
> regulators eventually respond by tightening rules and toughening
> enforcement; and local institutions ultimately 'comply' by adhering
> narrowly and legalistically to the letter of the law, which has become
> by then exceedingly intricate (Berman, 1986:46).

In other words, regulation or increasing bureaucratization has followed federal
laws on education, including PL 94–142. Political-administrative-bureaucratic
practices at both SEA and LEA levels have increased, following PL 94–142.
In schools too, administrative practices have increased and new arenas – teams
of people to decide on the IEP, and new committees such as the Eligibility
Placement Committee (EPC) – have emerged (see, for example, Mehan,
1983).

Practices since PL 94–142

There are some fairly safe generalizations which can be made about
educational practices since PL 94–142. One is the number of students called
handicapped and placed into 'special classes' has increased (Mehan *et al.*,
1981:408) and that this increase has varied by category: 'For example, there

has been a decrease in the number of students declared mentally retarded and a 119 per cent increase in the number of students declared learning disabled (Algozzine and Korinek, in press) (Ysseldyke, 1985:13). Figure 4.2 depicts these differences.

Forness notes that statistics for categories in California show marked discrepancies from the national profile for 'mental retardation', 'learning disability' and 'emotional disturbance' (1985). This is discussed below. Tweedie comments generally that:

> Several hundred thousand handicapped children have been brought into the public schools. Over 4 million children receive special education and related services in public schools. There has been an increase in placements of handicapped children in regular classrooms. More handicapped children are being given individualized education programs. Federal, state, and local expenditures for special education have rapidly increased (1983:65).

A second generalization is that while the Act sought to remove the educational inequities children called handicapped experienced, inequities remain: 'For instance, [the] Massachusetts law which was a model for PL 94–142 has not served as intended. About half the decisions under the law result in a

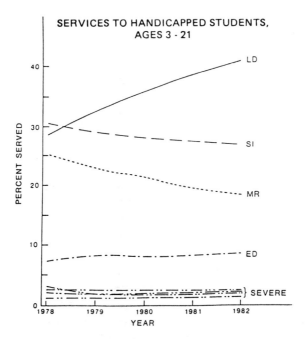

Figure 4.2: Numbers of students served by category (1978–1982)
Source: Ysseldyke (1986)

child being placed in a more restrictive environment' (Bloom and Garfunkel, 1981:379). According to Noel *et al.*, improving local practices has been hampered by 'a lack of specific guidelines and precise requirements for meeting the law' and the brief time within which a comprehensive array of practices was to be developed (1985:30). Where parent involvement is concerned, for instance, LEAs have developed *ad hoc* practices: these include seeking blanket approval from parents and getting parents to sign an IEP after it was developed. Thus procedural safeguards in the law have not been observed and the states have allegedly not provided technical assistance to school districts: because of the numerous procedural requirements states have focused efforts on monitoring and compliance (Noel *et al.*, 1985:30).

Thirdly, PL 94–142 has resulted in increased regulation thus bureaucratization at a variety of levels, including schools. Mehan *et al.* suggest referral practices have become more formalized, alongside wide variations in reporting procedures (1981:408). In the schools Mehan *et al.* observed, referrals increased as teachers became more aware of the referral system, and then 'flattened out' when teachers decided the administrative demands required of them in making referrals were too great. Fourth, the law appears to have institutionalized the *category* of handicap identity a student acquires rather than the IEP. This has occurred despite the fact that a student's needs are not described by such categories. Fifth, the issues surrounding free appropriate education have become increasingly politicized: the use of litigation in interpreting PL 94–142 attests to this (see for example, Yanok, 1986).

Beyond these generalizations, the analysis of whether or not practices conform to Pl 94–142 becomes more complex. Noel and Fuller cite a number of studies which suggest that there is a 'greater uniformity among states in special education practices [in the sense of litigation and procedures] than in any other major categorical education program area'; but they also note that there is 'great variability among states in the ways that policies are being translated into practices' (1985:27). This suggests states conform in their political-administrative (procedural) practices but vary in schooling practices; but this oversimplifies the multidimensional nature of practices.

Practices which have become bureaucratized, for example, decision-making in school committees, to decide which students should receive special education programs and what, both conform to some of the requirements of PL 94–142 and depart from them in other aspects. Institutional practices may conform superficially to the law's requirement and depart from the aim of ensuring a free appropriate education in a number of ways. As Mehan's work (1984) shows, firstly, *who* is called handicapped depends on administrative contingencies some of which follow from economic conditions (see above), including the number, thus proportion, of students already deemed in that school in that year to be 'handicapped'. Secondly deciding which special education option a student receives is contingent on how many student places are left in which special education programs in a particular LEA and does not depend on a student's 'needs', a highly problematic notion anyway. Thirdly, decisions about the category of handicap and the type of program judged appropriate (and available) are more frequently made in advance of the EPC meeting, so that these team meetings ratify prejudged decisions: professionals use techniques of linguistic persuasion to ensure parents agree to these decisions (Mehan, 1983). The notion that a team constructs an IEP, and that this constitutes an operational standard by which a free appropriate education is assured, as a matter of right, is thus illusory: it may happen or it may not.

Not surprisingly, given the complexity of the issues, those who comment on these practices or the 'outcome' of PL 94–142, focus on different aspects, and offer different 'solutions'. Some sense can be made of the diverse 'findings', comments and theorizing by putting these commentaries into various categories of approach.

There are basically four approaches in the literature commenting on PL 94–142: while there is some overlap they can be identified by their primary concerns. These concerns variously focus on:

(1) the law;
(2) disability or handicap as a real, natural, or medical condition (rather than as a social construct: see chapter 1 on this distinction);
(3) teaching practices in the sense of pedagogy and curriculum including school organization.

While all three of these approaches have theories of how the social world is constructed, the fourth approach is characterized by a primary concern theorizing the social world: these are sociological accounts.

Commentaries focusing on the law

Commentaries which focus on the Education for All Handicapped Children Act do so from a variety of perspectives and offer various solutions. Gerry, a lawyer, and an influential actor in arenas connected with education and handicap, notes that 'Federal regulatory provisions [PL 94–142] provide a superstructure within which numerous policy vacuums or gaps exist [which] if left unfilled become the subject of litigation' (1985:16). In this context, Gerry's view is that SEAs and LEAs can develop policies proactively, thus 'retain[ing] control over education decision making' and avoiding litigation. To do this they need to construct philosophically consistent and operational policies (Gerry has an analytic framework to help achieve this), and *behavioural measures of agency response* which can be used to assess the implementation of policy. Thus Gerry's solution is to fill policy gaps in the Federal legal superstructure by measurable, operationalized policies at other levels of the educational apparatus. This is to argue that a solution lies in *more regulation via legislation* and to work from the premise that legislative decisions have determinant 'reform' effects.

Yanok notes that the precise meaning of the legal phrase free appropriate education has become the subject of litigation and that two Supreme Court decisions (*Hendrick Hudson District of Education* v. *Rowley* 1982, and *Irving Independent School District* v. *Tatro* 1984) which ruled on the services necessary to provide a free appropriate education, interpreted the law as requir[ing] only that a basic *floor of opportunity* be provided which consists of access to specialized instruction and related services which are individually designed to provide *educational benefits* (p. 49). In his view:

> further litigation will be needed to compel the Supreme Court to address the broader question of what are the minimum legal enforceable levels of opportunity and benefit to which all handicapped children are entitled. Only when this matter is resolved unequivocally will the meaning of *free appropriate public education* be comprehended freely (1985:53).

This solution, based on further appeals to legislative conditions, excludes from its social theorizing struggles, thus the politics of educational policy; it also ignores inherent problems in defining substantive aims (an appropriate education) in law. In this context, Weber's distinctions between formal rationality and substantive rationality are relevant (Eldridge, 1972; Giddens, 1971). Yanok's suggestions appear to see legislation as potentially controlling or determining practices at other levels. But as the Introduction suggested, and as Mehan's Californian studies show, decisions at other levels, such as who is handicapped and what programs they will receive, are, to a degree, independent of federal and state legal decisions.

Noel *et al.* provide a more complex account of law and levels of decision-making in policy. As already noted, they see the relevant laws, rules and regulations which are part of special education policy *not* 'as an unalterable set of laws, or blueprints, but rather . . . [as] a set of guidelines which are continually being changed by those who put them into practice (Poster 1978)' (Noel *et al.*, 1985:13). Moreover, teachers are key policy makers:

> It is a long way from passage of legislation in the US Congress to a classroom, and while administrative policies and procedures determine the system for delivering the services, the success or failure

of the policy rests with the commitment and competence of the individual practitioner (1985:16).

Thus, implicit in Noel *et al.*'s discussion is a model of policy and practice very similar to that put forward in the Introduction. Their view is that to retain the 'critical support of the taxpayer', special education needs to show the public 'that its programs and practices work and produce performance changes', to integrate its services with medicine, rehabilitation and general education and to train its teachers differently so that they work in cross-disciplinary programs. This is to see special education as a technical medically related practice and in arguing for a focus in the 1980s on the efficacy of services and finance, to locate this selective view of handicap in a corporate discourse. Moreover, Noel *et al.*'s solutions do not seem to fit particularly well with their analysis of the politics of policy practices.

Bloom and Garfunkel argue that while the law 'was intended to force public schools to provide education for all children', and regulations on the appeals procedures were issued to 'effectuate' that law, in Massachusetts, parents have used the appeal process politically for objectives not foreseen by those drafting the legislation and regulations: 'the appeals process has performed a function radically different from the one for which it was designed. It has become a device that parents can utilize in seeking preferred placements in the private sector at public expense' (Bloom and Garfunkel, 1981:393). This practice may generate public hostility, absorb monies which are needed elsewhere, use private placements for students with 'mild handicaps' which may then become unavailable for children with more severe handicaps, a practice which may systematically disadvantage certain 'racial and linguistic minorities and adolescents', and it may use the services of skilled practitioners who:

> are now providing elaborate services to children who could be appropriately served in less comprehensive and less restrictive environments . . . within . . . public schools [as well as the services of] skilled advocates working to obtain private placements for mildly handicapped children of upper middle class parents, while disadvantaged children with severe disabilities, who are much in need of representation, have none (Bloom and Garfunkel 1981:394–5).

In sum, 'the annual appeals procedures allow important but less pressing problems to take precedent over a problem that is critical – the problem of directing scarce resources towards those children who are in most need of them' (1985:395).

Bloom and Garfunkel's comments are in line with Carrier's (1983a, 1983b) and Tomlinson's (1982) findings that those in an upper middle class position are able to use the educational system to attain their objectives. While PL 94–142 may have encouraged the provision of education for children formerly excluded from the education system, its legal safeguards are limited, and cannot achieve structural change of the kind intended: that of altering the power relationship between professionals and parents; especially it would seem, parents from minority or lower class backgrounds. Bloom and Garfunkel's solution is to refine the law so that 'Within the appeals process, a two-part procedure for public versus private displacement disputes might be instituted' (p. 398). This solution proffers a legal strategy to remove political action by parents who are better able to negotiate with professionals than are working-class parents.

Ysseldyke discusses the effects of the requirement in PL 94–142 that students first be 'identified' in terms of a handicap before funds can be allocated (1986). He argues that this requirement has affected the statistics for certain categories of handicap (see above) but, more importantly, it distracts attention from the central issue which is not 'identification' but *how to teach*. 'I think it may be time for professionals to quit arguing about how best to identify types of students and to get on with the job of teaching students who experience academic and behaviour problems' (p. 18). Thus Ysseldyke's solutions focus on instruction and he suggests that there 'be a major shift in the ways in which special educators are now trained; away from learning the characteristics of specific types of students to learning about how best to assess and instruct those who experience difficulty in school' (1986:18). In this solution, Yessldyke implicitly criticizes the medically based discourse on disability which has dominated special education practices and, in line with the argument put in chapter 2, argues for making teaching and pedagogical skills central to the schooling of those who experience difficulty.

Berman, in an interesting analysis of the intricacies and consequences of legalism and education policy, argues that legalism has emerged because 'central authorities have often tried to improve the law's effectiveness simply by tightening enforcement, increasing accountability, or clarifying guidelines' (1986:60). This is based on a 'misperception of institutional realities' whereby central authorities (legislator, regulator, judge) attempt to force compliance 'regardless of the . . . law's substance' (1986:47). '[T]he problem of legalization thus lies in deeply held, yet inaccurate perceptions of how law-like mechanisms can induce local institutional reform, [thus] the solution first of all requires a change in consciousness [a change in their social theorizing?]' (1986:47). This approaches the idea that policy fails where its social theorizing is inadequate (Introduction). The issue of legislators' models of how decisions are made at other levels is discussed below in the relation to Mehan's school-based studies. Berman's solution, however, is to attempt to use both the coercive conditions which legislators seek to impose, and 'help, in the form of a more sophisticated type of learning': his underlying concern is 'How can coercion to guarantee individual rights be balanced with assistance to help local systems learn how to realize the law's intent?' (1986:60). His view approaches a political view of the law, in that law makers must think strategically, and his social theorizing is less reliant on seeing laws as providing a determinant set of conditions than some other accounts.

Commentaries focusing on handicap as a real, natural thus medical condition

A key issue for those concerned with handicap as a natural, thus medical, condition is variability between states in prevalence rates. While there are others who enter the debate on this issue from an opposed position, in which all categories are seen as constructs and thus as arbitrary (in the English debate see Tomlinson's distinction between normative and non-normative categories (1982)), there is a substantial American literature which discusses this variability from a largely natural-science based discourse (this variability is a confusion we need to sort out), and which only occasionally allows for state policy conditions, including economic and administrative conditions, as influencing these rates.

Hallahan *et al.* analyze variability between ten categories and refute the claim by others that prevalence rates for 'learning disability' show the highest variability and the greatest growth. Their 'data . . . argue for the conclusion that the definition and identification criteria for learning disabilities are at least as well articulated, and perhaps more so, than those for other categories in special education' (Hallahan *et al.*, 1986:13). More recently, Kosc argues for a more sophisticated definition of learning disabilities, as a starting point for further discussion, and bases his proposals on the idea that '[l]earning disability represents structural deficiencies in one or more psychological abilities . . .' (1987).

Forness suggests that the discrepancies between the number of children classed as mentally retarded, learning disabled and emotionally disturbed 'served in' Californian schools and the national figures indicates that California's policy enacting PL 94–142 differs significantly from the federal legislation (1985). Table 4.3 (Forness, 1985:37) provides figures on these differences.

Forness attributes the 30 per cent loss in numbers of children defined as mentally retarded to California's 'relatively conservative approach to EMR identification and placement' following a number of lawsuits (in 1968, 1970, 1971, 1972) on mislabelling which led to changes in Californian law (see above). This decline in EMR enrolments began before the California educational apparatus responded to PL 94–142 and 'continue[d] to decline

Table 4.3   Changes in Numbers of Handicapped School Children Served, United
States versus California, 1976–82

	United States			California	
1976–77	1981–82	Difference	1976–77	1981–82	Difference
MR 970000	802000	17% loss	42900	29900	30% loss
LD 797000	1627000	104% gain	74400	190700	156% gain
ED 283000	342000	21% gain	22000	9200	58% loss

Numbers rounded to nearest thousand (US) or hundred (California)
Source: US Department of Education (1983)
Adapted from: Forness (1985:37)

by nearly one-third more during the first five years of Public Law 94–142
implementation'. Forness attributes these effects to the outcome of *Larry P.*
(1972) which struck down:

> the use of most IQ tests then used in California to decide diagnostic
> eligibility for the EMA category . . . [leaving] psychologists without
> clear alternative measures to determine a referred student's potential
> *vis à vis* his or her functioning level. There is considerable sentiment
> in California that *Larry P.* was the right case at the right time but
> directed at entirely the wrong target (Lambert, 1981; Macmillan and
> Meyers, 1980). The real villain was not the IQ tests but the lack
> of flexible alternative provisions in California for children who
> needed 'individualized' approaches or other help in regular classrooms
> (1985:38).

Consequently, Californian practices allow only the 'most obviously mentally
retarded pupils [to be] . . . judged eligible for services', others who fail to
meet the criteria for 'learning disability' as defined in the California Education
Code 'may be mainstreamed in the worst sense of the term, that is, without
accompanying support in the regular classroom' (Forness, 1985:38).

Forness also discusses the somewhat extraordinary history of changing
definitions of learning disability and related categories, such as educationally
handicapped, discrepancies between PL 94–142's original definition (which
was dropped and not replaced), as well as the way services to those changing
categories have changed. He suggests that the most recently proposed
definition in California for learning disability (a learning discrepancy . . .
related to disorders in one of the basic psychological processes (Californian
State Department of Education 1983a) 'represents attempts to keep even fewer
Calfornian children identified as LD' (p. 39). He concludes that 'California's
continuation of policies in both mental retardation and learning disabilities
may thus have rendered potentially large numbers of children, with serious
difficulties in academic performance, ineligible for special education services.
Emotionally disturbed children may likewise be affected' (p. 39).

Forness attributes these consequences partly to 'California's particular emphasis on non-categorical programming [which] has led to an unusual combination of marked increases in one category (learning disabilities) with marked decreases in two other (mental retardation and emotional disturbance)' (p. 39). His discussion illustrates one of the dilemmas in the objective to reform educational practices surrounding handicap: funding is based on category thus on labelling a student with a particular handicap, yet such categorization also initiates the politics of exclusion (chapter 1). As Tomlinson has noted, categories are at the centre of special education practices and its inequities (1982), yet removing categories may result, in Forness's view, in mainstreaming or teaching practices which also disadvantage these students.

Commentaries focusing on teaching

Within the commentaries which focus on teaching and handicap since PL 94–142, there are a number of concerns, approaches and solutions proposed.

Ferguson focuses on students with severe handicaps and notes that 'public policy' on appropriate education programs for these students increasingly requires teachers to employ 'a functional approach both in content and with the aim of preparing such students for futures in competitive employment' (1985:52). She asks how this new public policy 'for severely handicapped students [is] reflected in the curriculum-in-use in secondary public school classrooms' (p. 53) and concludes that the policy fails since 'functional teaching and functional learning has as much to do with how the teachers perceive their students in terms of *types* as with their content decisions' (p. 55). In the view of many teachers:

> Community-based living and participation in community domestic and recreational activities seem 'feasible' for most. But nonsheltered, competitive employment seems feasible for only a few. The teachers find that the policy reform does not accommodate all the students they know as severely handicapped. Its demands are too stringent for many students who have too few marketable abilities and too little time left to acquire them. The teacher's new categories and classifications reconcile students' ability with work, with the result that many become doubly damned as both severely handicapped *and* unproductive (Ferguson, 1985:59).

Thus the way teachers 'translat[e] the policy reform into practice reveals that the reform fails because it does not reform enough'. Ferguson argues that policy reform should take account of teachers' interpretations and attempt to 'create alternative commonsense meanings of work that do not newly stigmatize the work of severely handicapped people' (p. 59). This is not so much a solution as a protest against the morality of paid work and productivity: what would help 'would be to create notions of work and foster work settings in which the economic dimension is at least diminished and where membership and worth are less dependent on economic productivity' (p. 59). The connection between everyday morality and paid work was discussed in chapter 1.

In a discussion on mainstreaming, Johnson and Johnson argue that discrepant findings about the conditions for successful mainstreaming derive from a lack of theoretical models about the conditions for effective learning and positive interaction between those called handicapped and those not (1986). From their eight year study in a variety of education settings of the effects of cooperative, competitive and individualistic types of experiences on mainstreaming, they argue for cooperative styles of teaching and learning and conclude that:

> Both mainstreaming and desegregation are required by law and are being implemented through North America. In many classrooms, however, mainstreaming and desegregation are being conducted in a highly individualistic way. Students work on their own, on individualized material, and with a minimum of interaction with their classmates. This chapter provides some basis for recommending that cooperative learning procedures should be utilized in mainstreamed and desegregated classrooms if the goal of improved intergroup acceptance is to be achieved (Johnson and Johnson, 1986:241–2).

Thus they criticize the Individualized Education Program required by PL 94–142: an IEP is a practice which segregates.

The concern of Voelker Morsink *et al.* is to theorize the conditions of effective teaching for students classified as learning disabled, mentally retarded or emotionally disturbed (forthcoming). In a rigorous and comprehensive review of categorical and non-categorical programs and education settings, they cite research which shows that 'psychomatic categorization of students is limited in both reliability and practical applicability' (p. 5); moreover, 'the ambiguity in categorical classification is intensified by the fact that definitions of the three categories are neither consistent among states nor stable over-time' (p. 6). The argument for noncategorical programs is also reinforced by the 'lack of evidence that specific teaching methods are differentially effective for students labelled learning disabled, mentally retarded and emotionally disturbed' (p. 7) although there is some evidence of 'real difference among the categories' (p. 12). What they call teacher-directed instruction (p. 17) is effective across various settings (p. 20), so that the 'critical factor is not the setting, but rather the way in which instruction is delivered and managed'. Common elements characterize effective teaching across general education settings (p. 24).

They note extensive diversity between both categorical and noncategorical programs, which inhibits reliable comparison, and 'although current research synthesis does not provide clear directions for policy change', some directions are clear. *Economic and political-administrative-bureaucratic conditions* rather than theoretical issues affect placement decisions:

> The overall evidence suggests that multicategorical placement does not always follow decisions based on educational quality, but often reflects districts' responses to shrinking fiscal and personnel resources, as well as administrative convenience; the multicategorical resource room creates more students per teacher (Smith-Davis, Burke and Noel, 1984; Noel, Smith-Davis and Burke, 1985) (Voelker Morsink *et al.*, p. 44).

There is concern that 'the multicategorical resource room . . . [is] abuse[d] in practice' (p. 45) and about 'whether college and university training programs can adequately train cross-categorical and multi-categorical personnel in four years, and about the depths of training provided in higher education programs and the manner in which districts program for mildly to moderately handicapped students' (p. 47). '[C]urrent practice in noncategorical/multicategorical programs (particularly in resource rooms) is discrepant from best practices' (p. 51). They protest against administrative convenience and cost effectiveness taking precedence over benefit to students: environments may be 'theoretically less restrictive but actually not more facilitative. The long-range consequences of such policies are serious . . . [thus] policy should follow, rather than precede, careful study' (p. 55).

The work of Voelker Morsink *et al.* reveals both the educational consequences of political-economic expediency and the unintended effects of legislative 'reform': their works shows that legislative conditions are limited, in the case of PL 94–142, to formal rationality and that *substantive rationality in the sense of effective teaching or a free appropriate education is an issue outside legislative 'reform'*. Clearly too, *policy is made at all levels.*

Biklen notes that PL 94–142 is seen as mainstreaming law, although it does not use the term, that mainstreaming can take many forms and that 'schools have been relatively free to shape their own mainstreaming practices' within certain conditions. These are:

> administrative structure and leadership, funding mechanisms and funding levels, staffing patterns, attitudes of individuals, types of disabilities, a social history of the school or community, parent involvement, skill levels of teachers, the style of providing related

services such as speech therapy and physical therapy, diagnostic and assessment practices, and availability of special equipment (1985:60).

He suggests there are four types of integration: (1) *'teacher deals'*, which rarely bring any administrative support with them; (2) self contained classrooms in a regular school or *'islands in the mainstream'* in which there is no 'real social or programmatic integration for either the students or their teachers'; (3) a *'dual system'* where the states establish 'intermediate school districts' to service a multi-school district area; a system which is 'fraught with problems', and (4) *'unconditional mainstreaming'*. In the latter setting:

> teachers and staff speak about integration and learning as correlated goals. Staff do not try to disown certain children as another staff's responsibility . . . [and] what seems to make mainstreaming possible in these planned settings [is] . . . the presence of a problem solving attitude. People share an unconditional commitment to try and make it work, to discover the practical strategies to make it successful (1985:61).

Conditions of these programs include administrative support, a problem-solving attitude throughout the administrative and teaching staff, frequent discussions by teachers, administrators and parents on how to make mainstreaming more effective, and careful documentation within the school of progress with individual students (p. 61). Thus Biklen claims that we now know a great deal about how mainstreaming works: 'there are literally scores of practical methods, strategies and principles, nearly all of which can be implemented by public schools immediately at little or no additional cost' (p. 61).

For Biklen, successful integration is constituted by a commitment to mainstreaming (unconditional mainstreaming) and the conditions described above. His strategy includes moral and pedagogical dimensions (see chapter 2); it is an argument against professionalism, where this involves disowning responsibility or claiming responsibility for only *part* of a student's needs; or for only *some* students. His solution to the politics of professionalism lies in his emphasis on the central importance of a *problem-solving attitude*. But the analysis needs to be taken further: what precisely are the conditions and practices which sustain and maintain commitment and a problem-solving attitude on the part of teachers? While recognizing the multi-dimensional nature of meaningful integration objectives, Biklen attempts to sidestep the politics of educational practices surrounding mainstreaming or integration which *presently* are characterized by competing objectives.

Hargrove *et al.*, in a comprehensive review of the 'implementation' of PL 94–142, argue that 'Compliance with rules and regulations is necessary but not sufficient for the implementation of social programs' (1983:15) and ask 'What are the conditions necessary for, first, local compliance with federal law and, second, local implementation of program purposes that reach beyond compliance and engage the organizational cultures of schools and school systems?' (1983:17). Thus they pose a key theoretical issue: Weber's distinction between formal and substantive rationality.

Compliance occurs when an IEP is written to satisfy a bureaucratic requirement and is then ignored, when parents are brought in to sign their names to a decision about their child's schooling or a school decides, for the sake of bureaucratic neatness to leave children with mild handicaps in special classes in their school. In contrast, effective 'implementation' occurs when an IEP is used in instruction (but see Johnson and Johnson's comments above), when parents actively take part in decisions about their child's schooling, or when a school actively seeks to place children with mild handicaps in regular classrooms.

In order to examine as wide a range of 'potentially important influences on the implementation process' as possible (p. 24), Hargrove *et al.* studied three school districts, comprising ninety elementary schools, fifteen junior high schools, seventeen senior high schools, and seven special education schools, where there were approximately 72,000 students and 4000 teachers. This constituted a complex, bureaucratic system, the *key background condition*, in which responsibility for children called handicapped was divided between the department of special education and each school district, headed by a superintendent. This 'created an ambiguity about responsibility that has consequence for the implementation of policy' (p. 32). The three separate school systems differed in administrative style: 'different sets of administrative directions . . . shaped the implementation of policy in unanticipated ways' (p. 34).

There were legal and financial constraints on the school system's efforts to implement the law in regular schools (p. 39); economic conditions were such that school officials had to choose which aspects of PL 94–142 would receive most money (p. 102). Because the law gave priority to services for those with severe handicaps, and this area was the most highly litigious (advocates were well mobilized and litigation or its threat was mostly in this area) most was spent in this area. The organizational culture of each of the school districts affected the implementation of PL 94–142 (p. 48). Moreover, mainstreaming is an ambiguous policy – are children to be referred or put into regular classrooms?: 'Judgments about the appropriateness of such actions in any school are difficult' (p. 59). The literature on leadership styles was ambiguous (p. 65) yet important, given conventional wisdom that the principal's style is what really matters.

The overall data suggested such collegiality was critical to successful implementation of PL 94–142 in elementary schools (p. 69). While there seemed only a few ways to succeed in implementing PL 94–142, there appeared to be a number of ways to 'fail', in the sense of 'the most mechanical, low effort pro forma compliance' (p. 70).

The overall findings revealed that 'of the three independent variables considered in the analysis, the independent affect of teacher interaction was more closely correlated with performance status than either programmatic structure of the school or leadership style of the principal' (p. 75). However, 'this does not mean that leadership style of the principal [is] . . . unimportant'. Leadership style may 'foster motivation through increasing teacher interaction and increasing curricular options and support services available to their school' (p. 76). Educational philosophy possibly underlay leadership style (p. 77).

PL 94–142 was less relevant to secondary schools: historically few special education services had been available to secondary schools and referral rates were no more than 1 per cent, though there were reports from teachers, principals and guidance counsellors that a significant number of students who were struggling in regular programs would benefit from these services (p. 83). The organizational differences between elementary schools and secondary schools together with differences in their special education populations and the different practices of special education, constituted two very different implementation settings for PL 94–142 (pp. 97–8).

'Each school must be understood as a unique institution' (p. 107) and what succeeds in one school should become knowledge disseminated throughout schools. Conventional wisdom believes that principals are everything, but both the literature (which is ambiguous) and their findings suggested that:

> the central idea is that the principal provides a general set of standards and sense of direction for the school and then ensures that key personnel get their job done. This would include the provision of technical assistance from the outside – for example, special educators to help teachers. But, the chief theme that emerges from these studies is the importance of the staying power of the principal to ensure that ideas are implemented (p. 109).

Schools which performed low on implementing PL 94–142 were:

> likely to be poor schools academically . . . routinized bureaucracies that adhere to fixed, unexamined norms, leadership is weak, teachers are likely to be less competent than the average, and the socioeconomic environment is most likely adverse to education. Such schools require an infusion of strategies, such as new principals and lead teachers, workshops in schools, and a great deal of technical assistance; but such large resources are unlikely to be available in

a metropolitan school system that is run on a very tight budget and that must deal with severe and politically salient questions of desegration and problems of low student performance on achievement tests (p. 112).

In a list of recommendations, Hargrove *et al.* suggest that 'exemplary [school] practices learned from experience and research' should be disseminated, a clearly relevant strategy. Despite extensive evidence that different schools construct their own policy practices, their recommendations ignore this theoretically key issue:

We are not suggesting that the federal government permit state and local educators to develop their own paths to service delivery according to local necessities . . . We think of 94–142 as a national program that should be administered and evaluated accordingly.

Their apolitical view of government practices emerges in final comments:

American federalism oscillates between tightly administered categorical programs and disinterested federal involvement in social problems. The classic federal implementation approach for such programs has been that of compliance, egged on by the constituency to be served and fueled by distrust for the states. After the experience of several years illustrates the limitations of compliance strategies, and when the pendulum of national politics swings, the federal role shifts towards a permissive, *laissez-faire* attitude.

We reject both of these approaches and commend a steady policy of development within the continuity of programs that are so clearly designed that they can be evaluated and sufficiently flexible that they can be implemented. The development of programs of this kind is the best avenue toward agreement on a division of labour among levels of government within the American federal system in which responsibility is focused and each level of government does what it can best do by helping those beneath it do what they can best do. This great chain of helping begins in Washington and ends in the classroom (1983:120–1).

Thus Hargrove *et al.* are against legalism and for what might be described as cooperative development. Finally, they suggest that the:

technique of 'mapping backward' calls for discovering the behaviour that is required for implementing a law at the grass roots and then working up the intergovernmental chain to ask what each level of government might do to reinforce the conditions congenial to effective implementation below (1983:114).

This suggests their view is that classroom and school practices are of primary importance in achieving substantive educational aims and provide a basis for developing federal and state strategies 'that will strengthen local capacity and commitment' (p. 114).

In sum, the findings Hargrove *et al.* show that local conditions vary greatly, schools make their own policy practices, highly bureaucratic schools are not conductive to effective integration (chapter 6 discusses bureaucracy more fully), and collegiality between teachers and, finally, commitment are highly related to successful integration.

Nevin and Thousand also focus on teaching (1987). Their interest is in discovering conditions 'to increase the resourcefulness of educators in creating more effective programs to ensure academic and social programs of all students' so that '*inappropriate* or *unnecessary* referrals are reduced' (forthcoming:3). They note the 'gaps between what is known to be *researched* best practice and what is currently practiced' (p. 28). They argue for a strengthened single system of education rather than a dual system in that 'instructional needs of students fail to warrant separate systems' (p. 30), for more ongoing support and training for teachers to integrate general and special education practices, for new models of how humans learn and for further theorizing on how to change educators' beliefs and practices.

Sociological accounts of special education practices and PL 94–142

As in the other categories of accounts, sociological commentaries on North American educational practices and handicap and PL 94–142 derive from different perspectives and vary in the solutions they propose. What these accounts share is an interest in relating educational practices to wider aspects of social institutions and conditions; they differ in the concepts they use to do this.

Brinker and Thorpe's study is less clearly sociological than others but is included here for its conceptualization of policy-making at different levels (1985). In an analysis of nine states comprising fourteen school districts and 245 students with severe handicap (SH), two patterns of state policy emerged, an integrated and a non-integrated pattern. These patterns differed in the numbers of categories used, the type of training for teachers and the number of these students integrated with regular schools. The nonintegrative model is characterized by (a) more categories of exceptionality, (b) higher levels of in-service training, (c) separate certification requirements for regular and special teacher certification, and (d) a lower proportion of SH students integrated into regular schools. The integrative model was characterized by

(a) fewer categories of exceptionality, (b) regular education foundation for special education certification and special education courses for regular education certification, (c) more college programs for teachers of SH students, (d) more federally funded demonstration projects and specific allocation of PL 94–142 funds for SH students, and (e) a higher proportion of SH students being integrated into regular schools.

Brinker and Thorpe note that little research has been carried out on how large federal programs affect state policy, how state policy affects local policy and how local policy affects classroom policy and 'finally, the cummulative effect of all these policies and practices on individual students' (p. 18). They conclude that these patterns reveal state policy contexts which appear to provide factors conducive or not to integration but emphasize, from their previous work, that the 'more immediate contextual factors have considerably more explanatory power (Brinker and Thorpe 1984b)' (p. 25).

Shapiro draws on a Marxist framework, attributes the limits of special education reform to wider social forces, has no solutions to offer and theorizes at a high level of abstraction (1980). He focuses on secondary schooling and students with special needs. Shapiro's basic premise is that 'special education reform like other areas of educational change, may proceed only to the extent that is congruent with the needs or goals of the [social and economic] structure which is essentially a corporate economy' (p. 212). The extent of change achieved by potentially radical educational reform depends 'in the last analysis', not on the activities of 'educational pressure groups and innovators as catalysts' but 'on the parameters set by the social and economic structure'. Shapiro's form of theorizing (structuralism) was criticized in the Introduction, for its determinist view. Shapiro anticipates such criticism, places Gintis, Bowles, Carnoy and Levin in this category and suggests they have been important in identifying the extent to which they have shown 'how changes in educational practice and organization reflect changes in the needs of the corporately organized economy', but adds that changes in educational practices and organization also reflect 'demands that arise out of the dominant liberal ideology' (p. 213). This liberal ideology emphasizes 'the rights of the individual insofar as they operate in a bourgeois democratic state', and moves to reform educational practices which derive from this ideology conflict with the needs of the corporate economy and result in tensions and contradictions evident in these practices.

According to Shapiro, 'mainstreaming' demonstrates these contradictions especially well. While reforms may have provided access to the same building as students not called handicapped, differences between students in their key educational experience are maintained through stratifying educational practices such as 'tracking, homogeneous classes, ability grouping, and "resource rooms". These processes illustrate other contradictions of schooling in liberal-capitalism': the critical dilemma in school practices is between developing an individual's potential and:

> providing the differentiated experiences and socialization necessary for those who will fill different positions in the social and economic hierarchy. It is a conflict that pits the Durkheimian notion of education against contemporary conflict interpretations. The former emphasizes education's role as an agent of moral socialization. Durkheim shows the way education promotes group identification by participation in a ritual. It is this function that advocates of mainstreaming emphasize. By attendance and participation in the life of the school, hitherto excluded individuals will join the life of the community: they will become full members of society. Conflict interpretations of education, however, emphasize that it is the separation rather than the commonality of experiences that characterize schooling in America. The separation and differentiation of educational experiences (in the form of tracking, etc) resulting from the schools' role in the organization of our economic life, constitutes the real (though hidden) curriculum of schools. It is this which forms attitudes, self-concepts, peer-identification, and life-chances. Despite the increased physical proximity between students resulting from mainstreaming, the real sources of student identity and role-expectations – the educational organization of the school – are left untouched. While special education reform augurs the further fulfilment of liberal ideology in that it ensures a more complete equality of access to a public institution, it does so within the constraints imposed by a hierarchical social structure. The latter ensures that school remains a hierarchically organized institution dispensing educational (and hence social and economic) opportunities unequally. As Randall Collins has shown it is indeed the central function of schools to provide experiences that separate and stratify students. In this way, individuals are prepared to assume appropriate social and economic roles (Shapiro, 1980:215).

Shapiro cites the failure of comprehensive education policy in England to remove the socially segregating effects of a system where secondary level students went to schools of different statuses. His point is that educational streaming *within* a school ensures the continuation of social differentiation. This includes 'the remedial nature of much of the instruction in the high school resource room [which] serves mainly to reinforce the low expectations (and low self-image) of many special needs students. It also ensures those who use the room are stigmatized as being intellectually deficient' (p. 219).

In particular, he criticizes the notion of 'curricula diversification' (inherent in the notion of special needs and IEPs): 'viewed as educational change [it] . . . embodies the liberal notions of democratic pluralism and equality. Such a view, we believe, mystifies the real nature of the form' (p. 217). As he comments:

> [The] failure in the traditional school system is not viewed as the result of an environment that systematically alienates and excludes a significant sector of the student population. Instead, such students may be labelled 'learning disabled', 'emotionally unstable', or 'socially maladjusted'. We may see their problems arising from an indolent or apathetic disposition, broken homes, learning problems, mental retardation, or other 'handicaps'. In all of these ways we are able to ignore the educational process that is often responsible for school failure . . . Mental retardation and emotional illness are labels used to obfuscate the classic hostility and exclusion shown towards such students. In Massachusetts, four years after the introduction of the state special education reform law, a recently publicized report states that minorities are two or three times more likely than whites to be enrolled in special education classes (p. 218–9).

Shapiro's comments on individualization in education and the IEP illustrate the generality of his extensive critique. On the one hand, he is against curricula diversification, as in IEPs. Such instruction reflects the 'bureaucratic ethos' of high schools and rarely results in creative, flexible curricula innovations: it illustrates the 'quintessential bourgeois perspective' that 'handicap or disability of a student is the individual's problem'. 'It emphasizes individual activity at the expense of group work and support' (p. 222). This generalized critique of secondary schools provides no basis for educational solutions compared with other accounts which address issues of cooperative learning stragegies: for example, Voelker Morsink *et al*. However, Shapiro's aim is 'that these comments will provide special educators with a greater awareness as to the limitations and inadequacies of the present system' (p. 214).

In contrast to Shapiro's generalized account, Mehan and Milofsky are sociologists whose work reveals sustained attempts to study and theorize school practices organized around a notion of handicap. In an early study of Californian schools, Milofsky argued that special education was structurally marginal to regular schools, special teachers had limited access to children whom regular teachers controlled, and that 'Public schools are intensely political and, unless these politics are understood and accounted for in program planning, new programs which are organizationally subordinate will be exploited' (1974:455–6). While 'Special educators have a highly developed professional structure and elaborate technology' (p. 456), their 'programs have not been successful for the majority of their students' (p. 437):

'The problem is that their expertise can be used by school administrators to garner additional resources or take independence away from regular teachers' (p. 456). The attempt to solve these problems by integrating special education with regular education, as outlined in the then proposed California Master Plan for Special Education (California Assembly Bill 4640, 1973–1974 Regular Session) where it was anticipated mainstreaming would overcome these difficulties, was unlikely to work: 'unless special education teachers are carefully trained and are able to work with teachers as equals rather than as experts telling teachers how to do their job, it is doubtful that they would have fewer political problems with mainstreaming than they do now' (p. 456). In this 1974 work, Milofsky sees special education programs as potentially useful provided the political problems and differences between regular and special teachers and the structural marginality, thus relative powerlessness, of special education is eliminated.

In his later book (1976), Milofsky focuses on the formal organizational qualities of schools, particularly urban schools, which contribute to sustained failure for some children who are eventually seen as discipline problems, transferred out of regular schools and dumped in individualized special education programs which 'show little educational benefit to referred children' (1976:xi). Milofsky's concern is thus with the way regular schools socialize children into careers of failure rather than with a critique of individualized special education programs. His study examined practices following the California Educationally Handicapped Minors Program, 'one of the first large-scale efforts to intervene on slow learning suspected to be caused by specific learning disabilities or minimal brain dysfunction' (p. xi). Central to his theorizing is the argument that 'Schools are first and foremost authority systems . . . Children must accept the validity of the school as an institution and the competence and fairness of the teachers. None of this trust is assumed and in fact authority is always precarious in schools . . .' (p. xvii). Thus teachers are preoccupied with orderliness in their class and 'all other education procedures stem from the regular class' (p. xviii). Regular programs are politically dominant over all other programs: these are the 'roots of [the] marginality of special education programs to regular programs'. In this context, 'The main justification for keeping special education programs in many *urban* schools is that the "dumping ground" function is useful for maintaining order' (p. 152). Order appears to be the central concern: 'One senses that the only thing important to those who run the public schools is maintaining administrative order in the regular classroom. Specialized and individualized instruction are destroyed by those anxious to maintain business as usual and a good public appearance' (p. 153). Milofsky thus suggests that special education programs are useful to teachers whose concern is with order in regular classrooms. But staggering problems confront regular education:

Since all children must attend schools, society's problems must be confronted daily in the classrooms. Not only are public schools expected to supervise children; they are also saddled with the unfortunate myth that they are the major vehicle of equality in American society. Since no single institution can eliminate racial prejudice and economic discrimination in the society, public schools become apologists for the capitalist economic system, the front line in the provision of social welfare services, and unwilling agents for social control – and all this is to be done with a minimum of personnel and resources. It is no wonder that public schools provide individualized instruction so inadequately. How can services for any one child be justified when ten others also need assistance? How can therapy be provided when the welfare of all children in schools is threatened by the rebellion (even though justified) of a few? Whether schools ought to be agents of social control or not, educators are faced with the unfortunate responsibility of dealing with the universality of our educational system. It is impossible for schools to be anything but agents of social control, and the maintenance of order is a central issue. This is less true in middle class white suburbs, where schools do approximately what the public expects of them, than in low income, minority, inner city areas, where education is often much inferior to the ideal (1976:153–154).

Milofsky appears to argue that school is organized for failure for some students, both in regular classrooms and, for further organizational or structural reasons, in special education programs. The criticisms of special education practices, those of labelling, inadequacies in diagnostic methods, and ineffective teaching, and proposed reforms are a distraction from looking at how regular schools practices construct failure for some students.

Most school failure cannot be tied to true handicaps, however. In the majority of cases encountered in this research, the 'failures' who made their ways into special classes did not suffer detectable neurologically based learning problems. Student failures were most often byproducts of conflicts and rigidities in regular programs. Though the children's handicaps were generally secondary rather than primary (or true), their failure was nonetheless real. To close down special programs to all but the vanishingly small percentage of children who are demonstrably neurologically impaired might guarantee justice, but it would also eliminate the constructive role special education may play in intervening in secondary mental retardation, which is a product of the educational institutional structure (1976:156).

This is especially the case in what Milofsky calls *administratively disrupted schools* in which teachers 'come to see their students as increasingly disruptive over a period of years, are reluctant to admit they are unable to teach certain children, mistrust their principal' so that 'A cycle of frustration, anger, and failure forms between teachers and children; children may be damaged psychologically, and instruction may genuinely break down' (p. 157). Administratively disruptive schools are especially characteristic of inner city schools, whereas middle-class schools in suburban areas are less likely to be administratively disrupted.

Milofsky concludes that special education programs contain a major contradiction. While 'On the surface, special education is a sham and a source of considerable injustice and institutional racism in schools' (p. 163), 'special educators use the very inadequacies and injustices of their programs to ameliorate the central crisis in schools today; the eroding legitimacy of the institution in urban areas' (p. 165). This is a sophisticated analysis. Milofsky attributes a political awareness or discourse to Californian special educators. Given the political, cultural conditions of special education practices in North America and of PL 94–142 discussed earlier, this seems highly plausible. This political discourse amongst special education appears to contrast considerably with the dominant discourse in Britain and Victoria (chapters 5 and 6) which are largely constructed from themes from professionalism and its inherent argument that special education issues are 'technical' in the narrow sense of belonging to special educators.

Finally, Milofsky concludes that the dilemma of special education practices (labelling and stigma, yet a route to success for some children and a source of funds) are not easily resolvable. But since:

> Our schools do not adjust, do not teach appropriate lessons and use methods congruent with cultural styles other than the Protestant middle class values on which public education is based. The behaviour of children inevitably conflicts with the rigidity of the classrooms. Administrative disruptions occur, and failure follows. Special educators are simply one more group of victims of the institution.
>
> [Thus] failure and inequity are structured into our present educational system. Most poor and minority children will not do well. Partial solutions such as those provided by special educators will have partial success. They will never significantly alter the experience of poor children in schools. Only when the institution of public schooling is completely revised will we see greater educational equity (1976:164–5).

In his most recent work, Milofsky argues that research into special education practices provides a new angle in the argument that discipline is central to schooling (1986:173). The best available research on referral (Berk *et al.*, 1981) shows no relationship between referral and discipline problems: in the last two decades the centrality of discipline in urban schools has gone. Schools have become larger, more specialized and more bureaucratic and 'teachers have become less concerned with controlling decision making at the school level' (p. 174). Under certain conditions, neither regular teachers nor special educators accept responsibility for special education practices, so that 'Rather than being an example of social control motivated by organizational maintenance or class domination concerns, special education provides a lesson in bureaucratic irresponsibility' (p. 175).

Moreover, despite Durkheimian and Marxian theorizing which both provide bases for social control theories of special education practices (as maintaining a system's boundaries or as instruments of class control) 'social control is disorderly and unsystematic in special education programs' (p. 177). Part of this incoherence derives from the fact that teaching programs 'cannot be designed in keeping with federal law' PL 94–142 because most of the time 'special educators cannot diagnose students' physiological disabilities with any precision' (p. 175); practices depart from PL 94–142's requirement 'that measures other than IQ tests be used to evaluate children for placement', whereas 'intelligence test scores continue to be far and away the strongest predictor of whether or not children will be placed in classes for the retarded' (p. 177). Incoherence also derives from the fact that there are two school systems, 'the old bureaucratic, crisis-ridden school system of cities and the newer, wealthier suburban districts' (p. 178). Various conditions of schools means that teachers 'have power to make the most important policy decisions for the institution' (p. 182). Teachers are even more powerful than the other low-level, 'street bureaucrats' such as police officers, social workers, nurses – because 'teaching has definite products – the achievement level of students – which are inseparable from issues of social control' and, secondly, because teachers work in proximity with each other, share students and cooperate in *ad hoc*, informally organized ways. This cooperation contrasts with bureaucratic organizations, since 'much of this nonclassroom work is neither assigned to specialized staff nor routinized in the form of permanent administrative positions' (p. 182). Here Milofsky's analysis coincides with Hargrove's emphasis on the importance of collegiality among teachers as a necessary condition for meaningful mainstreaming practices or successful implementation of PL 94–142.

Teacher's work, instruction, is inextricably linked to control, 'which is unique among street-level bureaucrats' (p. 186). Since its inception public education has instituted various practices which support the authority of the teacher in the classroom. Special education practices, which Milofsky describes as the removal of the student from the school, constitute one such set of practices but 'institutionalizing removal . . . has serious consequences both for special education and for schools' (p. 186). Because there are two school systems, there are two special educational systems:

> It is not hard to find imaginative, therapeutic special education programs in suburban school districts. It is also not uncommon to find that the content of special education programs is in direct relation to the social class of parents. The lower the parental income, the more special education is likely to serve control purposes . . . [and] The social control model of special education works once one moves outside the cities (p. 198).

The notion that special education works as an instrument of class control against the interests of minorities and low income students is an illusion: 'schools are too disorganized to use special education as a device of social control'.

> Urban school systems seem unstructured and ungovernable, at least from the standpoint of special education, because those systems are old, large, and politicized. Suburban systems are more flexible and innovative. Unfortunately, they also enroll most of the white students in a state like Illinois or Pennsylvania.
>
> The denouement is that there is a subtle racism in pretending that there is one school system in this country when in fact there are two. In special education, there has been intense attention to guaranteeing children due process as they are reviewed for placement in special education classes precisely to protest against use of special classes for social control purposes. That due process sometimes works in suburbs as special educators fight against regular educators, trying to protect the right of psychologists and special teachers to admit to their programs only children who would profit from removal to a special class (Milofsky, 1984). Due process does not work in cities because it requires that someone in the schools be administratively accountable and responsible. If no one is, then the system does not work. Due process controls just become a wilderness of irrelevant paperwork, and members of the special education evaluation teams – the schools psychologists, social workers, nurses, and speech pathologists – simply become administrative functionaries who push papers. Since cities have the most children who are poor or members of ethnic minorities, the administrative ambiguity which prevails affects the children who need it most. Administrative rationality and accountable programs are provided to suburban

children who are otherwise better protected by wealthy, informed and caring parents (Milofsky, 1986:199).

Milofsky's discussion of different types of political-administrative-bureaucratic conditions in schools and their consequences for special education practices contrasts with the class-structural account from Carrier (1983a, 1983b, 1984, 1986).

Carrier notes the rising proportion of American school-aged children enrolled in special education programs. In 1948, this was just over 1.2 per cent; in 1958, 2.1 per cent; in 1968, 4.4 per cent; in 1978, 8.2 per cent, while in 1974–5, the US Office of Education estimated one child in eight, or 12.6 per cent, was in need of special education (1986:281–2). Carrier's main interest theoretically is to relate the sociology of special education to central debates in the sociology of education and thus to the argument that education 'reflects the class structure of Western societies' (p. 284).

Schools have class reproductive functions and thus 'have to differentiate children and allocate them to different curricula and pedagogies' (p. 303). Special education, in a contractualist system of education, one based in the belief that individual attributes distinguish children, is one such sorting device. This structural view goes beyond both interactionist and institutional accounts of special education. Interactionist accounts argue that:

substantialism is a mirage, that in many cases children are stigmatized as handicapped as a result of the merest social contingencies or the vagaries of administrative convenience. Consequently, those identified as handicapped are not uniformly and qualitatively different from normal people (Carrier, 1986:306).

Interactionist accounts, based on a contractualist, ideological concern for performance, a concern which encourages behavioural techniques in special education, are thus 'part of the extension of capitalist ideology and social relations in education' (p. 306). Institutional frameworks may provide detailed accounts of why educators and special educators do what they do but they do not examine the *wider social forces* which constrain the limits within which educators and special educators can manoeuvre. Structural accounts link special education to these broader social forces: these

forces emanat[e] . . . from the organization of labor and the nature of employment in capitalist society . . . [and] affect fundamental ways that human identity and merit are defined and so limit the socially acceptable ways in which schools can classify, educate and certify children' (p. 305).

Since schools must perform some class reproduction functions, they 'are caught in a bind' (p. 304) since 'the contractualist ideology [which now characterize both American and English systems of education] requires that sorting, if it is to be legitimate, needs to be explained in terms of individual attributes' (p. 304). It is here that Tomlinson's non-normative handicaps are convenient and:

> it is no accident that these are the largest categories by far in special education: about 55 per cent of English children in special education in 1977 and about 58 per cent of American children in special education in 1978, rising to 85 per cent if the speech impaired are excluded from the total figure. It is no accident that these categories have increased much more than special education generally over the quarter-century in both countries, and it is no accident that, with the possible exception of learning disabilities, these categories predominate among the lower class of society, the subordinate position of which, reproduction theory indicates, the schools endeavour to reproduce by relegating the lower classes to less desirable streams (Booth, 1981, p. 194; Chandler 1980, p. 20; Dunn, 1973, pp. 119–20) (Carrier, 1986:305).

Finally, Carrier argues that special education, which has focused on 'the [alleged] discovery of substantial pathologies or abnormalities that affect educational performance . . . may very well be an artifact of the gradual and uneven move to contractualism' in education systems. His evidence for this lies not only in the ideologies he proposes underlie the (uneven) development of the American and English educational systems, ideologies he calls substantialism and contractualism, but in the growth of individually oriented curriculum and pedagogy which he claims has been recently 'gaining ground in both American and English education' (p. 307).

Mehan's work on handicap and educational practices in Californian schools extends over a number of years and involves a number of colleagues (Mehan, 1983, 1984; Mehan *et al.*, 1981, 1982, 1985; Cicourel and Mehan,

Table 4.4 American data and English data on the proportion in special education *

	North America**	England
1940	1.1	—
1950	1.2	0.75
1970		1.1
1975	8.2	6.5***

*   see text on the American figures as including those in special classes and special schools attached to regular schools earlier than the English figures
**   includes kindergarten-aged children
*** Warnock estimate, according to Carrier
       Source: adapted from Carrier (1986:301–2)

1985). A 1981 paper examining school practices and PL 94–142 focuses on institutional processes of decision-making which 'creates' referrals 'handicap' and students' career paths. These institutional processes respond to conditions at other levels but are also practices which, to a degree, are independent of these other conditions. The law provides incentives to seek out students who may be called handicapped; economic conditions also act as an incentive in that funds are made available for each such student until a proportion of 12 per cent of the school population is reached. Thus institutional processes of decision-making are constructed within local and wider conditions; these Mehan *et al.* refer to as 'practical circumstances': they are '"practical" in that they make their appearance day in and day out' (p. 390. The 'social forces' which influence the referral system include informal screening procedures outside the mandates of PL 94–142 (principals may confer with teachers privately), scheduling of appraisal meetings which, in turn, depend on the availability of an itinerant psychologist and of testing materials which were in short supply (funds were short) and the time delays which occurred in completing an assessment as opposed to 'the smooth processing intended by federal law' (p. 401). '*These vagaries in scheduling, not student characteristics, influenced the placement and treatment of students*' (p. 403). Overall, these 'practical circumstances that operate at a structural level ... constrain the decision making involved in identifying, assessing, and placing students in regular and special education programs' (p. 407). This view of the sources and contingencies of referral oppose other theories. Mehan *et al.* argue that:

> inequality in educational opportunity is not a function of genetically endowed intelligence (Jensen, 1969, 1980; Herrnstein, 1974), 'cognitive styles' (Bereiter and Engleman, 1972), or social class backgrounds (Coleman *et al.*, 1966; Jencks, 1972; Bowles and Gintis, 1976); it is a consequence of unintended institutional arrangement, such as classroom assignment (Mehan *et al.* 1981:397).

Moreover, 'it is not possible to be a "special student" in the absence of institutionalized practices for their recognition and treatment' (p. 396).

Mehan *et al.* question the rational view of decision-making which appears to inform legislators' views: 'the law assumes that school districts are rational organizations' (1981–417) yet 'a wide range of evidence is accumulating that indicates human beings rarely adopt this maximizing decision-making posture' (p. 417). Nevertheless:

> we find educational decision makers to be acting rationally, *given the constraints they face*. The educators are operating in contexts that make it impossible to conform to the tenets of the rational model. The litany of practical circumstances presented in this chapter

suggests that school districts do not have the unlimited access to the unlimited resources presupposed by the rational model (1981:418).

Finally, Mehan *et al.* discuss the 'dialectic' between federal policy and school practices. They draw on two competing accounts of the 'failure' of policy: the view that government policy becomes ineffectual in the face of local exigencies and the 'diffusion of power' (Pressman and Wildavsky's 1973 view) and the view that policy contradictions lead to failure (Attewell and Gerstein's view). Mehan *et al.* argue that elements of both views are present. 'These "practical circumstances", which are inherent features of the presentation of education in a bureaucratic mode' (p. 420) parallel 'local exigencies' but Mehan *et al.* reject the notion of the diffusion of power as a source of 'failure'. In this, Mehan *et al.* adopt a highly apolitical view of institutional practices. But PL 94–142 does show evidence of 'contradictory interests' for instance:

> school personnel must strike a delicate balance between children's right to be 'normal' and their rights to be 'exceptional', which has inherent contradictions. Thus, not only must the school district deal with contradictions within the law itself, but they also must deal with the relationship between this and other laws and respond to social movements, such as the protest against evaluative devices (1981:421).

In a related paper, Mehan *et al.* report how teachers initiate referral of students and arrive at their categorization of students (1982). They concluded that neither of the two competing theories of how people construct categories were accurate. The mentalist perspective on category formation argues that people construct order out of chaotic reality 'in their heads', whilst the realist perspective argues that the structures of perception reside in the particular stimulus object. Mehan *et al.* found that teachers used both perspectives in categorizing students:

> The teacher's decision to refer students is only partially grounded in the students' behaviour, it is also grounded in the categories that the teachers bring to the interaction, including the expectations for academic performance and norms for appropriate classroom conduct. But what the teacher brings to the interaction is not independent of student's behavour, as some versions of expectancy and labelling theory would lead us to believe. Rather, what the teacher brings to the interaction with students seems to be as important as what the students do with the teacher in the classroom interaction (1982:314–15).

This interactional perspective 'maintains that perceptual structure exists neither in the head of the perceiver nor in the object of perception' but is constructed from both.

Mehan *et al.* emphasize, however, that teachers, in this categorization, and in the context of PL 94–142, are forced to move from what he calls an educational practical project of classifying children to more and more stable institutional categories.

> When the teacher asks special educators for help, the 'puzzling student' becomes a 'referral student', a member of a loosely defined, but institutionally consequential category. With the administration of standardized tests and decision by a placement committee, the 'referral student' becomes a 'learning disabled' (LD) or 'educationally handicapped' (EH) student. The official category LD or EH becomes both a social fact about the child and an object with a fixed, stable meaning for the school. The official category takes on a life of its own, its origins hidden (Bourdieu & Passeron, 1977) even though it is a social product of its own practices (1982:317).

A solution lies in the knowledge that communication is 'context specific':

> if teachers could see students in school-related contexts and in out-of-school contexts, they may be less susceptible to adopting a generalized deficit view of children who are not succeeding in classrooms. The teachers in the Kamahamaha Early Education Project (Au & Jordan, 1978; Jordan, 1977) and in the Odowa classroom project (Erickson & Mohatt, 1982) have been successful in this respect. By incorporating information about students' performance outside of school, mutual accommodations in curriculum organisation have been made to the advantage of students' improved school performance (1982:318).

Mehan takes up the issue of rationality and decision-making again in a 1984 paper:

> What rationality adds to the concept of purpose is consistency: consistency among goals and objectives and their relation to a particular actor, and consistency in the application of principles to select optimal behaviour . . . [but] in naturally occurring decision-making situations it is not clear just what the variables are that need to be weighed, or whether people employ such an algebra in actual practice (pp. 46–7).

Furthermore, 'Decision makers make mistakes and errors because they cannot keep enough information in their heads or because they are innundated with too much information' (p. 49). PL 94–142 is however 'based on the comprehensive version of the rational model of decision making'. Its primary purpose is '"to ensure that all handicapped children have available to them a free appropriate public education which emphasizes special education and related services designed to heed those needs" [Sec. 601c]. The . . . student's needs are to be met by the IEP', and 'needs are the first, foremost, and primary basis upon which the educational decision-making concerning placement is to be made' (p. 50). The rational model informing 94–142 thus assumes a student's needs can be unequivocally identified, that the knowledge exists to design a program to meet these needs and that the resources required to run this program are readily available. As discussed in chapters 1 and 2, the notion of 'need' and 'educational need' are highly problematic, and the shortage of resources was discussed earlier in this chapter.

In the 1984 paper, Mehan describes further aspects of 'placement meetings' practices which are not consistent with rational decision-making:

The entire range of possible placements was not discussed during these placement meetings. At most the possibility of placement in one or two closely related programs was considered, such as an educationally handicapped classroom or a learning disability program. And these possibilities were seldom debated or discussed. An alternative was presented to the committee by the school psychologist without question or challenge by other members of the committee, including the parents.

These observations point to a gap between the rational model as conceived in the ideal and the real decisions observed in actual practice (1984:53).

Thus 'decision-making' in institutional settings confronts people with a number of economic, legal, and practical considerations (conditions) that constrain placement decisions and the process by which such decisions are reached (p. 54), so that 'This practice of making placements by available category contrasts sharply with the theory of decision making inherent in special education law and rational models of action' (p. 56).

The law envisions a sequence ('temporal order') in placement meeting practices but:

The variation between the expected and the actual order of events in placement meetings demonstrates that the goals and objectives for the individual child were not written first, and then the services suggested to meet these goals. Instead, placement was selected in the context of available services.

The explanation of the parent's rights after the placement

decision but before the goals and objectives were written is particularly telling, in this regard (1984:57)

In contrasting actual practices in IEP meetings compared with the rational model and temporal sequence envisaged by the law, Mehan concludes:

> it is more productive to think of the E&P committee meeting as a culmination, a formalization, of a lengthy process that originates in the classroom. The construction of an educationally handicapped student's career or educational biography starts when the teacher makes the initial referral. Often, the teacher has only a general notion that a student 'is in trouble' or 'needs help'. This initial, rather general attribution establishes the presumption of a handicap. This attribution becomes refined as more and more institutional machinery (e.g. tests, committee meetings, home visits) is applied to the case, until finally, by the placement meeting, only a parent's refusal to sign the documents during the placement meeting would be likely to change the assumed placement. The fact that all but one of the cases brought before E&P committees resulted in special education placements is further evidence that early actions were being ratified at this stage in the process (1984:60–1).

Finally, Mehan argues for a new perspective on decision-making in organizations which, in turn, provides a different perspective on how student's acquire a particular category of handicap.

> What occurs here is a shift in perspective – really a shift in metaphor – for viewing organizational behaviour. When organizational behaviour is examined from the perspective of the rational model, one sees 'acts' and 'choices', and searches for 'reasons' and 'motives'. When organizational behaviour is examined from the perspective of the organizational process perspective, one sees end results, and looks for the routine practices that constitute them. As a consequence of this shift in perspective, organizational behaviour can be understood less as deliberate choice and more as *end results*, or as a consequence *of organizations functioning according to standard operating procedures*. For this case study, the shift in metaphor means that the placement of a student is more a function of organizational procedure than of organizational choice. The placement of a student in a special education program is not so much a decision made as it is an *enactment of routines* (1984:66) (emphasis added).

In work published with Cicourel, Mehan's concern is with how teachers make judgements about children's cognitive and linguistic skills and how this affects students' school careers (Cicourel and Mehan, 1984). These judgments constitute stratifying processes in schools: these practices occur 'when a teacher places students into ability groups, or when students are segregated into different academic programs, tracks or streams . . . [or] when counsellors meet with students to design curricular choices' (p. 13). Teachers' practices are bureaucratically constrained: there are too many children with too little time to teach them all (p. 14).; they must not only teach children how to read but they must produce children with certain kinds of reading skills, by a certain date and in a certain form' (p. 16). Their practices respond to 'organisational imperatives to conform to legal guidelines and [are] not based on students' talents or socioeconomic backgrounds' (p. 16); these organizational imperatives include policies such as 'children must read by age six or end of grade one and must demonstrate their reading skill on a standardized test' (p. 16). Teachers perceive some children, when they enter school, as being of lower ability and the studies Cicourel and Mehan cite show that teachers' adaption to this low performance and organizational constraints works to lower these children's performance *vis-à-vis* other teachers perceive to be of higher ability: teachers actually spend *less* time with children who need more of their help, compared with the time they spend with others who are performing better.

In theorizing organizational settings as having 'their own agendas, practices and constraints', Cicourel and Mehan argue against generalized Marxist accounts, including accounts based on the notion of 'cultural capital' owned only by middle-class children (as Bourdieu and Passeron theorize, 1977). In showing that organizational practices construct policy practices Cicourel and Mehan identify some of the conditions within which teachers work (with varying degrees of discretion). This approaches the model of theorizing put forward in the Introduction but differs from it in locating responsibility for outcomes not with those who make decisions but in 'social forces' such as organizational practices.

In this institutional practices view, Mehan *et al.* argue against assigning responsibility to individuals for the outcome of decisions which construct students' educational career paths. The practical circumstances which constrain decision-making 'seem to be beyond the control of the people involved' (1981:390) so that 'Differential educational opportunity seems to be more of an unintended consequence of bureaucratic organization than it is a matter of individual or collective intentions' (p. 391): 'institutional practices are responsible for the distribution of students into these educational categories' (p. 390). This is an interesting philosophical stance which contrasts with Hindess's view that assigning responsibility to those who make decisions is central to confronting the politics of practices. Furthermore:

This institutional practice idea contrasts with the view that there is a real world of troubled children 'out there', waiting to be identified, assessed, and treated. The institutional practice view of disability does not separate the problems of children from the process of their discovery or procedures for their assessment or treatment (1981:406).

The institutional view both accords with everyday discourse and departs from it. On the one hand, the practical circumstances Mehan systematically describes appear commonsensical; on the other hand, locating responsibility in the exigencies of these conditions, rather than with the people who make decisions within these parameters, departs from the dominant individualistic discourse which characterizes much of everyday life in late twentieth-century capitalism.

In sum, Mehan's work shows identities of handicap reflect institutional practices rather than students' needs (1981), those in special education programs are not necessarily in the type of program which is thought to be specific and appropriate to a particular handicap (those called 'learning disabled' may be in a class for 'mentally retarded'); the practices educators deploy in making decisions about a category a student is put in and about what to teach (IEPs) are constrained by legal, economic and political-administrational-bureaucratic conditions and depart signficantly from the rational model of decision-making and practices legislators theorize as characterizing schools and school districts. Finally, the conceptual distinction he makes between the *practical* nature of tasks teachers face (how and what to teach, etc.) and the *institutional* nature of categories (which are part of special education practices and policies outside school) implies that higher level conditions and decisions play a major part in constructing a student's school career. But this is to have an undialectical and hierarchical model of educational practices. From other sociological accounts teachers initiate the politics of exclusion through their practices of labelling students.

In a quantitative study which used a multivariate analysis across fifty states and the District of Columbia on patterns of identification of students called learning disabled, Noel and Fuller found that the 'identification and mainstreaming of mildly handicapped students is a socially constructed problem influenced by certain state fiscal demographic factors' (1985:28). States varied in the amount of federal funds received, in their state resources, in the number of children living in poverty, in the proportion of children called learning disabled and in the extent to which these students were integrated into regular classes. While Noel and Fuller point out that 'the interpretation and application of policies at district or building levels remain extremely powerful determinants of special education practice', the correlations between certain state educational characteristics and numbers called LD and the patterns of placement suggest that:

state socioeconomic factors are exerting significant influence on those practices. While states establish regulations and standards to guide the operation of special education programs, local schools bend and shape these 'rules' to accommodate their needs and capacities. However, these local rules are in fact shaped by the fiscal and social context in which the schools must operate. The results of this investigation suggest that the social and budgetary policies set at a state level define the categorical program called special education (1985:34).

Noel and Fuller deduced these conclusions from finding that there is a strong 'positive relationship between poverty [rather than minority groups] and relative increases in the percentage of LD children identified between 1976 and 1982' (p. 33). This suggests poor school districts use special education programs 'as a means of supplementing their education programs' (p. 33); wealthy districts 'are more successful in obtaining maximum reimbursement from a broad range of federal and state sources to support their programs' so that 'wealthy states could have less need to rely on special education programs for their marginal children' (p. 34). Finally they comment that:

> From its beginnings, special education has included those children whose only handicap was that they stayed outside the mainstream of what was expected or tolerated in the schools (Lazeron, 1983). Special education's response to this problem has been to develop complex definitions and eligibility criteria and to refine the objectivity of assessment instruments. Nonetheless, as the profession attempts to maintain the purity of the field, it is evident that local schools are striving to provide services to the greatest number of students possible, and the poorer a school district, the more difficult it becomes (1985:34).

Conclusions

For a variety of reasons, embedded in North American cultural, political and historical practices, those intent on redressing perceived inequities in educational practices surrounding 'handicap, deployed a legal strategy in an attempt at reform. This resulted, in 1975, in the passing of The Education for All Handicapped Children Act (Public Law 94–142). This was first fully enacted in the 1981–82 school year. This law sought, despite a tradition of local control in State educational apparatuses, a control which had been especially strong in schools and school districts, to ensure that each child called handicapped received 'a free appropriate education'. The law required individualized education programs (IEP) to be developed by a team of people for each such student, in which parent 'rights' to refuse a particular placement and to take part in making decisions on programs were to play a significant part.

Research has shown that PL 94–142 has had a number of effects which, while significant, have failed to guarantee 'a free appropriate education' for students called handicapped. Inequities remain. Procedural safeguards have failed: while they are undoubtedly deployed by some parents to achieve their objectives the law has not protected less political parents. Procedural safeguards are especially likely to fail, Milofsky suggests, in cities, in the older crisis-ridden school systems 'because it requires that someone in the schools be administratively accountable and responsible' (1986:199). The law cannot achieve extensive structural change of the kind envisaged: that of altering the power relationship between bureaucrats and teachers and parents, especially those already disadvantaged by class or minority group positions. Nor can the law achieve substantive educational aims, that is, substantive rationality, in the sense of effective teaching or a free appropriate education: these are beyond legislative reform. Such matters belong to *teachers* who, as a variety of commentaries note, *are the key policy-makers in educational reform*.

A primary effect of PL 94–142 has been to increase the *bureaucratization* and *politicization* of special education practices; this reflects a general bureaucratization in recent years of educational practices at federal, state, and local education agency levels (Kirp and Jensen, 1986). Increased litigation was part of these effects. Bureaucratization, policitization and increased litigation appear to illustrate Offe's claim that state policy initiates *conflict* at other levels of state apparatuses. Moreover, where apparent compliance with the law occurs, and mainstreaming takes place, a number of commentators note that this does not necessarily mean that *social integration* occurs, especially where teaching practices, such as the IEP requires, are highly individualized.

An increase in the number of students receiving special education services has also occurred, particularly in the number categorized as learning disabled. This lends support to the idea various sociological accounts put, that special education practices have served control functions for regular classrooms and teachers, in the maintaining of particular types of order. Milofsky suggests this view needs refining in light of the fact there are two school systems in North America, those in the inner urban areas which are administratively disrupted and in which more children from poor and minority backgrounds go to school, and those in suburban areas where special education can work as control and therapeutically. Hargrove *et al.* note that highly bureaucratic schools are not conducive to effective integration. Special education programs, whether categorical or noncategorical, are extremely diverse (Voelker Morsink *et al.*). Overall, this evidence thus demonstrates that *schools devise their own educational programs, or policy practices*, within the limits of 'practical circumstances', which are both local and wider (Mehan).

Theorizing varies as to the nature of these wider conditions: Shapiro, for instance, locates them in the structure of corporate economy and in the ideology of bourgeois capitalism. Carrier suggests they lie in the organization of labour, the nature of employment in capitalist society, and the way these construct definitions of human worth and merit. In contrast to this abstract theorizing or what Hindess calls a reductionist position, a number of researchers identify the sources of these wider conditions as variously emanating from PL 94–142 (through its emphasis on procedures: due process, team decisions, SEA and LEA reporting procedures) or from SEA and LEA conditions.

Where local, school practices are concerned, research suggests that commitment (Biklen), collegiality among teachers and the 'staying power' of principals (Hargrove *et al.*), are significant factors in what some call 'implementation' of the special education law, but which, following the model proposed in the Introduction, is more accurately seen as *policy practices being made at all levels of the educational apparatus*. Johnson and Johnson argue cooperative styles of teaching are necessary if social integration is to occur; this parallels Shapiro's implicit view that non-divisive school experiences would overcome the different identities and statuses school practices, including those called 'mainstreaming', presently engender (but this differentation is also necessary, Shapiro argues, so that students get to occupy different positions in the occupational hierarchy). Voelker Morsink *et al.* state that the way instruction is delivered and managed is critical, what they call teacher-directed instruction is effective across a range of settings, while Nevin and Thousand argue that the instructional needs of students do not warrant a dual system of schooling.

It is clear that the pedagogical issues raised above cannot be regulated by legal fiat. PL 94–142 has had substantial *formal* effects in rationalizing schooling practices surrounding handicap, rationalizing them in Weber's sense of constructing organizational practices which are more accountable procedurally than formerly. Since PL 94–142, extensive formal reporting practices have emerged at SEA, LEA and school levels, some of which do not comply with the law. But this regulation, bureaucratization and politicization, has clearly failed to achieve the ambitious aims of guaranteeing a free appropriate education for all children called handicapped. Some parents may have used the law and litigation to achieve this end but clearly the law cannot systematically control *substantive* educational aims, such as those implied in the vague phrase free appropriate education. The substance of educational aims, including those of teaching well, however this is defined, are clearly matters for educators not legislators. In this context, advocates whose objective was to reform education practices organized around a notion of handicap appear to have seen legislative decisions as more effective than they are, thus to have worked with an inadequate social theory (Introduction).

Moreover, as Mehan's careful work demonstrates, legislators, at least those involved in PL 94–142, have theorized decision-making at other levels as a rational process: but this is not how decisions are made. Everyday decisions are contingent on administrative, fiscal and bureaucratic conditions and tempered by less than full information; and parents may be controlled by linguistic processes of persuasion, thereby eliminating democratic ideals of shared decision-making. Clearly, legislation is a limited site of decision-making where substantive school practices and educational aims are concerned. As Milofsky comments, teachers are more powerful than other street bureaucrats and have the power to make the most important decisions for schools. Thus a central concern in reform should be pedagogical issues, including training teachers somewhat differently.

Finally, legal strategies have been the main means deployed in struggles to reform educational practices surrounding handicap in North America. Clearly these strategies have resulted primarily in an increase in regulation, via political-administrative-bureaucratic practices at State, local and school levels. But increasing bureaucracy opposes democratic control, a core value, if not practice, of American political culture: 'The growth of regulation removes issues from democratic control turning them over to bureaucracy' (Kirp and Jensen, 1986:9). (This issue is discussed in more detail in chapter 6 on Victoria.) These effects clearly oppose the self-conscious democratism in American political culture, a discourse which encouraged the objective of removing inequities in the first place.

Theorizing policy and its 'implementation' has been a concern in American academic policy analysis. The two main competing theories argue, on the one hand, that policy 'fails' in the face of local exigencies and because there is a diffusion of power among decision-makers (Pressman and Wildavsky, 1973); and, on the other hand, that policy fails because it is, initially, contradictory and inconsistent (Attewell and Gerstein, 1979). The first theory appears accurate empirically (there is a diffusion of power in state apparatuses and there are local exigencies) but this is how government written policy *works* rather than 'fails': As Offe theorizes, it is the role of state social policy to initiate conflict at other levels of state apparatuses and the outcome depends on who holds power. The second theory appears to envisage policy without contradictions, thus a social practice in which policy is formulated 'consistently' and neatly: the consensus model of politics? This is to have an apolitical view of policy. Government written policy is the outcome of political states of play (Fulcher, 1986) and is based on theories of how the social world works (Introduction) including how 'policy' might be 'implemented'. A critique which attributes the failure 'of policy at lower levels in a state apparatus to contradictions in state policy implies a utopia' (or Orwell's 1984?), in which politics or protest no longer exist. It thus implies an absence of politics at other levels of state apparatuses. This contrasts with the view that (government?) policy fails because there is a diffusion of power and with theoretical claims such as Offe's, that the role of state policy is to initiate conflict at other levels of state apparatuses. It contains a reductionist view of power and politics: that only government has power and is political. It is difficult to see how this can be sustained empirically. The contradictions in PL 94-142, between rights and judgement about what might be free appropriate education merely formalize a struggle inherent in educational practices organized around handicap; this struggle occurs at all levels, given the past exclusion of many children called handicapped from North American schools and a profession, special teachers, who have historically both argued for, and been given, the responsibility of teaching these students outside regular schools.

To argue that struggle, politics, occurs at all levels challenges a number of theoretical frameworks, including Mehan's allocation of responsibility, for the construction of student identities and careers, to 'institutional arrangements'. His position, like the more abstract forms of Marxist theorizing, locates explanation and responsibility in 'social forces' though what these are differ: in Marxist frameworks these forces are class struggles or hegemonic ideology (see Shapiro, 1980, for example), or the organization of labour and the nature of employment in capitalism (Carrier, 1986) whereas, in Mehan's ethnographically grounded research, the social forces are institutional arrangements, rather than people with limited knowledge and limited views of the consequences of their actions and discourses. This is, interestingly, to raise substantial moral issues of the kind the Eichmann trial raises: I was only following orders. In this context, as with Castles' view of the hopelessness of sociology's dismissal of politics, Mehan's position, while clearly researched and cogently argued, avoids key moral issues.

References

Attewell, P., and Gerstein D.R. (1979) 'Government Policy and Local Practices', *American Sociological Review*, 44, pp. 311–27.
Benveniste, G. (1986) 'Implementation and Intervention Strategies: The Case of 94–142', in Kirp, D.C., and Jensen, D.N. (Eds) *School Days, Rule Days*, Lewes, Falmer Press, pp. 146–63.
Berman, P. (1986) 'From Compliance to Learning: Implementing Legally Induced

Reform', in Kirp, D.L., and Jensen, D.N. (Eds) *School Days, Rule Days*, Lewes, Falmer Press, pp. 46–62

Biklen, D.P. (1985) 'Mainstreaming from Compliance to Quality', *Journal of Learning Disabilities*, 18, 1, pp. 58–61.

Bloom, M., and Garfunkel, F. (1981) 'Least Restrictive Environment and Parent Child Rights: A Paradox', *Urban Education*, 15, 4, pp. 379–401.

Bourdieu, P., and Passeron, J.C. (1977) *Reproduction in Education, Society and Culture*, London, Sage Publications.

Brinker, R.P., and Thorpe, M.E. (1985) 'Some Empirically Derived Hypotheses about the Influence of State Policy on Degree of Integration of Severely Handicapped Students', *RASE*, 6, 3, pp. 18–26.

Carrier, J. (1983a) 'Masking the social in educational knowledge: the case of learning disability theory', *American Journal of Sociology*, 8, 5, pp. 948–74.

Carrier, J.G. (1983b) 'Explaining Educability: An investigation of political support for the Children with Learning Disabilities Act of 1969', *British Journal of Sociology of Education*, 4, 2, pp. 125–40.

Carrier, J.G. (1984) 'Comparative Special Education: Ideology, Differentiation and Allocation in England and the United States', in Barton, L., and Tomlinson, S. (Eds) *Special Education and Social Interests*, London, Croom Helm.

Carrier, J.G. (1986) 'Sociology and Special Education: Differentiation and Allocation in Mass Education', *American Journal of Education*, 94, 3, pp. 281–327.

Chambers, J.C., and Hartman, W.T. (Eds) (1983) *Special Education Policies: Their History, Implementation and Finance*, Philadelphia, Temple University Press.

Cicourel, A.V., and Mehan, H. (1985) 'Universal Development, Stratifying Practices, and Status Attainment', *Research in Social Stratification and Mobility*, 4, pp. 3–27.

Cummins, J. (1986) 'Empowering Minority Students: A Framework for Intervention', *Harvard Educational Review*, 56, 1, pp. 18–36.

Eldridge, J.E.T. (1972) *Max Weber*, London, Nelson.

Ferguson, D.L. (1985) 'The ideal and the real: the working out of public policy in curricula for severely handicapped students', *RASE*, 6, 3, pp. 52–60.

Forness, S.R. (1985) 'Effects of public policy at the state level: California's impact on MR, LD, and ED categories', *RASE*, 6, 3, pp. 36–43.

Fulcher, G. (1986) 'Australian State Policies on Special Education: towards a sociological account', *Disability, Handicap and Society*, 1, 1, pp. 19–52.

Gerry, M.H. (1985) 'Policy development by state and local education agencies: the context, challenge, and rewards of policy leadership, *RASE*, 6, 3, pp. 9–17.

Giddens, A. (1971) *Capitalism and modern social theory: an analysis of the writings of Marx, Durkheim and Max Weber*, Cambridge, Cambridge University Press.

Guthrie, J.W., and Koppich, J. (1987) 'Exploring the political economy of national educational reform', in The Politics of Excellence and Choice in Education, the 1987 PEA Yearbook, a Special Issue of the *Journal of Education Policy*, 2, 5, pp. 25–47.

Hallahan, D.P., Keller, C.E., and Ball, D.W. (1986) 'A Comparison of Prevalence Rate Variability from state to state for each of the Categories of Special Education', *RASE*, 7, 2, pp. 8–14.

Hargrove, E.C. *et al.* (1983) 'Regulation and Schools: The Implementation of Equal Opportunity for Handicapped Children', *Peabody Journal of Education*, 60, 4, pp. 1–126.

Jensen, D.N., and Griffin, T.N. (1986) 'The Legislation of State Educational

Policymaking in California', in Kirp, D.L., and Jensen, D.N. (Eds) *School Days, Rule Days*, Lewes, Falmer Press, pp. 325–42.

Johnson, D.W., and Johnson, R.T. (1986) 'Impact of Classroom Organization and Instructional Methods on the Effectiveness of Mainstreaming', in Meisel, C.J. (Ed) *Mainstreaming Handicapped Children: Outcomes, Controversies and New Directions*, Hillsdale, New Jersey, Lawrence Erlbaum Associates, pp. 219–50.

Kirp, D. (1983) 'Professionalization as a policy choice: British Special Education in Comparative Perspective', in Chambers, J.C., and Hartmann, W.T. (Eds) *Special Education Policies: Their History, Implementation and Finance*, Philadelphia, Temple University Press, pp. 74–112.

Kirp, D.C., and Jensen, D.N. (1986) (Eds) *School Days, Rule Days*, Lewes, Falmer Press, pp. 1–17.

Kosc, L. (1987) 'Learning disabilities: definition or specification? A response to Kavale and Forness', *RASE*, 1, pp. 36–41.

May, D., and Hughes, D. (1987) 'Organizing Services for People with Mental Handicap: the Californian Experience', *Disability, Handicap and Society*, 2, 3, pp. 213–30.

Mehan, H. (1983) 'The role of language and the language of role', *Language in Society*, 12, pp. 187–211.

Mehan, H. (1984) 'Institutional decision-making' in Rogoff, B., and Lave, J. (Eds) *Everyday Cognition: Its Development in Social Context*, Cambridge, Massachusetts, Harvard University Press.

Mehan, H., Meihls, J.L., Hertweck, A., and Crowdes, M.S. (1981) 'Identifying handicapped students', in Bacharach, S.B. (Ed) *Organizational Behaviour in Schools and School Districts*, New York, Praeger, pp. 381–422.

Mehan, H., Hertweck, A., Combs, S.E., and Flynn, P.J. (1982) 'Teachers' Interpretations of Students' Behaviour', in Wilkinson, L.C. (Ed) *Communicating in the Classroom*, New York, Academic Press.

Mehan, H., Hertweck, A.C., and Meihls, J.L. (1985) *Handicapping the Handicapped*, Stanford, Stanford University Press.

Milofsky, C. (1974) 'Why Special Education Isn't Special', *Harvard Educational Review*, 44, 4, pp. 437–58.

Milofsky, C. (1976) *Special Education: A Sociological Study of California Programs*, New York, Praeger.

Milofsky, C.D. (1986) 'Special Education and Social Control', in Richardson, J.G. (Ed) *Handbook of Theory and Research for the Sociology of Education*, New York, Greenwood Press, pp. 173–202.

Nevin, A., and Thousand, J. (1987) 'What the Research Says About Limiting or Avoiding Referrals to Special Education', *Teacher Education and Special Education*, 9, 4, pp. 149–61.

Noel, M.M., Burke, P.J., and Valdeviesco, C.H. (1985) 'Educational Policy and Severe Mental Retardation', in Bricker, D., and Filler, J. (Eds) *Severe Mental Retardation: From Theory to Practice*, Lancaster PA, The Division on Mental Retardation of the Council of Exceptional Children, pp. 12–35.

Noel, M.M., and Fuller, B.C. (1985) 'The Social Policy Construction of Special Education: The Impact of State Characteristics on Identification and Integration of Handicapped Children', *RASE*, 6, 3, pp. 27–35.

Offe, C. (1984) *Contradictions of the Welfare State*, edited by John Keane, London, Hutchinson.

Pressman, J.L., and Wildavsky, A.B. (1973) *Implementation*, Berkeley, University of California Press.

Shapiro, H. (1980) 'Society, Ideology and the Reform of Special Education', *Educational Theory*, 30, 3, pp. 211–23.

Stone, D. (1984) *The Disabled State*, Basingstoke, Macmillan.

Swidler, A. (1986) 'The Culture of Policy: Aggregate versus Individual Thinking about the Regulation of Education', in Kirp, D.L., and Jensen, D.N. (Eds) *School Days, Rule Days*, Lewes, Falmer Press, pp. 91–108.

Tomlinson, S. (1982) *A Sociology of Special Education*, London, Routledge and Kegan Paul.

Tweedie, J. (1983) 'The Politics of Legalization in Special Education Reform', in Chambers, J.C., and Hartman, W.T. (Eds) *Special Education Policies: Their History, Implementation and Finance*, Philadelphia, Temple University Press, pp. 48–73.

Voelker Morsink, C., Chase Thomas, C., and Smith Davis, J. (forthcoming) 'Noncategorical Special Education Programs: Process and Outcomes'.

Weatherley, R., and Lipsky, M. (1977) 'Street-level Bureaucrats and Institutional Innovation: Implementing Special Education Reform', *Harvard Educational Review*, 47, 2, pp. 171–97.

Yanok, J. (1986) 'Free appropriate public education for handicapped children: Congressional intent and judicial interpretation', *RASE*, 7, 2, pp. 49–53.

Ysseldyke, J.E. (1986) 'Current U.S. Practice in Assessing and Making Decisions About Handicapped Students', *The Australian Journal of Special Education*, 10, 1, May, pp. 13–20.

Zigler, E., and Hall, N. (1986) 'Mainstreaming and the Philosophy of Normalization', in Meisel, C.J. (Ed) *Mainstreaming Handicapped Children: Outcomes, Controversies and New Directions*, Hillsdale, New Jersey, Lawrence Erlbaum Associates, pp. 1–10.

ACTS AND REGULATIONS

Education for All Handicapped Children Act, 1975 (Public Law 94–142)

Regulation 34 CFR.300–EHA

United States Code Annotated, Title 20 Education, SS1001 to 1680 chapter 33 Education of Handicapped, pp. 485–543

Chapter 5

English policy practices

While the documents which constitute writtten national education policy
on disability in England and Wales can be readily identified, neither their
intent nor effects are immediately clear. The documents are the 1981
Education Act, the White Paper *Special Needs in Education* 1980, and the related
Regulations and Circulars the Department of Education and Science (DES)
has issued to the Local Education Authorities (LEAs) and other bodies: these
include Circulars 8/81, 1/83. Circulars are described as interpretations of
government written policy rather than policy as such and 8/81, for example,
contains the caveat: 'A Circular cannot be regarded as providing an
authoritative legal interpretation of any of the provisions of the Act as this
is exclusively a function of the courts.' In addition to these documents, the
Warnock Report *Special Educational Needs* (1978), is central to any discussion
of this policy since the 1981 legislation is widely seen as embodying major
recommendations in the Warnock Report.

None of these documents emerges from a policy or political vacuum;
they relate to wider concerns and practices in the English educational
apparatus (Goacher *et al.*, 1986). Thus the 1981 legislation and the other
policy documents have close links with the 1944 and 1970 Education Acts,
with Circular 2/75, and with wide ranging practices of including in, or
excluding from, regular classrooms, children called disabled. In addition,
national education policy is part of social policy in Britain (Finch, 1984).
Shifts in the welfare state arena are part of the political and economic
conditions in which national education policy is made and remade.

In England and Wales the educational apparatus consists of the
Department of Education and Science (DES), and 104 Local Education
Authorities (LEAs) and their schools. Historically, LEAs have been seen as
relatively autonomous organizations, as having a fair degree of discretion
in the provision each makes, although officially these authorities have been
accountable to DES for 'implementing' national policy. LEAs have diverse
practices (Evans, 1986a): thus there is 'no uniform national pattern of

educational provision' (Goacher *et al.*, 1986:47). Who controls educational practices organized around a notion of disability in the authorities also differs (Goacher *et al.*, 1986); however the way this control is exercised, according to Kirp (1983), is via professionalization. Following the terms outlined in the Introduction, professionalism is used here to refer to the discourse that experts know best: professionalization is then the historical struggle in which occupational groups attempt to control areas of occupational life. In this struggle, professionalism is the key discourse and tactic.

Wider institutional conditions

In the 70s, policy in the British welfare state included concerns about equality and social welfare (Wicks, 1987), although Ball notes that the early 1970s also saw a general attack by the 'Conservative Party . . . on socialism, trade unionism and egaliterianism' (1988). A theme of equality also characterized education policy: thus Finch notes that in the 70s equality of educational opportunity was still a central issue, though she notes too, citing Halsey, that 'the essential fact of twentieth century educational history is that egalitarian policies have failed' (1984:135). This was the context in which the Warnock Committee was set up and in which it deliberated for four years, on a brief which many felt, or hoped, would improve educational opportunities for children described as disabled.

By the mid-1980s, social policy concerns in the British welfare state have shifted to issues of economic performance and security for the economy as a whole, rather than, say, for those who are unemployed or outside the paid labour force (Wicks, 1987). This shift reflects a crisis in capital and its restructuring, and its effects were felt in the British educational apparatus, as they have been in North America, Australia, and elsewhere. In Britain, the effects included substantial cuts in funds for education and the emergence of a corporate discourse on education whose themes were efficiency and effectiveness (Ball, 1988). This view sees the economy as providing the principles which should shape educational practice. In the US, Apple describes how national reports on education contribute to this discourse:

> The major national reports on education in the United States have acted to alter the very discourse of education. They shift the terrain of debate from a more social democratic concern to the language of efficiency, standards and productivity . . . the ultimate effect may be eliminating from our collective memory why inequality in education, the economy and in politics was of public concern (Apple, 1986:171).

In Britain, Ball describes similar effects from, for example, the Black Papers (1988). Despite the shift in social policy concerns to themes of efficiency and effectiveness, some educators have resisted the effects on educational discourse. For instance, in 1986, the *British Journal of Sociology of Education* devoted an entire issue to inequality, its editor, Len Barton, arguing that inequality should be returned to the centre of educational debate.

A number of writers argue, however, that the restructuring of capital has had significant effects on educational practices in Britain. For instance, Gordon suggests that one effect has been to demolish any possibility of a comprehensive education policy (1986). As chapter 2 noted, a policy on comprehensive education, or education for all, as Fish puts it (1985), is where a debate on integration belongs, though Booth suggests that comprehensively organized schools provide only the *potential* for integration (1983). If Gordon is right, the restructuring of capital provides a potentially hostile context for an integration policy which is concerned with equality. But Gordon's theorizing reduces educational practices to the action of the 'state': she argues school practices should be understood as mediating the relations of capital and as containing 'oppositional spaces' in schools, through which this mediation might be changed, though what courses of action should follow Gordon does not make clear.

Other writers reject a level of theorizing which reduces policy and its effects to determinate effects of 'state' action; they thereby reject its essentially pessimistic stance. Thus the outcome of a comprehensive policy is debated and some remain optimistic about the possibility of achieving comprehensive practices (for example, Barker, 1986). In contrast, Ball suggests the discourse of comprehensive education in the 1960s was 'inchoate, fragmented and contested' and that in the late 1980s, 'The meaning and practice of comprehensive schooling in Great Britain are currently at the centre of a set of political processes which have profound implications for the definition of what is to count as education' (Ball, 1988). Booth is also less hopeful that comprehensive schooling will emerge and says that 'the nature of comprehensive education has never been defined by government'. He asks whether it implies grouping mixed by ability, or 'curricula adapted to the interests and backgrounds and cultures of pupils' or 'power sharing of education with committees of the school' and notes that 'the present government favours selection by ability and a return to selective schooling. It is also opposed to mixed ability grouping ... whether or not this orthodoxy percolates through the DES and LEA administrations or to the schools is another matter, but the intentions are clear' (Booth, 1983:265). Government policy practice on 'comprehensive' schooling has implications for segregated schooling ... obviously a Conservative Government with such views about selective education would not control segregated schooling for children with mental handicap *because* of adherence to a comprehensive ideal' (Booth, 1983:265).

Clearly there is a continuing struggle over whether or not schools in Britain should be 'comprehensive': Ball and Booth suggests this struggle will be lost to conservative forces, whereas Galloway and Goodwin argue that schools are generally comprehensive and that 'The principle of comprehensive education is now accepted throughout the country, except in a tiny minority of LEAs. Attempts in some Conservative controlled LEAs to abolish comprehensive schools, reverting to a selective system, have been abandoned following public outcry' (1987:1). Yet they also note that 'in our comprehensive school system a higher proportion of children than ever before is being removed from the mainstream for schooling in separate schools, classes or units' (1987:1). Thus interpretations of the extent and significance of comprehensive education for integration are inconsistent. Part of this may be due to different writers using different definitions of 'comprehensive education' but it also seems likely that the conflicting interpretations derive from a failure to conceptualize educational policy practices as *political struggles* whose outcomes vary in different arenas and in the various levels of the educational apparatus and at particular points of time. A diversity in practice is predicted in the model of policy outlined in the Introduction.

Clearly, however, the wider context – the possibly widespread dissolution of the comprehensive project in education, substantial cuts in funding, and a corporate discourse of efficiency and effectiveness replacing the theme of inequality – are likely to have a significant influence on policy struggles in various arenas in the educational apparatus concerning children described as disabled. This is the case for educational practices in general. Thus there have been struggles over key objectives in the British educational apparatus for some time. Evans describes this as follows:

> what we see is a system which is diverse: a system which has for ten years been forced to respond to the problems of falling rolls, expenditure reductions and rationalization; been required to accommodate to the questioning of entrenched views on the control of the curriculum and teacher autonomy and to engage in exercises of public accountability with facets as diverse as the reform of school management bodies, effectiveness studies of input and output, whole school curriculum evaluation and teacher appraisal.
>
> Within this diversity, within the ferment of educational debate which reaches for the roots of established practice, the new legislation for children with special educational needs was conceived, gestated and born (1986a:3).

Evans thus describes intense political struggles in the educational apparatus in the decade to 1986. The key struggles he identifies are who should control the curriculum, the extent of teachers autonomy, and public accountability (an administrative-political term for external control of various types) of schools; all of which occurred in a context of reduced spending on education and a decline in school pupil numbers.

These are the wider political-economic and wider educational conditions in which the documents constituting government written education policy on disability emerged. In addition, special educational practices of inclusion and exclusion of children called disabled had been part of educational practices for several decades. For some observers, this constituted 'integration' (Goacher *et al.*, 1986, for instance), in that children with a range of disabilities were in regular classrooms: this practice has coexisted with extensive segregation throughout this century. We need to recall, too, that integration has a wide range of meanings (chapter 2), that the issues are far from new (see Nix, 1981, on a policy for integrating children who were deaf in regular schools in Germany in the early 1800s) and that other commentators, such as Booth (1983), provide evidence to the contrary, that despite central government documents since the 1950s claiming that integration was government policy *and* was being implemented, no such 'general national move towards the development of an integrated education system' was occurring between the 1950s and early 1980s (Booth, 1983:264). But Booth, in contrast to others' notions of integration, refers to a process of increasing participation by children called disabled in the social and educational life of regular schools. Integration, in this sense, was not occurring in this period at an overall level; the available statistics show that segregation was increasing throughout this period. 'Between 1950 and 1977 there was a substantial growth in the proportion of children placed in special schools' (Booth (1981) cited by Swann, 1985:1). The trend towards segregation was also confirmed by Hegarty and Pocklington in their analysis for 1971–80 (cited by Swann, 1985:1). Moreover, this segregation appears to have been unevenly spread amongst different sections of the school population: the evidence available up until 1972,[1] suggests that children of West Indian parents were disproportionately likely to be referred for special education and that the majority of parents of children excluded from regular schools were working-class (Tomlinson, 1981, 1982, 1985).

Despite the statistical evidence on these overall trends, or practices, discourse on integration was clearly occurring before the Warnock Committee met in 1975 and had been the subject of government policy in Scandinavia and the US. In Scandinavia and the US, there had already been extensive debate on the issues and various legislation, seen as integration and mainstreaming, had already been enacted. The US had issued federal law PL 94–142 in an attempt to control special education. Conversely, in

Denmark, special education legislation had been repealed in an attempt to normalize conditions for those called handicapped.

In Britain, the 1970 Education Act is seen as part of the debate on integration. According to the 1970 Act, the notion of 'ineducable was to disappear from educational thinking, responsibility for those children deemed severely educationally subnormal (ESN(S)) was transferred from the health to the educational apparatus and some saw the 1970 *legislative conditions* as giving 'every ESN(S) child . . . the same right to education as ordinary children' (Spencer, 1983:17). Spencer also claims that before the 1970 Act these children were largely 'shut up in hospitals' but that since the 1970 legislation there was 'a gradual move . . . to get them more involved in the outside world' (1983:17). Despite Booth's national figures, there are clearly views that integration practices in the sense of a move from segregation were already occurring before the Warnock report. Thus there are claims that Warnock's recommendations merely legitimized already existing practices (Goacher *et al.*, 1986, for example), while others claim that Warnock made integration easier (Pritchard, 1980, for instance). The extent to which this claim can be sustained is examined below.

It appears, then, that a debate on integration, in its various senses, was taking place in the British educational apparatus since at least the 1970s (Evans, 1986a:2), while Booth says this happened in the 1950s (1983:264). It seems unlikely, therefore, that Kirp is right in his observation that special education policy has been a topic of concern to only a few (1983), even prior to the policy under consideration. Certainly there has been widespread comment since the policies presented in these documents were issued.

Overall therefore, the *political* and *economic conditions* of the British welfare state in the 1970s, when the Warnock Committee met, and in which the 1981 Education Act (the Warnock Act) was framed, were considerably different from those in which struggles over disability in the educational apparatus now occur.

National policy practices

There has been extensive comment on both the 1978 Warnock Report and the 1981 Education Act, which 'came into force' on 1 April 1983. What are the main statements and underlying principles in this written policy? And how should we interpret them?

The Warnock Report recommended the term 'special educational needs' replace the existing eleven categories of disability defined in the 1944 Education Act. It talked, too, of special education *provision* rather than treatment and it asserted that approximately one in five, or 20 per cent of the school population, would, at some stage in their lives, require special education provision. This contrasted with the previous, officially endorsed view that approximately 2 per cent of the school population was handicapped. The Report was clear that 'special educational needs' were relative:

> Whether a disability or significant difficulty constitutes an educational handicap for an individual child, and if so to what extent, will depend upon a variety of factors. Schools differ, often widely, in outlook, expertise, resources, accommodation, organisation and physical and social surroundings, all of which help to determine the degree to which the individual is educationally handicapped ... It is thus impossible to establish precise criteria for defining what constitutes handicap. Yet the idea is deeply engrained in educational thinking that there are two types of children, the handicapped and the non-handicapped (1978:37).

Despite this relative notion of special educational needs, which was seen as embracing 'learning difficulties' of a wide kind, a discourse on disability pervaded the entire Report; moreover the themes of guilt, suffering, burden, discovery, which belong properly, if at all, only to a discourse on severe disability, were a very clear part of the Report.

The Report recommended, too, that LEAs follow a statementing procedure for those with severe handicap for whom provision meant extra resources and it talked a great deal about specialist expertise, the necessity to expand this, and the role of specialist support services in providing advice, support and encouragement to parents. It talked much less about parents who, however, were to be seen as partners and to whom more information was to be provided than was the past general practice.

How shall we interpret these proposals? They were to have far-reaching political significance not only in the British educational apparatus but in Victoria, for instance, where the Warnock estimate of one in five was widely accepted in debate. This escalation of the proportion deemed to have special educational needs, was intended by many to have the effect of getting government to provide more resources: far from having this consequence, this officially endorsed notion and proportion was to provide the basis for *marginalizing* more of the student population (Tomlinson, 1985).

The Warnock concept of special educational needs, as relative, is undermined in the Report by the absolutist assumptions of its discourse on disability: a deficit is something a *person* – not the educational apparatus – *has:* thus the Report failed to provide a serious challenge to the political logic of disability, despite the relativity of its notion of special educational needs and the related discourse of professionalism was strongly endorsed: professionals via their expertise were to make decisions about special educational needs and about potential segregation and integration (seen as provision). The institutional bases for the educational version of a discourse on deficit, difference and professionalism, which lie in teacher training institutions which separate skills for teaching the 'able' from skills for teaching those deemed disabled, were reinforced: there was to be in-service training for regular teachers to gain the necessary expertise.

In line with its focus on disability, the Warnock Report gave little space to curriculum, on which it provided the shortest chapter and, for related reasons, it failed to ask the core question which should inform debate on integration, Why do children fail in school? There is, however, an implied answer in the Report: despite its concept of relative special educational needs, a relativity which includes the skills of regular classroom teachers, the Report's answer is that children fail because they have a disability. The politics of this is discussed below.

The Report also gave little space to discussing integration. While it distinguished social, locational and functional integration, its focus on provision as constituting integration, together with its endorsement of segregated practices, shows that the Warnock notion of integration is a new name for special education (Tomlinson, 1985). While it is widely seen as an integration Report, Warnock's view seems the more accurate: 'People say we fudged integration, but we fudged it as a matter of policy' (1978). As intended, then, it provides no political impetus to move from present practices of extensive segregation. *The actual procedures which constitute educational practices surrounding disability were,* however, *to be more highly regulated.* Thus the recommendation on statementing procedures endorsed bureaucratic management and effectively *bureaucratized* practices. This control was to be exercised by professionals.

The recommendations that parents be given more information and be regarded as partners, while weakly articulated and somewhat contradicted by the view that specialists should support, encourage and give these partners advice, was nonetheless seen as significant. This response makes sense only in the context of the well-entrenched professionalism Kirp sees as characterizing social welfare policy practice in Britain.

Overall, Kirp's view that professionalism pervades the Warnock Report is sound (1983). But to that should be added its strong discourse on disability, its conservative and politically expedient notion of integration and the gesture at reformulating the relationship between parents and professionals in the educational apparatus. Moreover, the recommendations on statementing suggest, as against Kirp's view, that consistent with its position on professionalization, bureaucratization was also chosen as a policy solution by the Warnock Committee. The Report's discourse on disability was clearly informed by medical and charity models (chapter 1), and obscures the fact that, for *most* of the 20 per cent of pupils described as disabled, impairment or individual deficit is an inappropriate way of conceptualizing their failure in school. Describing special educational needs as relative is a first step in clarifying the obscure and political debate which constitutes an educational discourse on disability but the Report failed to go further. It thus legitimized the political logic of disability for 20 per cent of the school population, thereby deflecting attention from the need to change school practices, including pedagogic skills.

The 1981 Act is seen as the Warnock legislation and came into force on 1 April 1982. It, too, has been widely discussed. Much of this comment has been concerned with the content of the legislation but before looking at this it is worth raising some questions about the general relevance of legislative conditions to the questions this book tries to answer. While I have argued that policy, as a form of social practice, occurs at, or is made at, all levels in the educational apparatus, this does not mean that policy made at, say, government level, in the form of legislation, has no influence on the policy at other levels. It means, rather, that it does not have a determining effect and that it may merely provide some of the conditions in which practice at other levels occurs.

What effects have the legislative conditions of the 1981 Act had on policy practices at other levels in the English educational apparatus? Goacher *et al.* suggest that:

> It would be misleading, then, to see the [1981 Education Act] as the starting point for a series of changes in local authority administrative and professional practice. Such changes were taking place before the legislation was enacted and were part of the evolving view of special needs which brought about the change in the law. At the same time, many other policy changes, not directly connected to special education, or even to education, were influencing the way in which local authorities could respond to the 1981 Act. These included central government economic policies, MSC initiatives, moves towards 'care in the community' by health and social services and, more recently, the signalling by the Government of certain priorities by the allocation of the Education Support Grant . . . *A new law may be seen as just one significant event in the general process of service and policy development* (Goacher *et al.*, 1986:22–3, emphasis added).

Welton and Evans also provide an answer to the role of legislation and suggest that the 1981 Act has become just one of the structural conditions or constraints within which local authorities and professionals evolve their own policies about meeting special needs (1986:224). This view appears to draw on a model of society 'as a totality governed by necessary structural requirements' (Hindess, 1986:119), a framework rejected in the Introduction; another interpretation is that the 1981 Education Act created institutional conditions for policy practices at other levels.

The Education Act, 1981 sought to direct practices concerning children with 'special educational needs'. A child has 'special educational needs if he has a learning difficulty which calls for special educational provision to be made for him'. A learning difficulty is defined as occurring when 'a child . . . has a significantly greater difficulty in learning than the majority of children of his age; or [if] he has a *disability* [emphasis added] which either prevents or hinders him from making use of educational facilities of a kind generally provided in schools'; 'Special educational provision' means . . . educational provision which is additional to, or otherwise different from, the educational provisional made generally for children of his age in schools unassisted by the local education authority concerned.

These few sentences reveal key aspects of the 1981 legislation. The Act retains a discourse on disability, despite an attempted shift to educational discourse via the notion of special educational needs; it defines special education as provision; in the context of a state apparatus this means resources in general, rather than specifically educational provision such as appropriate curriculum; and, importantly, the Act generalizes about provision in schools ('provision additional to, or otherwise different from, the educational provision made generally . . .'). It thus obliterates Warnock's relative approach, where a child's needs depend on the school he/she is in. The Act establishes a generalist discourse and provides a basis for negotiating over, and focusing on, resources rather than examining the educational and social context in which particular 'needs' might emerge. This provides a base for retaining the distinctions between normal and special (related to deficit, different, disability) provision.

Statementing is the procedure for obtaining special provision. All children with special educational needs, by definition, require additional provision, yet statements are only to be made for those with severe disabilities. Thus the Act is inconsistent. Where statements of a child's special educational needs are made, LEAs are required to make special provision in 'ordinary schools', provided the necessary provision is made *and* that this allows '*efficient education for the children with whom he will be educated; and the efficient use of resources*'. Here we see a corporate discourse (chapter 1 and above) which submerges concerns for equality of access to regular schools. In this context, Tomlinson's judgment that the 1981 Act legitimizes more of the same (1985) that is, no change from present practices of segregation and integration, seems accurate.

The Act is widely seen as an attempt to change the relationship between parents and the education apparatus. Section 3 states that where a local education authority believes it 'inappropriate for the special educational provision required for that child . . . to be made in a school, they may after consulting the child's parents arrange for it . . . to be made otherwise than in a school'. Authorities are to judge (professionally) whether special provision in an ordinary school is appropriate or not; they are required to consult with parents but the Act does not make their decision subject to parental approval. Wherever a parent disagrees with an Authority, he may discuss the matter with the Authority's respresentative. None of this indicates a serious approach to rights. Moreover, authorities are to 'determine the special education provisions that should be made'; and to serve notices on parents (section 5(3)). Despite wide interpretation that the 1981 Act confers new rights on parents whose child is deemed to have special educational needs, it is clear that the Act retains the language, hierarchy and politics of professionalism:

(1) The Secretary of State shall by regulations make provision as to the advice which a local education authority is to seek in making assessments.

(2) Without prejudice to the generality of sub-paragraph (1) above regulations made under that paragraph shall require the local education authority to seek medical, psychological and educational advice and such other advice as may be presented (Schedule 1).

Parents may make representations to the authority, but the Act makes no provision for appeal to bodies outside the educational apparatus. Parents can appeal to a local Appeals Committee. But this has no power to overrule the LEA's recommendations in the statement, but can ask the LEA to reconsider them (Galloway and Goodwin, 1987:18). The Act also refers to special educational treatment (Section 21) thus reinforcing a medical discourse on disability.

Circular 8/81 describes the Act as establishing a new framework for the education of children requiring special educational provision. In contrast with the Act's view that special educational needs means a child requires special educational provision additional to, or otherwise different from, that generally provided, in a school for others of his age, the Circular states that:

The majority of children with special educational needs as defined in the Act will continue to be educated within the resources of their ordinary school and will not require the LEAs to determine how their needs are best met. However, for a small percentage of children who have severe or complex learning difficulties it will be necessary for authorities themselves to determine the appropriate provision to be made in respect of individual special educational needs. The deciding factors here are likely to vary from area to area depending on the range of provision normally available in an authority's schools. As a general rule the Secretary of State will expect LEAs to afford children the protection of a statement of their special educational needs in all circumstances where extra resources in terms of staffing or equipment would be required to cater for those needs in an ordinary school (1981:3).

These statements suggest only those with severe disabilities will require extra provision and thus 'statements': but this sits oddly with the Act's definition of special educational needs as special provision. The concept of special educational needs conflicts with the recommendations on who is to be 'statemented' and to receive extra provision: not the majority of the 20 per cent with special educational needs, according to the Circular. This ambiguity thus provides a context whereby authorities can interpret and use statementing procedures differently: in fact, this is what occurs (Goacher *et al.*, 1986:125–7). Given the Act's ambiguity on key issues as well as the varying practices which connect LEAs, the DES, and schools, this diversity is hardly surprising. But it challenges the view that policy should direct (Booth, 1983:263) and that national policy, such as education policy on disability, can provide 'uniform national policy'. It is relevant then to look more closely at LEA policy practices.

Local Education Authority policy practices

The 104 LEAs in England and Wales differ in a number of important respects. Some are inner urban authorities (notably the Inner London Local Education Authority) while others operate in rural, dispersed communities. They have different histories, and this includes the educational arrangements they have made for children formerly described as disabled, or with a synonym, or as having special education needs. Overall these practices are diverse but they are characterized by professionalism and by a variety of professionals.

The connections LEAs have with social service departments and the voluntary sector, also differ. Moreover each of the social service departments and agencies 'has its own history, paradigms, policies, structures and procedures' (Goacher *et al.*, 1986:55). In the social service departments 'There does not appear to be a very clear idea . . . of the role they should play in the assessment procedures, and there have been differences in perceptions of responsibility for financing resources for children with special needs' (Goacher *et al.*, 1986:43). Goacher *et al.* suggest this detracts from the efficient use of resources (1986:43), though such efficiency is seen as important in the Act (see above).

LEAs have responded differently to key aspects of the Act: to statementing, to the percentage of children for whom statements, thus special provision, are seen as necessary: to the requirements to relate to parents and partners (provide more information, consult and involve in decision-making) and in the extent to which they integrate and segregate pupils. There is wide comment on these differences and while this comment describes a potentially confusing array of practices, they exhibit two clear characteristics. One is *diversity* and the second is conflict or *struggle*. Thirdly, LEAs provide a local level (as do schools) in which these struggles take place.

Specific practices in LEAs include withholding information from parents (Sharron, 1985; Vaughan, 1986:119): and giving inadequate information (Goacher *et al.*, 1986:137). Goacher *et al.* report that parents are relatively unconcerned about the formality of bureaucratic procedures (1986:131). In contrast, professionals criticize the procedures as time-consuming, formal, bureaucratic and therefore not good clinical practice (a revealing comment in itself). Appeals about the provision for children with special educational needs are concentrated in particular LEAs (Goacher *et al.*, 1986:131). Bookbinder reports conflict between parents and professionals (1986); while Newell points out that professionals are gagged by the LEAs (1985) Goacher *et al.* found little evidence of professionals thwarting 'the intention of policy makers by refusing to implement the spirit of the legislation': 'the majority we talked to were very much in agreement with the legislation's aim'. They suggest their research confirms

> Weatherley's argument . . . that those charged with delivering resources operate a kind of rationing system when resources are limited, and it is this which distorts practice . . . [since] we found that the main reason for poor services and bad practices was not a lack of commitment to the legislation, but difficulties in meeting the level of demand (Goacher *et al.*, 1986:199).

In this context, LEAs are faced with difficult decisions, and professionalism appears less a means of advancing the interests of a particular profession and more a way of legitimizing practices as authoritative, in order to contain protest. 'The Act required a redistribution of resources in favour of children with special educational needs. Within a fixed level of resources this inevitably implies a reduction of resources for the remainder of the school population' (Goacher *et al.*, 1986:199). Goacher *et al.* then go on to suggest that 'Policy makers will have to decide whether this is what they intend. Furthermore, policy makers must look more closely at the funding implication of major policy initiatives' (1986:199). This however is to have an apolitical concept of policy and to assume rationality rather than political behaviour on the part of (national level) policy writers. Those who have been closely involved with key decision-makers in a policy writing process at government level know that the funding implications of a policy may be well understood and that these may be kept from others in this process in order to contain the politics of decision-making in writing a policy.[2] These political reasons include both the expedient (we don't really intend and we wish to head off protest in Committee about the likely lack of necessary funds) and the realistic (we don't have the power to make decisions on how funds should be allocated). How then shall we theorize this diversity, struggle and localization?

The evidence fits Offe's view of the role of state social policy: that it sets up conflictual interaction at other levels. We could also 'theorize' the diversity as an instance of 'poor planning' or implementation: this was rejected in the Introduction. Thirdly, we can theorize the diversity, struggle and localization as showing that *policy is made at all levels* in the educational apparatus. Moreover, seeing this locally made policy as inevitably political both anticipates Offe's view of state social policy on initiating conflict at other levels and incorporates Hindess's point that decisions at national level may have a more extensive effect than decisions made at other levels. The notion of extensive effect clearly applies to the complex statementing practices the 1981 Act requires LEAs to undertake for (an ambiguous proportion of) children described as having special educational needs. This fits Evans's view that the 1981 Act 'required LEAs to review their arrangements in respect of the obligations placed on them to identify and meet the special educational needs of all children whenever and wherever these occur' (1986a:1) and that the main effects of the legislation appear to have been to create 'a flurry of activity relating to statutory obligations' (1986a:8).

The 1981 Act thus appears to have intensified struggles over integration in a number of arenas and to have made procedures for providing services *more bureaucratic,* thus potentially more controlling, both of its employees (professionals largely) and the recipients of services: parents and their children described as disabled. How does this flurry of activity, increased struggle and bureaucratization relate to what goes on in schools? Is it the case that, since the 1981 Education Act, children described as disabled are being increasingly *integrated* in regular schools in the sense of sharing in the social and educational life of their peers who allegedly do not have disabilities?

School policy practices

School policy practices on integration are extraordinarily diverse. Schools can integrate but schools also have the power to exclude: the opportunity to exclude is given in the 1981 Education Act in the procedures for statementing and assessing the provision deemed necessary. Clearly this opportunity provided by national policy is used in schools when those in power want to do so or feel they have no alternative. As Booth notes:

> Examples of the successful integration of children with almost any given disability irrespective of severity, can be found somewhere in the United Kingdom . . . The overwhelming conclusion is that where integration does not happen it is because people with the power to make the changes do not want children with disabilities in our schools (Booth, 1983:263–6).

Galloway and Goodwin confirm the wide disparity in school practices: behaviour and progress one school interprets as indicating the need to review curriculum, another sees as a case for referral (1987:172). There is evidence that some schools 'are providing education of an outstanding quality for their most vulnerable pupils' and that other schools 'are identifying a large number of pupils as having special needs, and giving these pupils a separate curriculum'. (Galloway and Goodwin, 1987:xiii). Evans asserts that the 1981 Act has merely created a legal framework for advancing the cause of children with disabilities, but that 'administrations and *teachers* will ultimately determine the benefit derived by the children' (1986a:3). These comments suggest that it may well be that decisions in classrooms are crucial. Regular schools are clearly critical sites where the process that leads to segregation begins (where labels of 'different' are applied) and its opposite, the process of integration takes place. Given this book's interest in assessing the effects of written national policy on school policy practices, whether written, stated or enacted this raises the questions of how far and in what ways national policy decisions, both written and enacted (no extra funding) may have influenced school policy practices, or, more specifically, what teachers say about what they do and what their actual practices are concerning pupils called disabled. Such effects might include encouraging integration in regular schools, encouraging segregation or merely politicizing practices surrounding students described as disabled.

There are no clear studies of the extent to which written national policy has encouraged integration practices in schools or politicized them. There are, however, statistics available on segregation both before and since national written policy. But what has clearly happened is that teachers and their teaching practices have become a focus for a debate on how to change existing practices in a way which might encourage integration. Evans (1986a, 1986b) and Galloway and Goodwin (1987) exemplify this position: implicitly they theorize *teachers as key policy makers*. Before looking at their theorizing and the courses of action they suggest, it is relevant to ask two questions: while school practices are diverse, has the segregation of schoolchildren called disabled decreased since national written integration policy? And has it altered the class, race and gender composition of children segregated from regular classrooms?

Swann's analysis of statistics reveals that between 1978 and 1982, children with sensory handicaps have increasingly found a place in regular schools while those with learning difficulties are being increasingly segregated (1985). The specific effects are that in the five year period between 1978 and 1982, that is, since the issuing of the Warnock Report, 'the proportion of children aged 5 to 15 in special schools grew by 4.9 per cent' (p. 4) but that:

> different categories followed different courses . . . In the case of sensory impairments (blind, partially sighted, deaf and partially hearing) there was either little change, or a decrease in the proportion of children in special schools, but in the case of the much larger groups of the physically handicapped, maladjusted, educationally subnormal (moderate) [ESN(M)] and educationally subnormal [ESN(S)] there was a clear trend towards segregation (Swann 1985:1).

Further, the increases for those in primary schools was at a much higher rate than for those in secondary schools (p. 7). Examining these figures more closely, Swann states that in 'a period when the school population of primary age fell by over thirteen per cent, numbers in ESN(M) schools *rose* by nearly eleven per cent.' Given the widely stated claims (Tomlinson, 1981, 1982, 1985, for instance) that children in the largest former categories of ESN(M), 'maladjusted' and 'disruptive' are 'almost exclusively from manual working class parentage' (Tomlinson, 1982:69) the increasing segregation of these groups suggests that national written level policy has had no effect in reducing the class and race bias in which children are selected out of regular classrooms. Thus Galloway and Goodwin, in 1987, confirm that:

> nationally schools for learning or adjustment problems
>
> (1) cater . . . almost exclusively for the working class,
> (2) cater . . . disproportionately for children from ethnic minority groups [West Indian largely, according to Tomlinson (1981, 1982)] and for boys,
> (3) lack . . . the confidence of many parents, especially those from ethnic communities (ILEA, 1985a) (Galloway and Goodwin, 1987:131).

How do the various writers theorize increasing segregation and the class and race effects?

In attempting to explain the trend to segregation, Swann notes Booth's point that 'screening procedures focus attention on the difficulties of children rather than on those of the teachers or the curriculum or the organization of schools', that this focus on a child 'for whom there are no extra resources may lead to pressures for special education'; and that a change in policy on the role of special schools (as providing a support service for mainstream schools) has been shown in one study (Goodwin, 1983) to increase the number of students referred for special education. In Goodwin's study, 'over the 3 years following the introduction of this support service, special school placements grew by more than fifty per cent' (Swann, 1985:11). Swann's view is that 'the changing role of special schools and a widening of their activities may account for such figures as the eleven per cent increase in segregation of children classed as moderately or mildly educationally subnormal rather than a lowering of tolerance amongst primary school teachers's (1985:11).

Swann's comments reinforce the view taken in chapter 2, that disability is the wrong discourse and that the central issues are curriculum, including teachers' skills. He suggests that the increased attention on children with disabilities, and on the need asserted for further support services for regular schools from special schools, has the counter effect of enhancing control via special education practices rather than encouraging integration. This is in line with Tomlinson's recent view that the effect of integration policy has been to expand special education practices, to marginalize increasing numbers of schoolchildren, and that this will be in the interests of advanced industrial societies which will require high rates of unemployment (1985). In this last comment, Tomlinson provides a structuralist account of special education practices.

At other points, however, Tomlinson's theorizing approaches the framework outlined in the Introduction: that social life is political and that people use strategies in struggles to achieve their objectives. In the case of struggles concerning integration, the current and opposing strategies are those of professionalism and democratism. In her chapter on issues between professionals and parents (1982: chapter 7), many of Tomlinson's observations fit this framework; she notes that working-class parents will have more difficulty in negotiating with professionals. She sums this up by saying that dominant interest groups (professionals) are able to shape educational practices for their own purposes (1982:107). But her point on negotiation is in line with Mehan's findings on linguistic processes of persuasion used by professionals in arenas where decisions are made about selecting children for segregated education (1983). Also relevant is Carrier's analysis of middle-class parents in the US negotiating for a label of difference they saw as preferable (1983b). While both Tomlinson and Carrier provide class-structural accounts of these processes, their evidence fits a discursive social practice model, in which people use the discourses available to them. But in this model, as Hindess points out, classes as decision makers are not a theoretical category though social actors may have discourses about social class.

Galloway and Goodwin discuss the issues of race and class in conjunction with the question of why segregation is occurring rather than integration, despite widespread statements and belief that children are being increasingly integrated into regular schools. They explore these issues by looking at the fate of Sheffield Education Committee's policy to integrate children with special needs into ordinary schools. They suggest the best possible political and economic conditions were present for making policy happen: the Committee had had a clear policy since 1976; they had given generous financial support to special education and were committed 'to the welfare of children living in socially disadvantaged circumstances' (1987:129).

> Yet in the decade after this humanitarian, politically radical council committed itself to integration, there was no noteworthy drop in the proportion of children, predominantly from working-class backgrounds, placed in long-term special schools or units. If we take into account the short-term special school placements, the unit for disruptive pupils, the 'home' tuition units and the school attached to a hospital child psychiatry unit the proportion of children receiving separate special schooling for at least some of their education may even have increased (1987:130).

How did this happen? How can such counter-effects or the failure of intended effects be explained? Galloway and Goodwin suggest that 'The apparent failure of Sheffield's policy resulted from the lack of any coherent plan to implement it'. The Introduction suggested that 'poor implementation' is an inadequate way of theorizing policy's apparent failure and that policy as practice may be theorized as occurring at all levels. We then have to look at the objectives of those involved in decisions: the objectives of individuals and actors which have decision making powers. This means, as Hindess suggests, locating responsibility for policy practice with the individuals and actors who make those decisions. At school level this means teachers, head teachers, committees and support staff, and at the LEA Education Committee level, members of the Committee. While not articulating these levels of responsibility clearly, Galloway and Goodwin suggest there was little guidance given to teachers to change from existing practice:

> Lacking any clear, firm, direction from the administration, teachers in ordinary schools and members of the support services had to

evolve their own solutions to the day-to-day problems they encountered. Inevitably these solutions reflected the special education network that actually existed, not the network that might have existed if the council had recognized the implications of its own policy. Consequently, many of the developments in special education services for children with learning and adjustment difficulties merely extended the existing network. The effect was to strengthen the identity of this network as separate from the mainstream, effectively deepening the divisions between mainstream and special education rather than integrating them. 'Integrated resources' constitute the one possible exception, but even they regarded children with moderate learning difficulties as beyond their remit (1987:130).

This view suggests that the Education Committee's policy was *inadequately theorized:* 'it failed to take into account existing practices and how these needed to be reoriented'. This also appears to be Galloway and Goodwin's view of why the Committee's policy decisons also failed to reduce class, race and gender basis: the 'plan to implement Sheffield's integration policy was not based on any clear analysis of the class, race and sex implications of the special education facilities for pupils with learning or adjustment difficulties. (Galloway and Goodwin, 1987:131). Poor social theorizing at LEA level does not mean, however, that teachers do not make policy: merely that, with clearer directions, they might attempt to integrate rather than segregate. Implicitly, however, Galloway and Goodwin have a top-down model of policy and appear to locate responsibility for its 'failure' with LEAs rather than with teachers.

However, in suggesting how a policy on integration might be implemented, Galloway and Goodwin focus on teachers and teaching practices and what needs to change here:

teachers in the mainstream should receive the training and the support to enable them to teach pupils with learning or adjustment problems successfully. We knew from our own work with teachers that this could be done. We also recognized that it had implications for teacher training at initial and in-service levels, for the support services and for local education authority (LEA) policy towards children with special needs. Our argument, then, was that special education, in its literal sense, could and should be provided in ordinary schools (1987:xi).

But they note, too, that integrated provision 'places considerable demands both on teachers and on LEAs. At a time of economic recession, when many teachers feel that not only their employers but also their pupils' parents are unreasonably expecting them to achieve more and more with less and less, it would be suprising if such demands went unchallenged.' (1987:152). Thus they locate a degree of responsibility for integration not happening with teachers. 'Effective integration requires a high level of expertise [which] cannot be achieved merely by political or administrative *dictat.*' (1987:154). They argue that:

> support services should share responsibilities with teachers. To be successful this requires definition of the scope of each person's responsibilities. Teachers are fully justified in demanding specialist help in their work with pupils with learning and adjustment difficulties. The relationship we envisage is described by Galloway (1985b).

> A teacher may say to an educational psychologist: can you suggest some activities I can use to help Helen learn to read? The teacher here is making clear that he retains responsibility for choice of activities. By implication, if the suggestions do not prove successful the teacher and the psychologist can together work out some other approach. This is quite different from saying: We've already done everything possible for Helen in this school, so now we're referring her to you. Here, the teacher is explicitly passing responsibility for the child to the psychologist, effectively absolving himself from further involvement (p. 64) (1987:167).

In this view, Galloway and Goodwin point out the moral dimension in integration and implicitly argue against the view, that draws on professionalism, that those with special educational needs belong to others, and not to the regular classroom teacher.

Evans' critique is detailed and somewhat inconsistent on professionalism. He argues for professionalism in that he sees teachers are insufficiently professional but argues against some of its techniques. His view is that 'schools *matter significantly* in respect of the quality and success of pupil learning' (1986a:2). Some schools contribute to learning difficulties: 'Learning difficulties of a great many children are *acquired,* in as much as they are so identified *during* the process of schooling and often as a consequence of their experiences at school' (1986b:3). The reasons lie in teaching practices which are poorly theorized: 'Being frequently eclectic, practice risks being incoherent and inconsistent. Untied to developmental theory, pragmatic and curriculum decision making becomes determined less by the needs of the child than the exigencies of the situation' (1986b:3). Here, Evans' critique is not so much of teachers themselves as of teacher training institutions that have failed to provide trainee teachers with coherent theories of learning and teaching.

Thus he draws our attention to a *key institutional* base which while promoting a notion and strategy of professionalism (about separate areas of competence: teachers of the able and teachers of the not-so-able) fails to provide a theoretically based technical competence and discourse on which these future teachers may draw. He also criticizes professionalism in noting that 'It is a matter of common experience that many teachers *keep* extensive records but have difficulty in interpreting their significance for children's learning' (1986b:3). Again, Evans draws our attention to what is clearly a technique of professionalism (record keeping) which is then an artifact for which teachers have no real use.

Evans also seems to argue against professionalism in suggesting that 'An effective policy on special needs would in one sense or another, require the participation of *all* teachers in primary and secondary schools if these contexts were to respond appropriately' (1986a:5). This is because 'in all mainstream schools, barriers to innovation are potentially linked to idiosyncratic interpretation of the new concept of special education needs and not insignificantly to the professional mystique which many teachers associate with the pedagogy of learning disabilities' (1986b). This is due to:

> The development and modes of operation of local authority advisory remedial and support services for over two decades [which] have had the unfortunate effect of *restricting the class teacher's vision of her professional role* and contributed to the evolution of a pedagogical paradigm which focuses on organizing the teaching of classes rather that organizing the learning of individuals (1986b:6, emphasis added).

In sum, 'For many children with special needs, teachers, in the past, have been part of the problem. Developing their professional skills may ensure that in the future they become an effective part of the solution' (1986b:8).

Evans's message is clear at one level: pedagogic practices, including school climate, generally need to change if teachers are to enact a policy of successful integration. This message is supported by others, including Hegarty of the National Foundation for Educational Research (for example, 1982a, 1982b). But Evans's insightful comments are undermined by the lack of an adequate critique of professionalism, such as Welton and Evans provide: 'professionalism is a strategy of job control in which one of the main prizes is the right to define and determine the situation in a given sphere of work' (1987:218).

Nevertheless, much of Evans's critique is relevant: that teachers lack the theoretical framework which ought to underpin their pedagogic practices, that teacher trainee institutions are clearly implicated here, and that the way in which LEA support services have operated has been to encourage a fragmented professionalism: our child not yours, or not mine, yours. It may seem pedantic to criticize Evans for urging the development of professional skills of regular teachers. But profeessionalism, as discourse and tactic, is clearly associated with separate areas of presumed expertise. This is the essence of bureaucratic mentality, as Weber showed, and a means of avoiding responsibility. Thus what needs developing, as Galloway and Goodwin suggest, is regular teachers' sense of competence so that they can accept responsibility for a wider range of children. This is not to argue for professionalism.

How does national policy relate to educational practices surrounding disability at other levels?

Before we can answer this question we need to summarize briefly the nature of national written policy, especially the 1981 Act, as well as educational practices generally in this area, as these are reported by Evans, Galloway and Goodwin, Swann and Tomlinson and outlined above. We can then ask how all this interconnects.

The 1981 Education Act defines special educational needs in deficit terms and as indicating a need for additional provision. It is expedient about whether pupils with special educational needs should be in ordinary schools; this is to occur only if it is compatible with effective education for other children and the efficient use of resources. Statements such as these are classic escape clauses in legislation; moreover, they are framed in a corporate discourse on special educational needs (chapter 1). The Act is ambiguous about who requires a statement to acquire a special provision and while it is seen as providing a framework for altering the relationship between parents and the educational apparatus, professionals have the responsibility for decisions at key points in statementing procedures. Thus the Act is framed in discourses on disability, professionalism and corporate concerns and while it implies extra funds should be allocated for this policy, this has not occurred; enacted policy and written policy conflict.

In many respects the Act is ambiguous and, at points, *absolutist:* children have special educational needs (deficits) whereas Warnock emphasized that needs are *relative* to particular schools. Others have gone further than Warnock and have suggested that schools create learning difficulties for the vast majority of these children (Evans, 1986b; Galloway, 1985) and that policy on exclusion is idiosyncratic to each school (Galloway *et al.*, 1985). In this context, the 1981 legislation, far from reflecting current thinking, is reactionary.

The Act has nothing to say on key educational issues, such as curriculum. The nearest it gets is to require LEAs to make provision for children 'protected' by statements. But the educational effects of such provision are another matter and where this is in segregated schools the evidence is that this provision disadvantages those who receive it: 'research . . . at the most charitable interpretation fails[s] . . . to support the view that children benefit . . . educationally from attending special schools rather than ordinary schools' (Galloway and Goodwin, 1987:x).

Local Education Authorities have a wide range of practices concerning special educational needs, practices which are diverse both between and within authorities. Authorities have responded differently to the Act on key issues such as the proportion for whom statements have been issued, the extent to which they use segregated facilities, and so on. But *the Act* has imposed some uniform effects: First, it *has increased the bureaucratic regulation of practices* concerning special education needs. This follows from the statementing procedures it requires of LEAs. It has also legitimated a *discourse* on integrating children with special education needs; and the practices which accompany this discourse have become increasingly politicized. Issues of rights versus professionalism are now openly debated, a debate which may well have been unthinkable before this national policy, given the deeply entrenched professionalism that has characterized social policy, including education policy, in Britain. But given the fictitious nature of these rights, a fiction which appears not to be widely perceived, *the basic effect of this discourse is a politicization of practices,* rather than a real move towards democratization.

Thus there are four main effects of the 1981 legislation: (1) increasing bureaucratic regulation, a regulation which is controlled by professionals; (2) an increase in the proportion of students marginalized through their being described as having special educational needs; (3) the legitimation of a discourse on disability, which underlies a notion of special educational needs; and (4) the politicization of practices where parent rights are largely a fiction. The Act has not curtailed various practices of exclusion in separate schools, classes and units, nor the race, class and gender bias in who gets excluded from regular classrooms. On the contrary, there are concerns that the Act may deepen race and class division (Galloway and Goodwin, 1987:172; Tomlinson, 1985) and that it may increase the number of pupils removed (Galloway and Goodwin, 1987:xiii). Segregation has increased since the Warnock Report for the largest category of children. This indicates the extent to which policy is made at other levels in the educational apparatus and that it is practices at other levels which construct these effects.

Conclusions

The 1981 Education Act and its associated Circulars and Regulations constitute national education written policy on disability in England and

Wales and are widely seen as integration policy and as representing many of the recommendations in the Warnock Report. There are differences between these documents, as outlined above, but at the heart of this policy lie a number of contradictions, or more accurately, struggles. It is informed by concerns about social justice (Stobart, 1986) but clearly it is also informed by concerns about professionalism (Kirp, 1983): professionals are to oversee assessment and statementing procedures. This professionalism characterizes social policy in England and Wales: in educational practices surrounding an expanding notion of disability it has legitimized a discourse on an historically increasing proportion of children as different and thus as not belonging in regular classrooms; it has also legitimized the establishment of institutional bases for separating educational practices for those called disabled, namely separate (special) teacher training institutions and courses. Professionalism has been the key control strategy used in educational practices called 'special education' and its dominance has not been challenged by any of the conditions created by national written policy, including legislation.

Under professionalism, extensive exclusion from regular classrooms and the marginalization of students have occurred; an exclusion which was theorized in chapter 1, following Paul Abberley, as oppression. Segregation in special schools, which has been a consequence of professionalization, has not benefited children excluded from regular classrooms (Galloway and Goodwin, 1987). The politics of this exclusion has been obscured by a discourse of professionalism (in the child's best interests).

A second struggle is related in the Act's position on parents rights. Government written policy has altered the discourse about education and 'disability' to include a theme of rights but it fails to provide the political means of achieving these, so that the power professionals hold remains.

The themes of redressing inequalities in the educational apparatus for children called disabled and of integrating pupils in ordinary schools had been present in debate and educational policy at a national written level since the 1950s and include the 1970 Education Act. Legislation seen as about integration and mainstreaming had been enacted in other countries, notably in the US.

In the English context, the Warnock Report (1978) emerged in social and political conditions where equality was still a policy issue and it was widely seen as breaking new ground, whereas it is, on closer examination, expedient about integration and contains a deeply entrenched professionalism as well as a medical- and charity-based discourse on disability. In fact, it is a highly political document. The main effect of the Warnock Report is to have established significant political conditions, in that it legitimized 20 per cent of the school population as having needs outside the facilities ordinary schools generally provide. Thus it failed to make clear — a general failure of debate in this area – that *for a very large proportion of this 20 per cent, the notion of an impairment as underlying whatever labels of difference a student acquires, is inappropriate, and that to imply it is present, as any discourse on disability and its synonyms does, is an extremely political act.* The 1981 Education Act further legitimizes these political conditions by establishing them also as legislative conditions.

These politics are submerged by the British version of professionalism where issues are presented as technical, rather than political. As Kirp notes,

> The British [version of social policy is of] . . . *enabling professionals through the exercise of benign discretion, to offer the highest level of service on the least stigmatizing terms possible, given available social resources.* This model of social welfare does not recognize conflict; it is silent concerning politics, and actively antagonistic toward law. It contemplates professionals and administrators working on behalf of an ever-expanding clientele toward an agreed–upon common good (1983:106).

A further struggle characterizes the 1981 Act in its alleged concerns for equality and economic themes of efficiency and effectiveness. Finch summarizes these antinomies as follows: 'In the egalitarian position, the idea of social justice is much more important than a consideration of national efficiency or the needs of the economy. It treats education as a valuable commodity in itself and recognizes that effective access to it should not be denied to any citizen' (1984:120). But the 1981 Act is also concerned with efficiency: the education of children with special needs is only to take place in regular classrooms if this is consistent with the efficient education for others and with the efficient use of resources. These corporate objectives are inconsistent with concerns for equality.

The 1981 Act was also seen as providing a legal framework in which the relations between parents and the educational apparatus might be changed. Nevertheless it reinforces professionalism and is, in a number of ways reactionary to, rather than reflecting, newer practices in this area. The diversity of practices in LEAs and schools provide a fluid context in which LEAs and schools can make their own policy practices within the increased formality the Act requires on making and reviewing statements. It is clear that the Act 'directs' policy practices in LEAs only in the sense of increasing bureaucratic control via the statementing procedures. It did not refer to the class, race and gender bias in who gets excluded from regular classrooms, a failure shared by an LEA which was outstanding for its commitment to integration and to reducing race and class discrimination (Sheffield LEA). Both government written policy, including the 1981 Act, and Sheffield LEA's written and enacted (funding) policies, inadequately theorized the practices which lead to exclusion. Thus the notion of enabling legislation cannot be applied to the 1981 Education Act.

Finally, segregation for some children has increased despite the Warnock Report and the 1981 Act (Swann, 1985) and despite the growing critique of the effect of separate education, both in its immediate educational effects (Tomlinson, 1982; Galloway and Goodwin, 1987:x–xi) and its labour market consequences for those assigned to it (Tomlinson, 1985).

Notes

1 Official statistics on immigrant children have not been collected since then (Tomlinson, 1982:157).
2 This occurred in the policy process for *Integration in Victorian Education,* where the present author, the Chairperson and another member of the writing team met a number of times in a period of two weeks towards the end of the Review, to consider in more detail than was possible or desirable in Committee meetings, the funding implications of the policy and how the politics of this might be contained in Committee. This was not, at least for one of the participants, an entirely cynical process: a written policy where there was a clear intent to integrate was seen as a possible means of overcoming resource demands. The focus, at that stage, was thus in presenting a written policy with a clearly articulated intent to integrate. Resource implications were, in a reasonable sense, seen as belonging to agendas in arenas other than the Review. In reality this is what happens: the Cabinet allocates funds to education, and departments of education as state apparatuses make decisions at various levels, or in various arenas, on how these funds are to be allocated. Such arenas include other potential decision makers, such as teacher unions. Committees, such as Warnock, have no power to make decisions about resource allocation, though in times of economic restraint they might make recommendations about redeployment. In this context, it is significant that Warnock failed to make clear recommendations on *redeploying* resources.

References

Abberley, P. (1987) 'The Concept of Oppression and the Development of a Social Theory of Disability', *Disability, Handicap and Society,* 2, 1, pp. 5–20.

Apple, M.W. (1986) 'National Reports and the Construction of Inequality', *British Journal of Sociology of Education,* 7, 2, pp. 171–90.

Ball, S. (1988) 'Comprehensive Schooling, Effectiveness and Control: an analysis of educational discourses', in Slee, R. (Ed) *Discipline and Schools: a Curriculum Perspective,* Macmillan Australia.

Barker, B. (1986) *Rescuing the Comprehensive Experience,* Milton Keynes, Open University Press.

Bookbinder, G. (1986) 'Professionals – and Wrong Predictions', *British Journal of Special Education,* 13, 1, pp. 6–7.

Booth, T. (1983) 'Policies Towards the Integration of Mentally Handicapped Children in Education', *Oxford Review of Education*, 9, 3, pp. 255–68.

Carrier, J.G. (1983b) 'Explaining educability: an investigation of political support for the Children with Learning Disabilities Act of 1969', *British Journal of Sociology of Education*, 4, 22, pp. 125–40.

Department of Education and Science (1975) Circular 2/75 *The Discovery of Children requiring special education and the assessment of their needs.*

Department of Education and Science (1981) Circular 8/81 *The Education Act 1981.*

Department of Education and Science (1983a) Circular 1/83 *Assessments and Statements of Special Educational Needs* (Joint Circular with DHSS Health Circular HC(83)3 and Local Authority Circular LAC (83)2).

Evans, R. (1986a) 'Children with learning difficulties: Contexts and consequences', paper presented at the Australian Association of Special Education 11th National Conference, Adelaide, October.

Evans, R. (1986b) 'Responding to Special Educational Needs: Perspectives on Professional Extension', paper presented at The Australian Association of Special Education Conference, Adelaide, October.

Finch, J. (1984) *Education as Social Policy,* London, Longman.

Fish, J. (1985) *Special Education: The Way Ahead,* Milton Keynes, Open University Press.

Galloway, D. (1985) *Schools, Pupils and Special Educational Needs,* London, Croom Helm.

Galloway, D., and Goodwin, C. (1987) *The Education of Disturbing Children: Pupils with learning and adjustment difficulties,* New York, Longman Inc.

Galloway, D., Martin, R., and Wilcox, B. (1985) 'Persistent Absence from Schools and Exclusion from School: the predictive power of school and community variables', *British Educational Research Journal*, 11, 1, pp. 51–61.

Goacher, B., Evans, J., Welton, J., Wedell, K., and Glaser, D. (1986) *The 1981 Education Act: Policy and Provision for Special Educational Needs,* a Report to the Department of Education and Science, University of London Institute of Education, October.

Goodwin, C. (1983) 'The contribution of support services to integration policy', in Booth, T., and Potts, P. (Eds) *Integrating Special Education,* Oxford, Basil Blackwell.

Gordon, T. (1986) *Democracy in One School: Progressive Education and Restructuring,* Lewes, Falmer Press.

Hegarty, S. (1982a) 'Meeting Special Educational Needs in the Ordinary School', *Educational Research*, 24, 3, pp. 124–81.

Hegarty, S. (1982b) 'Integration and the "Comprehensive" School', *Educational Review*, 34, 2, pp. 100–5.

Hindess, B. (1986) 'Actors and Social Relations' in Wardell, M.L., and Turner, S.P. (Eds) *Sociological Theory in Transition,* Boston, Allen and Unwin.

Integration in Victorian Education (n.d. but 1984) Report of the Ministerial Review of Educational Services for the Disabled, Melbourne, Government Printer.

Kirp, D. (1983) 'Professionalization as a policy choice: British Special Education in Comparative Perspective', in Chambers, J.C. and Hartmann, W.T. (Eds) *Special Education Policies: Their History Implementation and Finance,* Philadelphia, Temple University Press, pp. 74–112.

Mehan, H. (1983) 'The role of language and the language of role', *Language in Society,* 12, pp. 187–211.

Newell, P. (1985) 'Backlash – Don't Gag the Professionals', *British Journal of Special Education,* 12, 1, p. 9.

Nix, G.W. (1981) 'Mainstreaming: a bend in the river', paper presented at the Association of Canadian Educators of the Hearing Impaired National Convention, Vancouver, British Columbia, August.

Offe, C. (1984) *Contradictions of the Welfare State,* edited by John Keane, London, Hutchinson.

Pritchard, D.G. (1980) 'The educational integration of handicapped children in the light of the Warnock Report', *Aspects of Education,* no. 24.

Sharron, H. (1985) 'Needs must', *Times Education Supplement,* 22 February 1985.

Special Educational Needs (1978) Report of the Committee of Enquiry into the Education of Handicapped Children and Young People, London, HMSO (Warnock Report).

Special Needs in Education (1980) White Paper, Cmnd 7996, London, HMSO.

Spencer, D. (1983) 'United we stand', *Times Educational Supplement,* no. 3483, 1 April 1983.

Stobart, G. (1986) 'Is integrating the handicapped psychologically defensible?' *Bulletin of the British Psychological Society,* 39, pp. 1–3.

Swann, W. (1985) 'Is the integration of children with special needs happening?: an analysis of recent statistics of pupils in special schools', *Oxford Review of Education,* Vol 11, no. 1, pp. 3–18.

Tomlinson, S. (1981) *Educational Subnormality: A Study in decision-making,* London. Routledge and Kegan Paul.

Tomlinson, S. (1982) *A Sociology of Special Education,* London. Routledge and Kegan Paul.

Tomlinson, S. (1985) 'The Expansion of Special Education', *Oxford Review of Education,* 11, 2, pp. 157–65.

Vaughan, M. (1986) 'Backlash – Caught up in the Act – or Caught out?', *British Journal of Special Education,* 13, 3.

Warnock, M. (1978) *Special Education Needs* (Chair: M. Warnock).

Welton, J., and Evans, R. (1986) 'The Development and Implications of Special Education Policy, Where did the 1981 Act fit in?', *Public Administration,* 64, pp. 209–27.

Wicks, M. (1987) *A Future for All: Do We Need the Welfare State?* Harmondsworth, Penguin.

ACT

Education Act, 1981, HMSO.

Chapter 6

Victorian policy practices

While I have pragmatic reasons for focusing on Victorian policy practices rather than those of other Australian States, the reasons are political and theoretical as well. Pragmatically, I had an insider's view of the production of what is now seen as 'Victorian policy', namely the *Integration in Victorian Education* report (1984). This is the report of the Ministerial Review of Educational Services for the Disabled. Established by the then Minister of Education, Robert Fordham, the Review was one of a number set up by the new Labor government, the first elected in Victoria for twenty-five years. The new government's policy was one of 'social justice'; it thus represented a modern variant of a vaguely defined set of ideas which, according to one Labour historian, has characterized policy making in Australia throughout its history (Macintyre, 1985). The Review was established as part of this 'social justice' policy. The insider's view came from a year's secondment to the then Department of Education as main policy analyst and writer for the Review.

Politically and theoretically, the 1984 report, like other education policy practices in Victoria,[1] raises a number of issues central both to the Victorian educational apparatus and to Australian society in general. Thus it represents a number of social democratic themes and concerns for the education of those called disabled, concerns which reflect written policy in the wider educational apparatus (see, for example, Ministerial Papers 1–6, 1982–1984) and which are central to Australian society. Some of the strategies proposed in the report to democratize this area of educational practices have failed. This raises critical political theoretical questions about the nature of Australian political and educational life. Secondly, at a substantive educational policy level, and in line with the policy of democratization in the Ministerial Papers (defined as participation in decisions by those affected by them, and implying a move to local control), the report's theme of school-based services appears to represent a move from central to local control. Again, Victoria is seen as the most advanced of the states in such a shift (Boyd and Smart, forthcoming:

introduction) but it seems clear that such moves are being overlaid by corporate restructuring (see Victoria, Ministry of Education, 1986a, 1986b, 1986c, 1986d) and that Hughes is correct in pointing out that 'Victorian initiatives ... while still retaining elements of devolution, also involve a clear central control, but a more explicitly political control' (forthcoming: 20). This corporate discourse Ciavellera (1987) calls a centralist discourse: corporatism and centralism clearly conflict with democratism as a discourse whose themes include the right to equal treatment, a say in decision-making, and a move to local control.

Thirdly, the report has been the most controversial of the recent special education policies the various states have issued (Fulcher, 1986a).[2] According to a review of Australian state policy documents on special education, the 1984 report[3] is the only document with what might be called a politically 'progressive' approach to integration (it contains the second objective outlined in chapter 2), compared with the qualified approach taken in other state written policies. Thus the Victorian report defines integration as referring to the increasing participation of all students in the social and educational life in regular classrooms. The qualified approach taken in other state written policies provides no direction for moving to such a process: their written concepts of integration are consistent with past practices of extensive segregation of children called disabled co-existing with the presence of *some* children thus described being in regular classrooms. While the Victorian concept directs practices to change, the versions in other states' documents allow the preservation of the status quo. Fourthly, the 1984 report has influenced the Victorian educational apparatus: new practices have emerged, many of which might be described as counter-effects, or not what many of the policy makers had in mind. Since the report was written with a serious intent to promote integration (understood as increasing participation), an intent which contrasts with Warnock's fudging the issue (chapter 5), this raises questions about the nature of government written policy, as action and intervention in the educational apparatus. Thus Victorian policy practices both illuminate, and are illuminated by, the model of policy outlined in the Introduction.

This chapter aims, as do the others, to assess the effect of government written educational policy on disability on practices in schools and at other levels of the (Victorian) educational apparatus. First, then, I shall outline the documents which constitute government written policy and discuss the main themes and discourses in the 1984 report. Secondly, the institutional conditions of educational policy practices on disability are examined. Here I will refer to national policy statements, discourse and funding practices both for education generally and 'special education', and to Victorian government written policy practices on education other than disability. I shall then look briefly at how the themes in the 1984 report fare in the wider Australian context. These themes are democracy, rights and disability. Later sections will examine the new practices which have emerged in the Victorian educational apparatus since the 1984 report.

Written integration policy practices at government level in Victoria

In Victoria, there is no legislation or Regulations on integration. However, there is very widespread understanding that the educational apparatus has an integration policy. The key policy documents are the *Integration in Victorian Education* report (1984), and various memoranda from the then Minister of Education, Robert Fordham, and his successor, Ian Cathie, and various officials in the former Department, now Ministry, of Education. These memoranda appear to be as follows:

(a) Minister of Education (Robert Fordham), memorandum to Presidents of Schools Councils, Principals and Staff, *Integration in Victorian Schools*, (no date).

(b) Deputy Director-General (M.K. Collins), memorandum to Presidents of School Councils, School Principals and Staff, *Integration in Victorian Schools*, 31 August 1984.

(c) Acting Chief Executive (M.K. Collins), memorandum to Executive Directors, Directors of Branches and Units, Regional Directors of Education, Principals of Schools, Presidents of School Councils, Officers-in-Charge of Student Services Centres, Teachers-in-Charge of Education Support Centres, *Guidelines for Schools: The Integration Teacher: Role, Rationale and Responsibility (Primary and Post Primary)* (no date).

(d) A/Director of Student Services (Alan R. Farmer), memorandum to Regional Directors of Education, O.I.Cs, Student Services (CG&CS) Centres, *Special School Placement Procedures*, 28 March 1985.

(e) Minister of Education (Ian Cathie), memorandum to Presidents of School Councils, School Principals and Staff, Regional Directors of Education, *Integration in Victorian Schools*, 20 May 1985.

(f) Acting Chief Executive (M.K. Collins), memorandum to Regional Directors of Education, Principals of Schools, Presidents of School Councils, Officers-in-Charge of Student Services Centres, Teachers-in-Charge of Education Support Centres, *Enrolment and Support Group Guidelines for Regular Schools*, 13 March 1986.

(g) Director Integration Unit (Bernard Lamb), memorandum to All Members Senior Officer Group Integration Committee, 29 April 1986.

(h)   General Manager (M.K. Collins), memorandum to Regional Directors of Education, *Delayed Admission to School of Parent's Choice*, 19 January 1987.

(i)   General Manager (Schools Division, M.K. Collins), Executive memorandum No. 144 to Regional Directors of Education, Principals of Schools, Presidents of School Councils, Officers-in-Charge of Student Services Centres, Teachers-in-Charge of Education Support Centres, *Integration Support Group Procedures for Regular Schools (Formerly Enrolment and Support Group Guidelines)*, 17 August 1987.

In the absence of legislation and supporting Regulations, these memoranda effectively *rewrite* aspects of Victorian government level written policy on integration as it has been negotiated following the report. The memoranda document and legitimize a number of new practices and are both responses to, and attempts to direct, policy practices at other levels: they indicate struggle over policy objectives surrounding disability and integration. There is extensive negotiation, struggle, between the Ministry and other levels in the Victorian educational apparatus; policy is *remade* rather than 'implemented'. This is in line with Goacher *et al.*'s (1986) observations on English policy practices following the 1981 Education Act, and with the model presented in the Introduction.

The 1984 report

A critical reading of *Integration in Victorian Education* reveals a struggle between professionalism (the discourse that experts know best) and democratism. Its main theme is the right of every child to a regular education (guiding principle 1). A key strategy to achieve this is the recommendations on participatory decision making structures at school, Regional and central levels. These are democratic concerns and strategies of the kind Demaine outlines (1981). This theme is supported by a lengthy chapter on legislating for these rights. There were intense struggles in Review meetings over legislation: some argued that legislation was the only means of protecting such rights: this group drew on American example (despite the difference between the American and Australian constitutions) and Australian legal opinion (for example, Hayes, 1984; Hayes and Macalpine, 1986). Others argued that there was no constitutional basis in Australia for the enactment of rights and that it was unlikely that legal remedies (a necessary mechanism for translating moral or in principle rights to legal rights) would be written into legislation since, given the emerging debate (in Review meetings) from protagonists of different positions on the need for extra resources, this would mean resources on demand. These struggles resulted in recommendations that the legislative issues should be passed to the recently established State Board of Education for further consideration.

Democratism also underlies the critique of the professionalism characterizing Victorian 'special education'; the critique in chapter 1 rejects key concepts and practices of the special education version of professionalism, including normalization, assesssment and identification. In the same chapter, a socially critical view informs the attempt to point out the limited relevance of a medically informed discourse on disability and it locates responsibility for children failing in school as potentially due to schooling practices: thus the report has a vague theory of how children might fail other than through 'deficits'. The concept it proposes to cover this is 'problems in schooling'.

However, the theme of criticizing educational practices makes only a brief appearance in the report; it is not followed, as politically and pedagogically it should be, by a discussion of curriculum, that set of learning experiences which undoubtedly contribute to some children's failing in school. The socially critical discourse on schooling practices is undermined by Extension Note 2, a last minute insertion by a representative of the Technical Teachers' Union of Victoria and the Victorian Secondary Teachers Association. Point 6 in this Extension Note effectively argues that the notion of 'problems in schooling' is a term and a problem which belongs to children rather than to schools. This Extension Note provides a basis for the notion of 'problems in schooling' becoming a new deficit label which can be incorporated into the political logic of a discourse on disability (chapter 1).

The report's chapter 5 continues the critique of a medically informed discourse on disability, putting the view that incidence and prevalence data provide a misleading basis for service requirements. The argument here is that there is no correspondence between an impairment a child may have and the educational services he/she may require, and also that the idea of the prevalence of disabilities ignores the *relative* (to schools) notion of how 'disability' is constructed – how social constructs such as disability and its synonyms emerge and are applied. But chapter 5 also provides a table on incidence based on American figures. The inconsistency in this chapter reveals the struggles between those with a medically informed discourse on disability, those with a social constructionist view (a minority around the Review table) and the external pressure from government to provide data for 'informed decision making'. This latter request, while rational in principle, when applied to educational practices in the context of a medical, natural science-based and deficit view of disability, reveals an inadequate theorizing of the social world; it merely reinforces this theoretically flawed and (from a social democratic stance) politically misleading discourse.

Despite its democratic discourse (its position on rights and the critique of professionalism), professionalism surfaces strongly in the report's recommendations that the membership of Enrolment Support Groups (ESGs) (the key structure and tactic proposed to ensure parent and student rights to participate in decision-making in schools) may include specialists who may then outnumber non-specialists and thus potentially, if this is the way a particular ESG works, submerge a parent's claim that their child has a right to a regular education. Extension Note 1 to the report, inserted also at the last minute, this time by the Review member representing parent organizations, which disputes the proposed membership of ESGs, reveals the struggle between democratism in this Extension Note and the professionalism in the report's recommended membership.

The integration objective in the 1984 report reveals a clear intent to move from segregated provision: it refers to processes of maintaining and increasing the participation of all children in regular schools.[4] Such a process could be monitored: the notion allows for accountability[5] (Gow and Fulcher, 1986) and it seeks to promote a shift from the extensive provision of educational facilities segregated from regular schools while retaining segregated schools 'for the time being'.

The report's discourse on democratism is thus undermined by professionalism and by not following through the pedagogical implications of a rights position and its socially critical view of school practices. These views should have taken it in the direction of a debate about comprehensive education and non-divisive curriculum practices. Its democratic intent is also undermined by the wider legal and constitutional conditions. These are discussed later.

While the democratism in the 1984 Victorian report is flawed and its dominance over professionalism is tenuous, it contrasts strongly with the entrenched professionalism in other state government-level written policies on special education, despite their token reference to parent rights and advocacy (Fulcher, 1986a). The controversial response the Victorian report received at government level in other states attests to the professionalism and medically informed views in these states. Levin's views on professionalism in Australian education apparatuses is discussed below.

Institutional conditions of education policy practices surrounding integration in Victoria

The institutional conditions affecting education policy practices in Australia are complex.[6] These conditions intersect in a variety of ways; while they may be divided into constitutional, legislative, administrative-political-bureaucratic and economic practices, the discussion will both cut across this division and refer briefly to policy statements at a written national level ('Commonwealth policy on education and special education'), to Victorian government written policy on education in general, and to the agencies who make decisions and whose practices construct the conditions of the 1984 report. Thus the focus is on 'the complex intersection of a variety of specific practices, policies and actors' and 'the conditions those practices sustain (or undermine)' (Hindess, 1986:120).

An important set of conditions derives from the state constitutions and the Commonwealth constitution; here I shall draw on an account by an American Professor of Law, Betsy Levin. This is a useful account despite its somewhat over-optimistic view of what legislative decisions can achieve (1985). As Levin points out, the state constitutions predate the Commonwealth's (1901); they 'empower their legislatures to provide for "peace, order, and good government", thus giving the states authority over all social services. Relying on such provisions, the states have enacted public instruction acts' (1985:222). Consequently the Commonwealth constitution does not provide the federal goverment with any direct authority over, or responsibility for, education in the states, apart from 1946 amendment which permits the Commonwealth Parliament to make laws with respect to benefits to students (Levin, 1985:223).

Despite the lack of a constitutional basis for direct responsibility for education in the states, the Commonwealth government has a Department of Education, Employment and Training,[7] and it has also sought, since 1974, to influence education policy concerning schools via the Commonwealth Schools Commission (CSC). The Commission[8] was established in 1974, following the Karmel Report (*Schools in Australia*) commissioned by the Whitlam government, the first federal labour government for twenty-three years. This government held office from 1972–1975 until the notorious withholding of Supply by the then Governor General, Sir John Kerr. It is useful to trace briefly here the Schools Commission's early discourse (policy statements) and funding practices both for schools in general and for 'special education', since these provide part of the complex array of political and economic conditions of the Victorian policy on integration, some of which derive from the constitutional conditions of education policy. This is to digress for a moment from Levin's account.

The Whitlam government agenda is widely seen as aiming to create a more equal and just society; thus, as opposed to the Hawke government's agenda of pragmatism and consensus, as a labour government with a 'social democratic project'. Its equity concerns for education entailed a focus on improving equality of opportunity in schools for disadvantaged groups. Under Whitlam, 'education was viewed as a central instrument for making society more equal and for promoting social reform' (Smart, forthcoming b:19 in typescript). The Karmel Report provided the Schools Commission with a democratic discourse. Its written policy principles or values were equality, diversity, devolution of authority, community participation and responsiveness to change. Where the education of 'handicapped' children was concerned, the Report had a relative notion of handicap (p. 109, 10.1), it retained the idea that 'within the limitations of present knowledge' some children 'are considered ineducable' (p. 109) and it did *not* have a discourse of disability: the Karmel Report's view was that intelligence testing as a basis for deciding who should be segregated was 'arbitrary' and it recommended that state Education Departments, and not health authorities, should take responsibility for educating children in institutions. It also recommended state governments should (democratically) take responsibility for educating children where this was presently under the auspices of voluntary bodies.

According to Hayes and Macalpine, the Karmel Report introduced a 'Renaissance' in special education which included legislation, especially the Handicapped Persons' Assistance Act, 1974, and the Commonwealth Schools Commission Act, 1974.[9]

The effect of this legislation on the education of children with intellectual disabilities has been less than Hayes and Macalpine claim: chapter 5 in *Integration in Victorian Education* provides some data for 1983 on the lack of educational programs for some children of school age both in the community and in some residential institutions. Like Levin, Hayes and Macalpine, both lawyers, seem over-optimistic about the effects of legislative decisions. Nor do they acknowledge reports such as those from the Human Rights Commission (1986a, 1986b) which document the extent to which those with disabilities have been unable to pursue their rights under the existing legislation. The limited effect of such legislation attests to the fact that legislation is only one site of decisions, while the ability of state governments sometimes to ignore Commonwealth written policy, indicates that policy is made at other than a national level of written policy statements.

Despite the Commonwealth's constitutionally weak basis for controlling or directing educational practices, the new Schools Commission made a number of economic decisions which clearly provided new conditions for regular and special education policy practices in the various states. Its key practice, here, was making 'specific purpose grants' to the states. The Disadvantaged Schools Program has been a major program, while the Special Education Program, which began in 1974, became one of the largest of these specific purpose grants: grants were made from 1977 for the Severely Handicapped Children's Program, and from 1981 for an Integration program and a Children in Residential Institution Program. In 1985 specific grant monies were provided for the Early Special Education Program.

The Schools Commission thus sought to enact the Karmel Report recommendations by funding 'specific purpose grants' to the states. A continuing theme has been the Commonwealth's inability to control how these funds are spent, despite their title 'specific purpose grants' (see for example, Ashby and Taylor, 1984). This shows the limited constitutional power exercised by the Commonwealth through the Commission in its attempt to influence state policy practices on schooling, even where it provides money for particular programs. This situation constitutes a dilemma for the Schools Commission and reports to the Commission suggest it should take a more clearly defined 'leadership role' (for example, Ashby and Taylor). But more accurately, it is clear that policy is made at a number of levels in the Australian educational apparatus (in the states, in schools) other than at national written and enacted (funding) levels. This is clearly the case, too, with the Schools Commission discourse. This discourse has consistently included relative notions of handicap (1975:167; 1978:111) and statements about the need for 'fundamental changes in school organisations, in roles and attitudes and in the ways in which schools develop their curricula' (Schools Commission, 1976:69), but the extent to which these suggestions are adopted at various levels in state educational apparatuses is extremely problematic.

While the Commonwealth government presently has a weak legislative basis for directing educational practices in schools, Levin takes the view that the Australian Parliament could use its external affairs power in section 96 to 'enact federal legislation guaranteeing equal opportunity for various special pupil populations'. (1985:272). In addition, 'Parliament has broad powers under section 96 of the Australian constitution to condition its specific purpose grants for education so as to protect the interests of children with special needs' (p. 272). While her view that legislation can guarantee effects is, from the model presented in the Introduction, determinate (and optimistic), her point that the federal government could draw on the external affairs power to write educational legislation is relevant. She sees such legislation as needing to include a civil rights objective: while the Australian constitution 'contains no guarantee of rights analogous to those articulated in the US Bill of Rights' (p. 219), there are international covenants and agreements on human rights which 'provide a sufficient nexus for such domestic legislation' (p. 272), in that Australia is a member of the organizations which have issued covenants or agreements concerning education (p. 246). Currently, school policy practices in Australia contravene these agreements and covenants, as does the federal government practice of funding private schools, a practice which significantly contributes to inequalities in education (Connell *et al.*, 1982) and, consequently, in the labour market (Jamrozik, 1986, 1987) and which a number of writers suggest will now exacerbate social division (Miller, 1986; Smart, forthcoming b).

Levin sees Parliament as unlikely to use the external affairs power to enact legislation, either to encourage 'equal educational opportunity for various special pupil populations' or to 'attach specific conditions on its federal aid to education' including that for disability. The reasons lie in Australia's traditions and political/legal culture where 'there is a strong preference for "states' rights" rather than a strong national government', where there is a tradition of deferring to professionals, and because the educational system 'is basically paternalistic: the power of educational decision making is entrusted to the professional' (Levin, 1985:272). Levin's account thus points up the limits of the constitution and of legislation as sites of decisions constituting conditions of the 1984 report and suggests that *power in decisions lies with professionals.*

Where Commonwealth legislation and educational rights are concerned, Sheehan notes that the Commonwealth Parliament rejected a Bill of Rights in 1985. Thus Parliament is unlikely to introduce 'federal legislation to ensure that all children [receive] an education' (Sheehan, 1986:16). Moreover, while a recent report to the Commonwealth on funding special education (Commonwealth Schools Commission *Report of the Working Party on Commonwealth Policy and Directions in Special Education*, 1985) suggested 'that resource agreements with the States should include the requirement that the States provide education for all at least to the cost of an average pupil . . . [this] is unlikely considering the decrease in Commonwealth funding for special education in the past two budgets' (Sheehan 1986:16). The decision to reduce spending on special education suggests that, as for education generally, the education of those called disabled is lower on the agenda of the Hawke government than it was in the Whitlam era. These decisions constitute both political and economic conditions of the 1984 report; further aspects of economic decisions are discussed below.

Where constitutional conditions of the 1984 report are concerned, the Commonwealth and state government constitutions allow an uneasy division of responsibility for education between federal and state governments, one where the state educational apparatuses can make political and pedagogic decisions about schooling practices, including those surrounding disability and 'integration', which are largely independent of direction by the Commonwealth but which are, nevertheless, paid for by Commonwealth.

Legislative decisions provide further conditions of the 1984 report.[10] These derive mainly, then, not from the Commonwealth Parliament but from the Victorian Parliament.[11] They include the 1958 Education Act, the Education (Handicapped Children) Act, 1973, the Education (Special Developmental Schools) Act, 1976 no. 8918, the Freedom of Information Act, 1982, and the Equal Opportunity Act, 1984. This last Act outlaws discrimination by educational authorities against a person on the ground of impairment, but it includes classic escape clauses; for example, in 5 (a) (b) (c): 'if by reason of his impairment the person requires special facilities'. In addition, there are two Acts relating to schoolchildren described as disabled, for which the Minister of Community Services has responsibility: the Community Welfare Services Act, 1970, and the Intellectually Disabled Persons' Services Act, 1986.[12]

There are a number of sections in the 1958 Education Act which relate to integration (State Board 1987:8). Section 61A of the 1958 Education Act concerns children deemed 'handicapped', an undefined identity which a Principal, amongst others, may confer on a child: 'where a child appears to a Principal to be handicapped'. Under this Section, the Minister may refuse a child to be enrolled, re-enrolled or continue to be enrolled in a state school (section 64(1)): clearly this includes regular schools. The Minister may also direct the parent to present the child for assessment (Section 64F (1)), and the Minister may determine where the child shall be educated (Section 64H (1)), and assessed by a Special Education Authority. (It needs noting that Special Education Authorities have never been established: assessments by Guidance Offices (educational psychologists) and/or by the Camberwell Ascertainment Centre have taken their place.)

The legislation thus allows the Minister more power to regulate the lives of schoolchildren labelled disabled than their peers not thus labelled. Part of that power derives from the undefinable notion of 'handicapped' in the legislation. While a cursory reading of the legislation might assume that 'handicap' is self-evident, such discretionary categories provide a basis for teachers to exercise their discretion in whom they call disabled or handicapped. This discretion constitutes a key practice in the political logic of disability and exclusion. Section 61A of the Education Act thus *regulates* children described as 'handicapped' (or disabled) and their parents *more highly* than their counterparts not thus labelled, and provides for their *exclusion* from regular schools. Thus the 1958 Education Act appears to confirm Hayes' observation that Australian education acts are contradictory: they both require parents to send their children of school age to school and yet also provide for extensive exclusion from attendance at any school. Hayes and Hayes assert that this has allowed the 'exclusion of unknown numbers of mentally retarded children from the education system' (1982:127).

Where educational rights and legislation are concerned, Hayes and Hayes note that:

> Putting the matter very broadly, Education Acts [in Australia] generally do not give 'rights' to school children. There might be a 'right' to some sort of education from the system, but the legislation generally imposes no right to freedom of choice of schools, and it generally does not impose any corresponding duty upon Ministers

to do the things which the legislation permits them to do. To move a child from a normal school to a special school, or from a normal class to a special class within a normal school, does not interfere with any *rights* of the child. It amounts to no more than the exercise of a more or less unfettered discretion as to the quality of the right to education (if indeed there is even that) (1982:116).

This 'unfettered discretion' refers to administrative-political-bureaucratic practices which are discussed below. The State Board argues against legislating for the rights of one group in the community since this 'tends to create negative attitudes and may harden existing prejudices rather than promote government policy'. It argues instead for 'writing a statement of principles into any reform of the Act' (1987:13-14). Thus the rights discourse in the 1984 report has no institutional basis in the Victorian Education Act, nor in the Australian constitution, as this is presently interpreted (but see Levin's arguments above). Its theme of rights is a moral discourse. Such rights are frequently described as 'fictitious' and clearly provide only moral arguments rather than effective conditions of the 1984 report.

Hayes's view of legislation and educational rights is somewhat different. While there is no tradition of the courts as educational policy makers in Australia and there are views that their 'impact . . . on Australian education is likely to remain subdued' (Birch, 1986:34), Hayes sees the courts and the development of administrative law as possible solutions for those pursuing the rights of children called disabled (1984). As Birch notes, equal opportunity legislation in various states may be seen as a means of state governments achieving rights legislation (1985:34). Relevant here is the Victorian Equal Opportunity Board which was established in 1977, following the 1977 Equal Opportunity Act. While its initial brief was to combat discriminatory employment practices, the Board now find that complaints about education, particularly disputes about integration, are forming the largest part of its work.[13] Thus some parents are taking the opportunity the Board provides to pursue their claims of 'fictitious' rights, perhaps as an alternative to the judicial process, which is 'slow, costly, inefficient, and prone to misconceive the public good' (Hayes, 1984:5).

Where the 1982 Freedom of Information Act is concerned, an Australia-wide study of professionals sharing information with parents is discussed in the section on new practices (Worthington, 1987).

In sum, the legislative conditions of the 1984 report derive mainly from the 1958 Education Act and the 1984 Equal Opportunity Act revising the 1977 Act. While the latter Act provides some opportunity for more assertive parents to pursue their claims, it is likely that these are a small minority of those who have disputes with schools. Clearly the 1958 Education Act guarantees little except that schools will be provided as the Minister thinks fit, that opportunities are provided for professionals to exclude children called handicapped from regular schools and that *those schoolchildren who are described as disabled are subjected to more regulation than their peers*. Finally, while legislation is often seen as a crucial mechanism in policy, and a key condition for guaranteeing outcomes (this is the assumption underlying chapter 11 in the 1984 report and one which Levin shares), the model in chapter 1 argues against seeing any site of decisions as determinate. Consistent with this, the present analysis of the Victorian legislation shows that legislative decisions in the Victorian educational apparatus are only one site of decisions which, far from being determinate, provide conditions which allow for a wide range of practices surrounding disability.

While there is a broad legislative basis for administrative practices in government departments, it may be argued that legislative decisions are open to a range of interpretations, that some administrative practices have a tenuous legal base and thus that *administrative-political-bureaucratic practices* are a site of decisions independent of legislative decisions. Hayes and Macalpine imply this is presently the case, in their comments on those called intellectually disabled, where they go on to argue for constitutionally based legal protection (1986).[14.]

In addition, there is evidence from other policy arenas that bureaucratic practices in the Victorian education apparatus may significantly inhibit a policy of educational reform. This evidence derives from the work of Rizvi *et al.* in their evaluation of the Participation and Equity Program in Victorian schools (1987). Funded by the Commonwealth government in 1984, the Participation and Equity Program (PEP) had a number of social democratic concerns, similar to those in the 1984 report on integration. These concerns included participation, interpreted in a number of ways: as representative decision-making and as the higher retention of students (their participation) in school years 11 and 12 (post-compulsory schooling).

Rizvi *et al.*'s theorizing of PEP policy shares a number of features of the model outlined in the Introduction, namely that policy is struggle and that it is remade in various arenas:

> Despite the views of those who see the world in rationalist terms, the institutionalisation of PEP in the wider field of education did not occur as a straightforward, two-stage, two-level process of (1) the articulation of theory or policy by some central group, followed by (2) a process of implementation of PEP policy in practice by people 'out' in the schools. On the contrary, the institutionalisation of PEP took place as series of resolutions of the contests which defined and redefined PEP (Rizvi *et al.*, 1987:9–20).

Moreover, almost all the participants in the Program as a whole were in a process of theorizing PEP (p. 11–13). The Program is struggled over, theorized by those involved, and interpreted differently in different schools. These interpretations resulted from processes of contestation between discourse, practice and organization. Such contests took place 'between specific individuals and groups who deployed themselves (or found themselves deployed) as advocates for and adversaries of particular ideas, practices and forms of organization' (p. 9–22). Schools made their own PEP policy:

> As we have argued in Chapter 4 (discussing the reception of PEP in target schools), in a few extreme cases, schools simply rejected the concern for participation and equity in the terms outlined by Commonwealth and State governments, though usually they did so quietly. They continued to develop their own ideas about how schools and society could be better adapted to one another through continuing programs of streaming and improvements to the competitive academic curriculum and its (low status) alternatives. More generally, schools responded with interest and concern to the Program's guidelines, and saw them as continuous with their own efforts at innovation and reform. Many, indeed, saw the guidelines as an endorsement of their efforts to reform schools and schooling (and were later deeply disappointed when the 'rescheduling' of the Program suggested a lack of Commonwealth commitment to the principles) (p. 9–24–5).

Also, and in line with Hindess's notion that social actors act on the basis of the discourses available to them:

> a range of alternative views and lines of advice were available to schools which were well-connected to teacher unions and/or parent organisations (the multiplicity of 'centres'), so that PEP could be treated as problematic because people within schools could influence and could be influenced by the debates between organisations (the Department/Ministry, the teacher unions, parent organisation) over what PEP was to be like, and how its work should be conducted (Rizvi *et al.*, 1987:9, 24–5).

Thus school practices organized around PEP were sometimes discrepant from the Commonwealth written policy statements and the overall outcome was not in line with the aims of the national written policy. While national written policy on PEP had a clearly democratic intent, and while people in the program theorized and discussed 'issues of participation and equity in education' (p. 11–13), the policy practices surrounding the program 'created, sustained and reproduced the very bureaucratic relationships [the program] sought to overcome' (p. 10–25). These practices were consistent with the bureaucratic nature of the Victorian education system – 'its hierarchical, formalised, rule-governed system of social relationships, institutionalised in an organisational structure' (p. 10–). What emerged was *representative bureaucracy* rather than *representative democracy*. Rizvi *et al.* distinguish the form of representative democracy from its content and argue that the 'representative committees' consisted of members who were advocates for particular groups. These committees then became arenas for the contestation of the interests of different groups, with the result that:

> rather than the establishment of forums in which substantial issues could be debated rationally and responsively on their merits . . . the 'political' life of the Program was interest group politics – something very different from the form of democracy promised in the Victorian Ministerial Papers with their notion of 'collaborative participative decision making'. In short, the Program in general adopted the mechanical (bureaucratic) forms of representative democracy (elections, attendance by representatives in committees, decision making by voting in committees) but not the substance of representative democracy. Its democratic aspirations were undermined, perhaps irretrievably, by its bureaucratic practice (1987:11–13).

Thus the Participation and Equity Program failed to resolve the tension between democracy and bureaucracy:

> in the event [the Program] was bedevilled by a contradiction between its democratic aspirations and rhetoric and bureaucratic practice characteristic of its day-to-day operations. Put another way, the promise of its new rhetoric of responsiveness was not redeemed in new forms of activities and practices. . . . despite its collaborative and rhetoric [sic], the Program's practices and forms of organisation remained highly bureaucratised. Indeed, as the Program developed, contradictions between the Program's discourse and its practice and organisation became more evident (1987:14–4).

While some of Rizvi *et al.*'s comments carry a deterministic note to them, they argue that 'Within schools, there is some evidence that PEP sponsored "anti-bureaucratic" attitudes, practices and forms of organisation, though not to the extent envisaged in the Program's ideals. In the relationship between schools and the centre, however, there is evidence of increasing bureaucratisation' (p. 14–31). 'Despite its best efforts, the Program became increasingly bureaucratised throughout the period 1984–86, and rather than registering a resistance to bureaucracy in Victorian education, it became an extension of the bureaucracy' (p. 14–11).

In sum, Rizvi *et al.*'s findings confirm that policy is made at all levels in the educational apparatus. The findings suggest that the bureaucratic nature of the Victorian educational apparatus provides and promotes conditions hostile to policy practices with a democratic intent. Clearly these conditions are highly relevant to the 1984 report on integration. What their study clearly conveys, though they do not say so, is that these bureaucratic practices in the Victorian educational apparatus provide an extremely strong institutional basis for the exercise and promotion of professionalism as a discourse which constructs hierarchical, bureaucratic forms of relationships. Bureaucratic relationships depend on the deployment of a discourse of professionalism.

Beyond these general bureaucratic practices in the Victorian Ministry, there are administrative-political-bureaucratic practices specifically organized around a notion of children having disabilities. Various practices had become established prior to the 1984 report. These included working conditions for special teachers different from those of regular teachers: low teacher/pupil ratios, a separate career structure, and non–credentialling curricula in special schools. These practices could be used in negotiations between agencies or social actors in their objectives surrounding 'integration'. Thus a discourse based on these practices can be deployed to block negotiations over proposals to redeploy special teachers in regular schools unless such conditions are maintained.

Other practices prior to the 1984 report were administrative-political practices of assessment by Guidance Officers and the Camberwell Ascertainment Centre in the absence of Special Education Authorities which had not been established. A further and significant practice is financing special schools at levels which, prior to the 1984 report, have been five times as high as per capita money provided for regular Primary schools (Table 6.1).

More recently, for 1984–85, this expenditure has approached four times that allocated per student in a regular primary school (Education Department,

Table 6.1   Victorian Education Expenditure 1983–84

In-school amounts	Primary		Special	
	Total	Per capita	Total	Per capita
Teacher salaries and allowances	527,911,700	1,595	35,906,000	8,016
Total recurrent	653,673,800	1,975	44,385,100	9,910
Provision of buildings and grounds	26,579,200	803	3,259,600	728

Source: calculated from Victoria Education Department *Compendium of Statistics* 1985: Tables 1.1.2 and 2.2.1, pp. 2 and 31.

Compendium of Statistics, 1986). Official figures on the proportion segregated in special government special schools between 1971 and 1982 is shown in Table 6.2. This shows an increase from 0.47 per cent in 1971 to 0.89 per cent in 1982. This may be interpreted as increased provision of services or as increased segregation.

Table 6.3, from a paper provided for the Review Committee, documents the number of special schools and their enrolments, according to official statistics in February 1983.

Thus there have been extensive administrative-political practices of exclusion from regular schools but in addition, and beyond legislative conditions, there have also been extensive practices of exclusion *in* regular schools where students are withdrawn on a full-time or part-time basis. On these latter practices, the Ministry of Education provides no information.

In addition, there are examples of integration practices in schools prior to the 1984 report which took place without system level support and despite community resistance. The notable example here is the closure of the Cobram Special Developmental School, a new, rural segregated school, with an official enrolment of fifteen students. Despite community resistance to the objective of integrating these students into Technical Schools, High Schools, primary schools and kindergartens – the community had recently built the Special Developmental School – the principal, Kevin Stone, with various parents who had previously not seen their children as having a great deal of potential, managed to persuade regular schools to accept these students. This process

Table 6.2 Number of Children in Government Special Schools as a Percentage of total Enrolment in Government Schools (Victoria)

Year	Total Enrolment in All Government Schools	Enrolment in Government Special Schools	Percentage of Children in Government Special Schools
1971	593,933	2,806	0.47%
1972	602,614	2,795	0.46%
1973	605,644	3,041	0.50%
1974	608,643	3,166	0.52%
1975	618,112	3,605	0.58%
1976	624,707	4,115	0.66%
1977	626,143	4,214	0.67%
1978	623,609	*5,363	0.86%
1979	614,419	*5,366	0.87%
1980	606,147	*5,428	0.90%
1981	595,042	*5,627	0.95%
1982	584,781	*5,230	0.89%

*Includes Special Developmental Schools
Source: Victoria Education Department, *Planning Report*, 1983: Tables 1, 3 & 9

Table 6.3 Enrolments in Victorian government segregated schools in February 1983*

School or centre	no. enrolled	no. schools
Day Special Schools for the Intellectually Disabled	2,408	19
Special Schools in institutions	496	6
Special Developmental Schools	900	24
Continuing Work Education Centres	91	2
Special School in Travancore	20	1
Special Schools in Welfare Institutions	197	4
Education Centres in Youth Training Centres	216	5
Education Centres in Prisons	Enrolments fluctuate	8
Day Special Schools for the Physically Disabled	464	5
Day Special Schools for the Deaf and Deaf/Blind	451	7
Hospital Based Schools	94	2
Totals	5,337	83

*These figures exclude those in withdrawal units and those in full- or part-time withdrawal classes in regular schools.
Source: adapted from Education Department of Victoria, March 1983:1

took two and a half years, between 1979 and 1981. This achievement is an exception, is widely quoted, and there are no other examples of such wholesale desegregation in Victorian segregated schools.

In sum, there is an extensive array of administrative-political-bureaucratic practices in the Victorian Ministry which given their bureaucratic character (hierarchical decision making and representative bureaucracy) undermine policy practices with a democratic intent. In addition there are a number of administrative-political practices organized around the notion of 'disabled schoolchildren' which may have a somewhat tenuous legal basis. These practices derive from negotiations between social actors or agencies with power, such as the Minister, teacher unions and bureaucrats, and may be used to regulate those with less power. The agencies involved in various arenas which make decisions on schoolchildren called disabled are discussed below.

Economic decisions provide a fourth set of conditions which affect Victorian educational policy practices surrounding disability. What these are, however, depends on one's theoretical framework. The Introduction argued that such decisions occur in a variety of arenas: thus we would expect decisions in political economic arenas outside the educational apparatus and in the Australian and Victorian educational apparatuses to constitute conditions of the 1984 report. There are persuasive accounts, however, which argue that *one* level of economic conditions (the 'restructuring of capital', for instance) has a (largely) determinate effect on education policy practices in Australia. These arguments come from sociological large-scale theorizing and educational policy commentators. These writers tend to talk of economic conditions or factors rather than decisions since, in general, they assign responsibility for social practices not so much with people, or social actors, as with 'entities' such as capital, or class, or external economic forces. Given the importance of economic arguments both from certain Marxist positions, from liberals and from educationalists, I shall discuss these accounts in some detail, as a basis for looking more closely at the levels and nature of economic decisions which constitute conditions of the 1984 report.

A number of recent, broadly Marxist accounts argue for the key importance of economic factors variously mediated through ideological shifts, class, etc., as affecting education practices in Australia. These include Kapferer (1987), Barlow (1986) and Kenway (1987). These three see the global economy or the global restructuring of capital as having a largely determinate effect on schools. Miller provides a more complex, comprehensive, historical account (1986).

Kapferer suggests that the gobal economy of international capitalism has produced 'non-determining' states (Australia among them) which now experience a legitimation crisis, particularly in their high levels of youth unemployment. This global economy has decreased latitude in planning and executing national goals, reduced the autonomy and independence of citizens, and has induced shifts in state ideologies (1987). Ideological state apparatuses, such as schools, become dragooned into the service of the technocratic state in the attempt to re-attach citizens more closely to its economic imperatives (p. 3). Kapferer's focus is on youth policies, including policies to increase school retention rates and to provide more training and vocationally oriented courses. She concludes that the ideological state apparatus have been largely successful in attaching 'young people to the commodity relations of the international capitalist enterprise' but that pockets of resistance remain (p. 23). According to Kapferer, schools in Australia now promote commodity relations. Thus underlying Kapferer's theorizing is a concern for the disappearance of school curricula which are not about job skills.

Kapferer's account, while provocative, lacks a theory of policy. She does not conceptualize policy as practice and intervention which occurs in many arenas and levels, rather than one or two (written government level and the international arenas of capital); nor does she distinguish types of policy. This allows her to praise the Victorian Blackburn report for its arguments, its discourse on the need to decommodify education, and not to recognize that this is written policy at one level, thus only one of many decisions and practices which will be contested around the issues the Blackburn report raises. It is clear, too, that despite such statements, other proposals in the report, such as the new curriculum area of Work in Society for the revised Victorian Certificate of Education, may well help commodify education through reinforcing the view that school is (mainly) about work.

Barlow also argues that the so-called commodification of education is directly related to the economic crisis that Western capitalism is currently experiencing (1986:1). The restructuring of capital in order to increase profit, largely through reducing labour costs, has meant that the state has also had to restructure. One means it adopts is issuing policies on effectiveness and efficiency. Educational reports with these themes have been issued at both federal and state levels including Victoria, and for both regular and special education.[15] Another means is to cut spending. Thus spending on education in Australia as a percentage of total budget outlay has fallen from 9 per cent in 1976–77 to 7 per cent in 1986–87. (While Barlow does not point this out, the high expenditure of 9 per cent in 1976–77 occurred under the Fraser conservative government which held office from 1975–83, while the allegedly socialist, Hawke government, in office since 1983, has reduced expenditure on education to 7 per cent. This anomaly is ignored in accounts such as Barlow's, perhaps because government is merely the mediator of economic determinants in her theorizing, whereas educational authors such as Smart almost apologize for the Hawke government's decisions (see below)).

Barlow states that another means by which the state restructures is by encouraging fee paying services (p. 8). The new Minister of Education, Employment and Training is clearly encouraging such practices.[16] Thus the major forms of restructuring in the educational apparatus which are aimed at reimposing 'more commodity-dominated social relations are in the areas of provision (funding), administration and control, and curriculum' (p. 13). Several recent policy documents in the Victorian educational apparatus appear to illustrate Barlow's thesis in their concern with changing administrative practices, a corporate model and tighter political control (for example, Ministry of Education, 1986a, 1986b, 1986c, 1986d; Allen, 1987; and see Smart, forthcoming a and b).

Since, by definition, capitalist relations (and its themes of effectiveness and efficiency) oppose democratic concerns, including egalitarian provision and cooperative learning, Barlow sees the increasing dominance of capitalist relations as hostile to egalitarian provision in schools. The major changes in education have derived, in her view, however, not from the state's need to increase the productivity of capital (via training and vocational courses) so that it may improve the accumulation of surplus value, but in a crisis of social relations and legitimation:

The major crises for education lie in the areas of reproduction of capitalist (and other) social relations, and the legitimation of its own actions. The education process is a major shaping factor in almost every family's life, and its potential to allow non-capitalist social relations to develop is enormous. Thus in times of social crisis the struggle to reassert those capitalist forms becomes quite intense. One can interpret the recent Federal Budget decisions regarding public education, and especially multicultural education and alternative resources centres as a reimposition of dominant social relations modes. What has been called the crisis in education, is actually a crisis of legitimation. Education has had to find a way of serving capital's needs in this economic crisis without abandoning its pretence of offering equality of opportunity (p. 14).

Like Kapferer, Barlow's account appears to lack a theory of policy, perhaps because, like others who take the position that the mode of production (in this instance, capitalism) constructs economic and class practices (the two are indivisible) and is the main determinant of social life, she believes that 'policy' (what governments say they will do and their funding practices) is a medium which merely maintains the social relations of capital.

Thus, drawing on Barlow's scenario, an economic crisis and hence economic decisions in the international arena of capital and at central levels in the Australian and Victorian educational apparatuses, provide an unlikely context for an integration objective if such a policy is seen as requiring additional spending and as dependent on non-capitalist relations.

Kenway is also concerned with 'changes in the economy and the deepening crisis of capitalism'. She argues that the deepening crisis has been accompanied by an ideological offensive by the New Right, which has included an attack on Australia's system of state schooling (1987). There has been 'a shift away from social democratic consensus characteristic of the Karmel era in the early 1970s, towards a Rightist position' and the 'Right has ... successfully colonized popular thinking on education', including the Hawke Labor government, since at least 1984. The debate, between 1983 and 1984, on state funding of private schools 'provided the Right with an opportunity not just to defend and even extend its educational privilege but to promote a restructuring of the education system in order that it might be more responsive to current economic circumstances' (p. 191). Thus Karmel's concepts have been redefined in terms 'of the logic of the Educational Right's discourse' (p. 194). Despite this hegemonic ascendancy on the part of the Right, Kenway is hopeful: 'the Schools Commission's Special Purpose Grants agenda indicates that the discourse of social justice has not been entirely dismantled' (p. 210).

While Kenway's analysis of how a Rightist discourse on education has become dominant is very useful, as with others from the Left whom she criticizes, the practical courses of action in 'sites of intervention' are left largely unsketched in her theorizing. Moreover, her analysis of policy may be queried. While a social justice theme does inform the Commonwealth Schools Commission's Special Purpose grants agenda (see *Commonwealth Programs for Schools: Administrative Guidelines for 1987* (January 1987)) and *Commonwealth Programs and Policy Development for Schools 1988* (May 1987), the opposing discourse on corporate themes makes a more dominant appearance.

These three sociological accounts theorize the shift from the social democratic concerns of the 1960s and 1970s in education largely, if not wholly, in international and federal level economic conditions and their associated discourses: Kapferer and Barlow assign responsibility to the global arena of the restructuring of capital, and Barlow to the resultant legitimation crisis. Kenway provides an account of the rise of a Rightist discourse on education which has discarded themes of equity and disadvantage for themes of cost-effective outcomes. These accounts appear to assign responsibility to a simple determinate level of effects (the global restructuring of capital, the economic crisis, the need to improve the accumulation of capital) or with closely related high levels of effects (a Rightist discourse but at what level?).

How far do these accounts outline economic conditions since 1986 for the 1984 report? There are a number of questions to be asked of these arguments and their theorizing. Firstly, while they see social democratic concerns as characterizing the Whitlam era (1972–75) of the Schools Commission, they do not analyze the extent to which these concerns characterized the educational apparatus more generally, including schools. This is not surprising, given they do not theorize policy as practice and intervention at many levels nor distinguish between written, stated and enacted policy.

Where democratic practices in schools are concerned, we might interpret these accounts as assuming that government political and economic decisions about, for instance, a social democratic project, are crucial determinants of such concerns in schools. This would be consistent with a view we would also expect these authors to hold of the 'limits to democratisation inherent in capitalism' (Jessop, 1982:251). Such accounts merely set out, however coherently and elegantly, to illustrate what (from their positions) we already know. Their level of analysis is high and it largely ignores schools as critical sites of decisions or policy practices.

There also appears to be an orthodoxy in these particular accounts from the Left of teacher union policies (as radical, or democratic). But this view conflicts with Castles' analysis of trade union politics in Australia (1985), with findings on Melbourne Primary School Council policy statements on integration[17] and with new practices on disability which unions have negotiated following the 1984 report (see the discussion below).

In her more detailed account, Miller suggests the connection between decreased resources and school practices and democracy is complex (1986). This position accords with the findings of Rutter *et al.* that schools, despite the same level of resources, do things differently (1979), with the findings of Ramsay *et al.* on successful, as compared with 'unsuccessful', schools in New Zealand (1983), and with Culley and Demaine's statement that, despite sharing similar economic conditions, individual schools matter (1983). To some extent, Kapferer, Barlow and Kenway, in that they allow for 'sites of intervention', 'pockets of resistance', or catch sight of a democratic discourse, make the same point although, ideologically, they would not want to agree on this.

Economic conditions are clearly relevant to the 1984 report. This follows not necessarily from the argument put in the accounts above, but from the existence of an extensive discourse on resources, disability and 'integration'. If we argue that economic decisions are made at all levels, we need to ask questions such as: Have enrolments declined, and if they have, have school costs declined in real terms? Has central administration absorbed more money than it did prior to the 'fall of the social democratic project'? Have teacher salaries effectively increased in real terms since the 1960s? If the answer to any is yes, then economic decisions at levels *other* than international and federal government arenas and capitalist corporations, and *other* than state government Cabinet allocation, constitute conditions of school resources and practices and of the 1984 report. Thus if there has been a reallocation of funds *away* from schools and *to* say, central administration, or elsewhere, then we need to assign responsibility not merely to global economic factors (as do Kapferer, Barlow, Kenway, Smart), but also to bureaucrats and unions, as well as to capitalists and others with Rightist or non-democratic concerns who have argued for reducing spending on education.

Answering questions about where, at what levels and in which arenas, economic decisions have been made, means sorting out education budget lines. This is a notoriously difficult task.[18] Teachers' salaries, their increase or decrease in real terms since the 1960s, would be easier to establish than other budget lines. Salary increases apart, however, it is clear that teacher unions make economic decisions which may affect a 'social democratic project' in education. As we shall see, following the 1984 report, union resource demands are an economic and political decision with far-reaching consequences for an objective of integration.

Despite their argument that economic factors are critical, the accounts discussed above lack some highly relevant data. Especially problematic for their theorizing is the fact that between 1973 and 1983, the Schools Commission made *a 50 per cent per pupil increase in funding* (Smart, forthcoming b:1 in typescript) and maintained a level of 3 per cent expenditure on education (as a proportion of total Commonwealth Expenditure) for the year 1976/77 to 1978/79, 2.6 per cent from 1979/80 to 1980/81 and 2.8 per cent from 1981/82 to 1982/83 (Smart, forthcoming b:Figure 1). The Fraser government held office from 1975 to 1982. In 1983–87, under the alleged socialist Hawke government, there was a 1.3 per cent decrease in the Schools Commission budget, where public schools received a 2.7 per cent cut and private schools 1 per cent and Commonwealth expenditure on education for 1983/84 was 2.7 per cent. These accounts are silent on the Fraser increase and suggest we are to understand the Hawke government's decisions to reduce monies for education variously as the ascendancy of a Rightist discourse (Kenway), as the commodification of education because states are now non-determining (Kapferer), and as reflecting the economic crisis (Barlow). Nevertheless, a Rightist discourse on education (Marginson, 1987) and global issues and economic restructuring began well before the Hawke government took office in 1982. These accounts imply that politics do not matter, since they argue that the political-economic aspects of a capitalist class structure are determining factors.

Accounts from educationalists also theorize economic factors as crucial: for example, Smart (forthcoming a); Boyd and Smart (forthcoming). While their policy analysis is often more illuminating than that of large-scale sociological accounts and contains more data (for example, Smart, 1986a, 1986b), their theorizing is even more general and couched in economistic determinate terms:

> A key constraint on the conservative and pragmatic policies adopted in the schools area by the Hawke Government has been serious concern about the state of the economy and in particular, worry about the massive federal budget deficit (currently estimated at about US 9 billion) (Smart, forthcoming b:1 2).

> Economic difficulties have increasingly led western governments of both the left and the right to perceive their education systems as predominantly aimed towards producing an international competitive workforce (Smart, forthcoming b:14).

Such accounts apologize for the disappearance of socialist policies under an allegedly socialist government and rightly point out that the Hawke government politics of electoral pragmatism and consensus have largely replaced the traditional socialist politics of idealism and reform.

But Smart's account also lacks a theory of policy. Thus he does not distinguish policy statements at one level and policy practices at another. This allows him to see the outcome of PEP as generally encouraging. This view contrasts with the detailed, clearly theorized study by Rizvi *et al.*, where key problems such as the conflict between bureaucratic and democratic practices is addressed, and whose findings indicate that schools make their own policy practices (whether they write, state or enact them) which may differ from Commonwealth written policy statements.

What is the contribution of these accounts to identifying the economic conditions of the 1984 report? It is clear that corporate themes have appeared in national policy documents (see, for example, the 1985 Quality of Education Review Committee report, *In the National Interest* (1987) and *Skills for Australians* (1987)) and in Victorian government policy documents, and that the Commonwealth has reduced its funds to schools. But we do not have to accept the arguments in these accounts of the effects of such decisions. For one thing, economic decisions may be made at other levels which, together with federal and state level decisions, may reduce the money and resources schools have. But the effect reduced funding has on egalitarian concerns or policy practices in schools is far from clear. Some of the key issues here are raised in a longer account by Pavla Miller (1986).

Miller's book, *Long Division: State Schooling in South Australia*, contains a detailed, historical analysis of social conflicts and the way in which schools are caught up in, and contribute to, social divisions of age, ethnicity, class and gender. A central theme is the social democratic project in education in the 60s and 70s. While Miller's approach is broadly that of political economy, it is difficult to unravel the connections she makes between schools, social conflict, political and economic decisions and the 'social democratic project'. One problem is what she means by the social democratic project. This is undefined. On p. 368 a democratic society is one in which work is a worthwhile part of all adult lives and in which people control technology.

> Should not the design of work in a wealthy democratic society attempt to cultivate the varied abilities of all? Should not schools prepare citizens to design and use technology in such a way that *all* will be able to make a worthwhile, sufficiently awarded contribution to society?

On p. 298, in a chapter on social democracy and schooling, the democratic project in education appears to be about reducing inequalities in education (of class, gender and ethnicity): however, there is a 'fatal flaw of the social democratic project in education. Since many fundamental inequalities in the distribution of wealth and knowledge were generated in an exploitative system of production, schooling could never fully compensate for society'.

Miller's point here is that democratic practices are severely limited under capitalism. While this seems indisputable, it merely raises a core issue, whereas a closer focus on individual schools might begin to identify conditions under which democratic practices can be sustained, despite the wider capitalist context. On p. 352, an aim of the social democratic project is to resolve conflicts: 'In the education system as in the society at large, many changes in government spending priorities helped intensify those social conflicts which the social democratic project had hoped to resolve' (Miller, 1986:352).

Here Miller attributes responsibility for social conflicts to government economic decisions. But while Miller clearly regards economic factors as important she is unwilling to be bound by clear connections between economic decisions and effects. Where spending cuts and schools, and social democracy, are concerned, she observes:

> Schools cannot change the world, and more money by no means guarantees better outcomes of schooling. Yet it remains true that what schools can or cannot do is closely linked to the amount of money that governments make available to them, and that government policies have a considerable impact on the magnitude of problems schools are supposed to deal with in the first place (1986:343).

Such plausible generalizations raise the need for more detailed research.

If there is a clear link between economic decisions and schools for Miller, it seems to lie in the extent to which schools get caught up in social conflict. The key conflicts which Miller identifies lie in economic decisions in the 1970s and 80s in both the international and federal government arenas. The global redeployment of capital to invest in countries where labour costs are cheaper (a reshaping of the international division of labour), which coincided with the election of the Whitlam Labor Government (p. 341), ended 'the last years of the long boom'. In the federal arena, between 1976 and 1982, the newly mandated Fraser government, with its 'increasingly confident conservative administration', was able 'the renege some of the concessions granted by federal Labor' (p. 347). Education was brought into the ensuing fray: 'it changed from a quiet and industrious battlefield to a visible and publicly contested site of struggle' in which 'schools would play a significant part in remaking the new order' (pp. 341–2). The Fraser government decision to increase state aid to non-government schools provided another source of conflict: 'In the period 1976 to 1983 general recurrent grants by the Commonwealth Government to state schools decreased by 1.9 per cent . . . [and] increased [to private schools] by 105.7 per cent' (p. 347).

The decision to reinforce the division between 'private' schools and government schools is one that several commentators regard as crucial. Miller appears to agree, since she notes that the effect 'according to the critics, was to lock the two ill-mated, contrary systems into a settlement which would allow the wealthy non-government schools to reassert, from a new basis, their erstwhile dominance' (p. 306). (This decision was part of the massive shift of resources from the public sector to the private sector (via cutbacks in welfare spending and a substantial reduction in corporate taxes) which occurred under the Fraser government.) But Miller also has some doubts whether the failure of the social democratic project lies in the analysis of the division between private and public schools, since she also asks 'Why does all this matter?'

Thus Miller's incisive, yet evasive, account reveals the complexity of issues in attempting to account for the connections between social division, economic conditions, and democratic practices in educational arenas. As she notes, economic decisions by the Commonwealth, along with the global restructuring of capital, have intensified social conflict over scarce resources. For example, in the South Australian education apparatus, one site of struggle over resources emerged in the introduction of program budgeting (linking inputs to outputs, a difficult endeavour in educational practices) and in changes in control in the form of corporate restructuring. We can argue that similar shifts have occurred in the Victorian educational apparatus which has also adopted program budgeting (first introduced in 1984) and a corporate restructure (see Victoria, Ministry of Education 1986a, 1986b, 1986c, 1986d) which was accompanied by statements about devolving responsibility for educational policy and resources (see *Taking Schools into the 1990s* (1986)). This site of struggle has resulted in extreme uncertainty, struggle, within the Ministry about the extent of this restructuring (Maslen, 1987), and has been accompanied by the Chief Executive's insistence that the Ministry must respond to 'economic imperatives' (Allen, 1987).

Miller notes that in addition to economic decisions, there was a debate on the size of the public sector in which it was argued that the public sector absorbed too high a proportion of annual expenditure. In fact, as Miller points out, this is mistaken: 'Of . . . the twenty-two OECD countries for which figures were available, seventeen . . . allocated a higher proportion of GDP in outlays of government in 1981 than did Australia. Australia's outlays were 6.5 per cent lower than the average of all OECD countries' (1986:343). This debate helped pave the way for government cuts in spending on education.

While Miller describes in detail the complexity of these events, her analysis evades clear deductions about the connections between political and economic decisions (the global restructuring of capital, the Fraser government massive shift of resources from the public to the private sector, the shift of resources from public to private schools and a debate about the size of the public sector) and the 'social democratic project'. What she clearly identifies is increased social conflict over scarce resources. As we shall see, conflict over scarce resources is a key condition of the 1984 report and this conflict is linked to the same conflict in other arenas but such a general connection outlines only one condition of the 1984 report: there is a resource struggle.

In sum, Miller sees the global arena of capital as influential but includes both economic decisions (spending cuts) made at federal and state levels and a debate criticizing the size of the public sector as factors contributing to social conflict. In Miller's analysis conflict is the key condition affecting school practices. Overall, Miller's theorizing implies schools cannot carry out democratic projects when resources are cut. But we need to interpret the nature of this conflict carefully: to argue that it emerges from economic decisions at largely one level is to argue for a single principle of explanation, and a focus on economic factors is an argument which comes from positions on the Left and the Right. From a more complex position, that institutional conditions are complex and can be reduced to neither the economic nor the political (which in Marxism, are combined), we need to extend the analysis and ask which schools had this project, and whether extra resources are a necessary and sufficient condition for democratic projects to be pursued. While the above accounts emphasize the effects of economic conditions, to a greater degree than a Hindess-based model supports, it is clear that economic decisions at a national level have had a wide effect on discourse and practice at other levels of the educational apparatus and that this includes arenas where there are integration objectives. But this does not negate responsibility for political decisions *in* the Victorian educational arena to deploy a discourse of professionalism, separatism and resources in struggles over integration. It is to this struggle that the discussion now turns.

It is relevant to look briefly at the agencies which are significant actors in educational policy practices in Victoria surrounding disability and which act as interest groups in various arenas of decision making: it is particularly necessary to look at those with power, since their discursive practices maintain particular conditions of the 1984 report. The most powerful actors and agencies are the Minister, senior bureaucrats and teacher unions. Other actors include the Cabinet (in its funding decisions), Regional Boards of Education, other bureaucrats, Guidance Officers (a lobby group formerly with a strong institutional base in the former Counselling, Guidance and Clinical Services section of the Education Department), individual teachers, School Councils, parents as individuals and in their associations.

Victorian teacher unions are highly powerful agencies in a number of arenas in which decisions are made about educational policy practices surrounding disability. In a context where Australian teacher unions are amongst the strongest teacher unions in the world ('if measured by organizational unity and level of membership support': most have over 95 per cent unionization), Victorian teacher unions have emerged as the most influential politically (Blackmore and Spaull, forthcoming). These unions 'deal with a highly centralized bureaucracy', a 'centralization . . . [which]

increases union power', so that they have become 'the *dominant* interest group to challenge the unilateral decision making of the education bureaucracy' (Blackmore and Spaull, forthcoming:2). Part of this power derives from their entering the state parliamentary process by contributing substantial funds to the state ALP campaign for the 1982 election. This power also constituted political conditions of the Ministerial Review Committee, affecting debate and decisions in that arena and establishing resources as the dominant issue in subsequent debate in other arenas. In the 1985 election campaign, teacher unions contributed less to the campaign. The unions are the Victorian Secondary Teacher's Association (VSTA), the Victorian Teacher's Union (VTU), the Technical Teachers' Union of Victoria (TTUV), and the parent union, the Victorian Teachers' Union (VTU). These three formed a peak council, the Teachers' Federation of Victoria (TFV) in 1984 (Blackmore and Spaull, forthcoming:6). Also relevant is the Australian Association of Special Education (AASE). As Blackmore and Spaull point out, professionalism is inseparable from these union politics and has been a key discursive means deployed in negotiations with the bureaucracy. But the 'interventionist' role of teacher unions in the political process, according to Blackmore and Spaull, appears finished: 'it does seem consistent that they will withdraw their support for the Labor Party. As such they will resume the normal political behaviour of the teacher unions in other Australian states' (forthcoming:17). Moreover, given the recent extensive restructuring in the Education Ministry, where a number of former Teaching Service positions have been reclassified as Public Service positions, it seems possible that the present dominance by the unions may diminish. The restructuring may be an attempt to break union power. Thus the extent to which unions deploy a discourse of professionalism and resources in arenas concerned with disability and integration may possibly decrease.

Teacher unions have, however, consistently deployed a discourse of professionalism and resources, linked to already established working conditions, in arenas concerned with disability and integration. Teacher–pupil ratios in Victoria are amongst the lowest in Western education apparatuses and are a key feature of negotiations between Minister, Ministry and unions. The ratios in segregated settings are a discourse teacher unions can and have deployed to argue against allowing children from segregated settings into regular schools unless these ratios are maintained. Categorization of school children thus becomes a key part of this discursive means and is reinforced by the institutional base of categorized special schools. This discourse lends itself very easily to arguments for additional resources for any child who disturbs teachers. Levin comments that integration is not much discussed in Australia because there is a fear that unions will ask for more resources (1985:264). While her view that integration is rarely discussed is wrong, the link she makes between unions, resources and integration is accurate. Such a discourse relates to what Castles describes as the 'laborist and economistic rather than social democratic and universalistic' position Australian trade unions have taken (1987b:97) (see below). This view contrasts with Blackmore and Spaull's claim that teacher unions have often developed radical educational policies (cited by Boyd and Smart, forthcoming:12 in typescript). As we shall see, teacher union resource demands are part of the political and economic conditions in which objectives in integration policy are struggled over in Victoria.

The Australian Association of Special Education (AASE) whose 12th National Conference was held in 1987, appears to be a powerful agency which has an increasingly powerful institutional basis in its Association[19] and a well-established institutional basis in the various segregated schools, separate units, special teacher training institutions and courses, and in its separate conditions of work. It is from these institutional bases that its members can deploy a discourse of disability, separatism and professionalism.

For example, the policy resolutions carried at the 1985 Annual General Meeting, recommended 'That Special Education course units should be offered by academic staff with: (i) postgraduate qualifications in special education; (ii) suitable experience as a teacher in both regular and special education'. This practice, which has had an institutional base in teacher training institutions, effectively excludes intending special teachers from exposure to discourses and themes other than those which have traditionally characterized institutions which teach intending special educators. Melbourne College of Advanced Education, the Institute of Early Childhood Education, Victoria College Faculty of Special Education and Paramedical Studies, and Monash University Faculty of Education have traditionally provided courses for intending special teachers which were based on deficit, difference and professionalism. Moreover, the Association pursues professionalism vigorously:

> A sense of pride and belief in our work as special educators comes with acknowledgment of our professionalism. Special educators must stand proud as a professional group. They must see AASE as being an essential part of their professional growth and development – the work of branches and state chapters in providing professionally stimulating and innovative interchange by way of meetings, workshops, seminars and conferences is a major aim of the association. The national conference *must* remain the focal point for Australian special educators each year. It is well recognised that our conferences are expertly organised and provide members with access to speakers of a high calibre who are leaders in the special education

field, both in Australia and overseas. I believe it is vital that the second generation of AASE concentrate their efforts on the above issues, if we are to fully mature as we move into the 1990's (President's report to the Annual General Meeting of the Australian Association of Special Education, 6–7 October, 1987:8).

Parent organizations are an agency whose views and representation are increasingly sought in debate and decision on policy practices in the Victorian educational apparatus. But they are much less powerful than teacher unions and, as Tomlinson notes for Britain (1982:chapter 7), Mehan for California (1983), and Worthington for Australia (1987), parents are unlikely to be able to negotiate with professionals: because of linguistic processes of persuasion Mehan suggests, and because of class (and implicitly a discourse of professionalism) Tomlinson suggests, so that working-class parents find it harder to negotiate (Tomlinson, 1982). In Victoria, the practice of seeking parents' views became written policy in the Ministerial Papers (1982–84): these Papers deploy a democratic discourse, and argue for a policy of devolution of authority to schools, for collaborative decision-making amongst those concerned, and for accountability to the community. The practice of including parents on School Councils and sub-committees and ESGs accords with this written policy but there is increasing evidence that such representation fails in a number of ways to achieve its intended democratic objectives (Worthington, 1987, Ciavellera, 1987).

While Worthington sees the practice of including parents on School Councils as the 'slow evolution in Australia towards the development of the rights of parents', his study showed that professionals work against parent 'rights': 'in education professionals in Australia . . . refer to the regulations and Government policy if [they] . . . are unable to dilute attempts by parents to gain certain rights' (p. 2), and even the most articulate of parents can be defeated by the complex regulations to which they are subjected and by the way professionals may use bureaucratic practices to withold information (1987:3). This suggests reasons for the reported failure (from a democratic stance) of some ESGs in Victoria.

Worthington's finding that parents saw 'one-off interviews and irregular interviews, as the least reliable and least useful method of communication' (p. 10) is not surprising, given Mehan's Californian findings that professionals use linguistic processes of persuasion and ratify decisions which have been made prior to meetings with parents. Worthington concludes that 'the policies of parent groups [on these issues] are generally in direct contrast to those of government departments' and that state departments, and states, vary in these practices. Since Worthington's study is Australia-wide, this suggests that legislative decisions such as the Victorian 1982 Freedom of Information

Act provides parents with limited access to information and constitutes a relatively weak condition of the 1984 report.

Ciavallera's small case study documents conditions which limit the extent to which the inclusion of parent representatives in School Councils constitutes democratic practice. Parent members did not represent the socioeconomic and ethnic backgrounds of their communities, women were under-represented, parents in two of the three schools studied felt incompetent to discuss curriculum matters with school staff and they lacked an understanding of the political process: *clearly they did not have available a social democratic discourse.* Some parents' comments show that they use a discourse of professionalism: the teacher knows best about teaching matters. These findings are consistent with Elkins' view (1985:181).[20] It would seem then, that parent groups, for a variety of reasons, may have a more limited effect on decisions on educational policy practices, including those concerned with disability, than they might like and than written policy, such as the Ministerial Papers and the 1984 report, may intend.

Democratism in the wider context

Given that democratism is a major theme in the 1984 report, how democratic are practices in other arenas in Australia?

While Australia is widely seen as a democratic state, it is a highly unequal society (Jamrozik, 1987)[21] and its performance on welfare provision is poor by comparison with others: 'Australia is amongst the least generous of modern welfare states and its institutional patterns and social policy preconceptions' are unlike most others (Castles, 1987b:91). Miller provides the facts: in 1981 Australia's outlays of government as a proportion of GDP was 6.5 per cent lower than the average of all OECD countries' (1986:343).

Castles notes that welfare provision has been based on selectivist principles, rather than the universal principle of citizen. This selection has favoured wage-earners (thus predominantly males of wage earning age) to the extent that Castles describes Australia as the 'wage-earner's state' (1985). Despite the image of Australia as an affluent society, the late 70's saw an increasing polarization between the rich and the poor (Miller, 1986:346) and it is now moving into an era of massively increasing child poverty (Castles) 1987:96), so that in the 1987 election, when Hawke's Labor Government was returned for a third term of office, the about-to-be-re-elected Prime Minister promised that by 1990 no child in Australia would live in poverty.

According to Castles, the institutional patterns and social policy preconceptions which distinguish the Australian welfare state from others are the lack of a social democratic project in working-class politics and in trade unions: trade unions in Australia have been 'laborist and economistic' (Castles 1987:97). This contrasts with the discourse of social democracy which has characterized some European states, notably Scandinavia, where the basis for social democracy extended beyond a working-class constituency. Castles traces this lack of social democratic project in Australian political life throughout this century and assigns responsibility for Australia's low level of welfare spending to a 'combination of long-term right-wing political hegemony and relatively poor economic growth' (1987a:94 and 1987b) and to the laborist and economistic discourses of trade unions.

In contrast, Macintyre argues that ideas of social justice have informed a wide range of policies throughout Australia's history since the arrival of Europeans (1985). But as might be expected, the debate on social democracy in Australia is complex (see, for example, *Arena* 78, 1987). In a more recent account, Macintyre summarizes a widely held view amongst a disenchanted left on the fate of social democracy under the Hawke Labor government, and thus of the fate of those groups, including those called disabled, who are most vulnerable when such concerns disappear:

> The key to the present success of the Hawke Government is surely the ALP-ACTU Accord, which incorporated the representatives of capital and labour in such a way that their support for the Government's economic strategy was assured. It has been said that corporatism is the highest stage of social democracy, and certainly it is true that the great advantage of a labourist or social democratic party in a period of economic recovery lies in its ability to command trade union acquiescence and dampen labour market pressures, thereby in turn winning the co-operation of big business. On the other hand, the terms of the Accord – notably in its commitment to wage indexation and tax cuts at the expense of public spending – are a reminder that this Labor Party still has a strong residual labourism. For the effect of the Government's policies is to benefit those involved in relations of production at the expense of those who are excluded from them. The Accord has marginalised the poor, the unemployed, the single parents and other welfare dependents who, to put it cynically, have nowhere else to take their votes. And within the limits of pragmatism and consensus, the Government seeks to balance the demands of special interest groups against the needs of private capital. The limits of change are narrow, the vulnerability to international economic conditions extreme. None of the conventional management of the mixed economy, comprehensive public welfare, abatement of inequality – are here to be found. It is unclear to me that Australia presents much in the

way of social democratic, much less democratic socialist achievement, from which other countries might draw (Macintyre, 1986:13).

Disability in the wider context

Disability is an important theme in the 1984 report. It is also a policy category in various state apparatuses including housing, health and employment. The position of those described as disabled in these other arenas in, for instance, paid work, may help us understand conditions of education policy on disability.

Struggles around disability in the Australian 'welfare state' deploy two main discourses: these are a medically based view and a rights view (Fulcher, 1989). These two discourses inform various legislation on disability made at both Commonwealth and state levels. The most recent, the 1986 Commonwealth Disability Services Act, draws on both discourses and seeks to improve the opportunities people called disabled have for full-time full-rate work. But as noted already, rights are fictitious where there is no Bill of Rights or no legal remedies available when rights are infringed. The extent to which the 1986 Act provides conditions which will limit discriminatory employer practices is therefore problematic. Such a view is in line with reports from the Human Rights Commission in 1986 that under existing legislation the rights of those with disabilities were unattainable (1986a).

Australian legislation on disability is complex in other ways. The complexity of 'provision' makes disability a *procedurally complex status and experience*: furthermore, *legislative anomalies encourage deception* (HRC, 1986a:89). The contentious nature of disability claims between, for example, injured industrial workers and employers, and the existence of the HRC, a watchdog mechanism (which has now been combined with another agency), to assess the extent to which those with disabilities (and others) are able to attain their rights, attest to the *contested* nature of disability. These contests occur in medical and health arenas and are played out in the context of the adversarial relations which characterize struggles in these arenas. These practices have politicized disability and confirm the theorizing in chapter 1: insofar as *disability* is a status and an identity struggled over, it *is a political category and construct*. This is so *whether or not an impairment underlies the use of the term disabled*. As noted in chapter 1, the practice of calling a person disabled, where an impairment may not be present, and where the consequence is exclusion, is particularly significant in education apparatuses (Chapter 1).

The main theme in Australian discourse on disability is that of an individual's inability to do something, particularly inability to work. But it is clear that 'inability to work' is both relative to particular tasks, to employer practices and to local demand and supply of wage labour.

There are further connections between work and disability in Australia. As Stewart notes, Australian legislation has favoured workers who have acquired disabilities as a result of impairments which are clearly work-related (injuries, for instance). Other forms of work-related disability, particularly diseases and illness caused by less obviously hazardous work practices, have been consistently underacknowledged in employer discourse and practice; this practice has favoured employers and reduced production costs, since benefits are then claimed from the welfare state as sickness or invalid pensions, rather than as compensation claims against employers (Stewart, 1986).

Commonwealth *funding practices* construct disability as *dependence*: the Commonwealth spends $10 on institutional care for every $1 it spends on assisting independent living for those with disabilities; it also constructs disability as *poverty*: 'At the end of 1985, 266,543 persons with disabilities were receiving the invalid pension, which is less than one-quarter of the average wage' (Meares, 1986:7).

In attempting to theorize these practices of exclusion and oppression in the Australian welfare state, and given their close connection with paid work and the alleged opposition to it of disability interpreted as 'needy', I have suggested that *paid work is the prime moral category in Australian social life* (Fulcher, 1989). Thus those excluded from paid work are deemed worthy of inadequate benefits. The view that paid work should attract better conditions of existence than those outside the paid, full-time production processes, a view which I have suggested is dominant, is consistent with Castles' analysis of the laborist and economistic position adopted by Australian trade unions (1985, 1987a, 1987b) and with welfare state practices of rewarding some (indisputably work-related) impaired, male wage labor more highly than those whose impairments do not derive from paid work.

These disability practices indicate some of the wider economic and political conditions of the 1984 report.

New practices since the 1984 report

New practices since the 1984 report are documented in the memoranda outlined above, in the little research that is available (Fulcher, 1986a, 1986e, 1988; Tschiderer, 1986), in various agencies' written responses to the report, in debate in the media and by observation at meetings. These sources confirm that 'disability' is contested at all levels in the Victorian educational apparatus: various objectives are struggled over in integration contests. Each source also adds to our understanding of these objectives and their politics.

Many of the responses to the report by key actors [22] and agencies [23] adopt a discourse of professionalism and, in opposing the democratism in the report, exemplify the continuing struggle between the two positions which began in meetings of the Review Committee. The response from the major teacher agencies began, and has continued, with arguments about resources (which are tied into log-of-claims negotiations[24]) and the discourse on curriculum makes only rare appearances (but see, for example, Varley and Howard, 1985). A key strategy in the discourse the bureaucracy presents is to outline the resources allocated to integration, a strategy which also reinforces the political logic of deficit, difference, separatism, professionalism, therefore extra resources, and which systematically deflects attention from curriculum. While a curriculum document has appeared on 'Students with Impairments, Disabilities or Problems in Schooling', this has the form of rhetorical device about ideals and 'oughts', rather than providing technical information on how to teach topics to cater for a range of students (Victoria, 1986e).

The memoranda outlined above are both 'effects' of the 1984 report and indicate new policy practices surrounding disability. The State Board describes them somewhat apolitically, as 'refined policy' (1987b). The memoranda reveal firstly, extensive negotiation, struggles around competing objectives which have resulted, secondly, in a resource discourse dominating the issue of rights, democratism and the central pedagogical issues of curriculum (see especially memoranda dated 31 August 1984, 20 May 1985, 19 January 1987). A third, highly significant, practice revealed in the memoranda is 'delayed admission', a procedure which applies only to students called disabled: this practice superficially conforms to the democratism of the 1984 report (the right to enrol) but yields to teacher union resource demands: 'If in the opinion of the Regional Director the current resource level at the school of the parents' choice does not match the educational needs of the child, it may be necessary to delay admission until such time as adequate resource provision can be arranged' (20 May 1985). The distinction between enrolment and admission was first intimated in the memorandum of 20 May 1985 (p. 3), and ratified in the diagram in the memorandum of 13 March 1986. This bureaucratically brilliant and politically significant practice has emerged from negotiations between the Minister and teacher unions. A memorandum some six weeks later (29 April 1986) directs Regional Boards to be careful not to infringe the 1984 Equal Opportunity Act by 'delayed admission'. A legislative base for 'delayed admission' might be sought in Section 61A of the 1958 Education Act but as the State Board (1987:14) and the 1984 report point out, this section of the legislation is inconsistent with an intention to promote integration, and it clearly borders on being illegal, given the 1984 Equal Opportunity Act: hence the memorandum of 19 April 1986.

The Ministry has not released figures on the numbers of students excluded from regular schools by delayed admission but in one region, where, in 1986, the official student population at primary level was 40,874 (excluding 640 in Special and Special Developmental Schools), the following exchange took place at a public meeting between parents, politicians and a representative of the Regional Board:

> What [it was asked] of those 383 children in the region who were not successful [in their application for a teacher's aide]? The official answer [was] that about 50 were judged not to need aides and that about 180 got shares of aides. When it was suggested this meant about 150 were being delayed admission to regular schools . . . the reply was that the figures were hidden because some of the applicants were from students already in regular schools. Round 5 to the bureaucracy for hiding the facts (Fulcher, 1987).[25]

Part of the Ministry's practice of power is therefore to withold information, despite the 1982 Freedom of Information Act.

In addition to the 'legitimate' practice of 'delayed admission', private disputes occur between parents and regular schools which do not appear in any statistics, whether hidden or revealed. In these disputes parents are variously unable to enrol their child or unable to attain the number of hours of admission they wish for their child in a regular school. The decision to exclude the student or to withold more hours of entry to that school appears to be made, in some instances, outside the Enrolment Support Group process. This is not surprising, given Mehan's research on Education Placement Committees (the Californian equivalent of ESGs); we can expect that processes of linguistic persuasion will occur outside ESGs, in less formal discussions between teachers and parents. But private disputes reveal unofficial delayed admission practices and the exercise of power via professionalism.

Also significant in the memorandum of 13 March 1986 on Enrolment Support Group processes is its length: it is nine pages long and has a diagram showing seven sequences for admission where extra resources are not required; for students deemed to require extra resources there are three subsets of procedures, each with subsubsets. The memorandum of 17 August 1987, revising these procedures, is nineteen pages long and more directive than that of 13 March 1986. The complexity and specificity of the procedures show that students described as disabled are not only *more highly regulated* than those not thus labelled but that *'disability' is a complex status and identity* which, given both its unclear status and the discretion professionals hold in practices surrounding disability, is *more than unusually contingent on those who hold power in these practices.*

The memorandum of 29 April 1986 shows that some schools have attempted to use the practice of 'delayed admission' to suspend students already enrolled in regular schools. The memorandum states that 'the situation of delayed admission can only occur as indicated in the Minister's memo of May 20th, 1985 . . .' The attempted deployment of a discourse on integration and disability to suspend students already in a school shows very clearly *the close connections between a discourse on disability and integration, and exclusion.*

The memoranda also document the *increasing control from central administration,* consistent with the corporate restructuring described earlier and despite the earlier discourse on devolving responsibility to schools (Ministerial Papers, 1983–85; *Taking Schools into the 1990s* (1986)). Thus the memoranda of 13 March 1986 convey 'guidelines on the operation of Enrolment and Support Groups which will assist in the implementation of the Ministry of Education's integration policy', whereas that of 17 August 1987 refers to procedures 'schools will follow'.

The allocation of substantial funds to special schools has continued. This includes capital expenditure: for instance, a new special school was opened in Burwood in April 1986 at a cost of $1.1 million and with a ratio of fifteen teachers and assistants to six students (*The Age,* 15 April 1986). Continued funding includes recurrent expenditure at four times that allocated for each child in a regular primary school (*Compendium of Statistics 1986*). Where parents would prefer their child to be in a regular school there appears to be no mechanism to redeploy such resources from the segregated sector (Fulcher, 1987). Responsibility for these decisions, to continue to provide substantial sums of money for both capital and recurrent purposes to segregated settings, we can hardly assign to 'capital'. It could be argued that the decision to maintain segregated institutions is not consistent with the bureaucracy's overall objectives of reducing costs, whereas it is consistent with teacher union objectives to preserve their members' present working conditions: special teachers thereby retain their career structures, lower teaching ratios, non-credentialling curricula and relative lack of accountability (as Tomlinson points out, 1982) compared with regular teachers, and regular teachers maintain their working conditions and present pedagogic practices. However, the bureaucracy's objective is to contain the escalated politics of disability issues in the educational apparatus ('ninety percent of the time we are doing nothing – we are doing politics') (Acting Director General of Education)), so that the bureaucracy also has an interest in deploying discursive means which maintain segregated settings. It is also the case that a number of parents use a discourse of disability, separatism and inability of their child to cope in a regular school, as a discursive means of supporting the maintenance of segregated settings.

The available research, while small in scope, clearly shows the *marginalization of more students in regular schools* as 'integration students' (Tschiderer, 1986). This marginalization is encapsulated by one teacher's reply to the question: What does it mean when you call someone an integration student? *'Watch him!'* she replied.

Similarly, the notion of 'problems in schooling' has been incorporated into the deficit vocabulary of disability discourse: students with problems in schooling is a phrase which appears on notice boards and pamphlets alongside the phrase 'Impairments or Disabilities'. The Ministry's memorandum of 17 August, however, refers to such problems as deriving both from curriculum structures and, in a small percentage, from a student's characteristics. Like the Warnock report's failure to convey to other arenas in the educational apparatus the notion that special education needs derive from school practices and only sometimes from deficits, it seems likely that the 1984 report's notion of 'problems in schooling', as a theme in a discourse which is critical of school practices, is not adopted in arenas such as unions and schools.

Research on Victorian Primary School Council written policies on integration also reveals the deployment of professionalism and the differing objectives surrounding 'integration' (Fulcher, 1986c). Forty-one policies were obtained: this was 68 per cent of the sixty School Councils contacted in a random sample. These policies overwhelmingly adopted a stance of professionalism concerning the entry of students described as disabled to their schools; only one of the forty-one policies used democratic terms. All the policies considered resources as equally, or more, important than rights. Only nineteen of the Councils proposed establishing the key democratic decision-making structure (as envisaged in the 1984 report) of an Enrolment Support Group, but only five of these Councils proposed a membership equally constituted of professionals and non-professionals. Seventeen Councils proposed establishing separate committees to consider resource issues and of the five who proposed establishing only an Enrolment Support Group, all weighted their membership towards professionals: the proposed ratios were 5:2, 3:2, 6:1, 5:2, 4:2. Only two Councils wrote that they included a parent advocate as a member of the Enrolment Support Group, despite such advocates being seen in government written policy as central to democratizing decision-making. The discrepancies between School Council written policies on integration and the 1984 report shows that *policy is made at all levels.*

The lack of democratic intent in these policies may be interpreted, as

Miller's theorizing would suggest, somewhat generally, as evidence of increased social conflict over scarce resources. But this is a politically convenient analysis: should we assign responsibility for School Council policies' lack of democratism to capitalism? The generality of such an analysis, which avoids locating responsibility for the non-democratic discourse of professionalism to people who deploy this discourse, is politically and economically evasive: it ignores discriminatory decisions in School Council arenas and it ignores economic decisions *in* the educational apparatus by unions that they would respond to integration struggles by deploying resource arguments.

There are no reliable statistics on how integration is progressing in Victoria. Not only is integration, in the sense the report defines it, a difficult process to quantify, even reliable head counts on other aspects of integration, such as the number of students who might have moved from segregated settings to regular schools, is not available. Education Ministry statistics suggest that in 1986, 0.9 per cent of the school population are in segregated schools (Table 6.2 suggests this proportion was segregated also for the years 1978–82). Ministry personnel argue, however, that as, since 1980, the Ministry has taken over as Special Developmental Schools sixteen former non-government agency schools whose students are allegedly more disabled than those in government special schools, this means that a number of former students in segregated schools have been integrated into regular schools, thus keeping the proportion static. There are two problems with that argument. The first is that we have no reliable data: even if some students have moved from government segregated schools they may have gone to non-government segregated schools, of which there are a number in Victoria. Secondly, this argument does not tally with evidence from a small State Board report in 1986 which cited special school personnel as reporting that since the 'official policy' of integration it was now harder to get their students into regular schools, even on a part-time basis (1986).

While both the collection of statistics on the proportion of students in segregated settings and their interpretation are highly problematic, the Victorian figures, which show no significant change in the proportion of students in segregated schools, are consistent with national figures (Table 6.4). These show a statistically insignificant increase in 1986 since 1984, from

Table 6.4   National statistics: proportion of students in special schools, 1984 and 86.

	1984	1986
government	0.85	0.92
non-government	0.66	0.39

Calculated from Table 2.2, Commonwealth Department of Employment, Education and Training *Schooling in Australia*, 1987, p. 7.

0.85 per cent to 0.92 per cent, compared with a drop from 0.66 per cent to 0.39 per cent for non-government special schools in the same period. However, there are many problems associated with the gathering of these statistics (see *Integration in Victorian Education*, chapter 5).

Conclusions

While there is evidence of good practice in integration in various Victorian schools (see especially Huish, 1986), these practices have existed for some time; many therefore predate the 1984 report. These instances of successful integration occurred because people wanted them to happen and despite the overall lack of system support (*Integration in Victorian Education*, p. 17). The notable example here is the closure of Cobram Special Developmental School, a rural segregated school, whose closure the principal achieved over a period of two and a half years between 1979 and 1981, despite community resistance. This was before the 1984 report. This raises the question: What are the conditions necessary for achieving an objective of integration?

Unless instances of successful integration follow in time, and follow politically from, the Victorian report they can hardly be seen as an effect of government policy. We need, as evidence that the Victorian report has encouraged integration, research on new and successful practices where links to government written and enacted policy can be empirically demonstrated and adequately theorized and which overall show increasing integration in the sense the report uses it. Such system level data is not available and the provision of additional though limited resources does not provide this (see below). Moreover a high level of recurrent funds continues to be allocated to segregated schools, a practice which emanates from economic decisions made *in* the Victorian educational apparatus. This evidence shows it is much more costly to retain students in segregated schools than in regular primary schools (Table 6.1). Given the Victorian Ministry's restructuring along corporate lines, and given reduced spending by the Commonwealth on schools, the decision to maintain such high levels of expenditure on segregated schools can hardly be seen as consistent with determinate effects of the 'state of the economy' as various accounts of Australian education discussed above would argue (for instance, Kapferer, Kenway, Barlow, Smart). Rather, we should assign responsibility for these decisions to those who made them, namely the Minister, high level bureaucrats and unions.

As the evidence stands, and in the absence of demonstrating these links between the 1984 report and successful integration practices, there are a number of counter-effects which have undoubtedly followed the issuing of Victorian government written education policy on disability. These counter-effects have emerged from *administrative-bureaucratic-political practices* which I suggest *are the dominant institutional conditions of the 1984 report*; these conditions have emerged from negotiations between the most powerful actors and agencies involved, namely the Minister, senior bureaucrats and teacher unions. Constitutional and legislative conditions appear to provide relatively weak conditions of the report. Economic conditions have led to a restructuring of the Victorian Ministry and the consequent organizational chaos (Maslen, 1987; Allen, 1987) constitutes conditions hostile to people being able to retain democratic objectives. In this context Miller is right in suggesting that schools get caught up in social conflict about scarce resources. But it is also the case that the major agencies in the Victorian educational apparatus — namely senior bureaucrats and teacher unions – have colluded, since 1984, and well prior to the present exacerbation of conflict over resources, to present integration as a resource issue to the less powerful actors and agencies, namely parents as individuals and as representatives of parent associations. This discursive means has almost excluded the theme of curriculum from debate and is well illustrated by one meeting between the Minister and parent representatives, when a list of disabilities was presented and it was asked: How can any one teacher hope to be qualified to deal with each of these disabilities?

The counter-effects which have followed the 1984 report include increased struggle over integration objectives. The *politicization* of integration issues and the degree of conflict suggest that Offe is right when he states that the role of state policy is to set the agenda and to initiate conflict at other levels of a state apparatus, although we do not have to agree with his reductionist theorizing, that the state is doing this. In this context, *government level written policy on integration*, or state policy in Offe's terms, *has no substantive program implications: rather it has political effects* in the educational apparatus. This seems the case where the 1984 report is concerned, not only because it has initiated struggles around disability at a number of levels in the educational apparatus but because central program issues, including, for instance, pedagogic practices of how to teach a non-divisive curriculum, were not addressed in the report. The new practices of delayed admission, attempted suspension of students already in regular schools via invoking delayed admission practices, the emergence of private disputes, all indicate the escalation of conflict and the *increased politicization* of practices surrounding disability and integration.

These new practices, and others, such as the marginalization which follows being identified as an 'integration child' (Tschiderer, 1986), indicate that the political logic of a discourse on *disability*, even when framed within an objective at a government-level written policy of integration as increased participation, remains not only intact but has resulted in *increased regulation* of more students than before the 1984 report. Further, this increased regulation derives from *increased control from central administration* and is inconsistent with the discourse on democratism as increasing local control, which appears in the Ministerial Papers.

The new, extensive and protracted practices surrounding admission of a child called disabled to a regular school, indicate the *increased bureaucratization* of this arena of educational practices. This bureaucratization is constituted not only by the regulation via specific practices which follows calling a child disabled but also, it seems, judging from reports about Enrolment Support Groups, in Enrolment Support Group processes.[26] These reports suggest that techniques of linguistic persuasion occur, similar to those Mehan found professionals used in similar settings in California, and that interest group politics, such as those Rizvi *et al.* found in committees struggling over the Participation and Equity Program (1987), have also emerged in ESGs. The reported failure of many ESGs, despite the use of parent advocates, suggests that the written policy that democratism should prevail via collaborative decisions has been overtaken by the interest group politics of representative bureaucracy. This indicates that collaborative decision making as a means of achieving increased participation in regular schools by students called disabled has failed and that the democratic strategy recommended in the 1984 report cannot be taken as an unproblematic condition of integration, or as necessarily facilitating the context in which decisions about integration are made.

The failure of collaborative decision making processes means, secondly, that the *social theory underlying the 1984 report was inadequate*. This seems to be true in a number of ways and despite the fact that the Schools Commission described the report as the first of its kind based in a social theory: while this is, at one level, a naîve comment, since all policy as practice involves theorizing, it also points up the limits of certain forms of social theory in suggesting courses of action for redressing oppression and exclusion, a major theme and concern in social theory. In this context, we need to extend Beilharz's arguments (1987). He suggests that social theory helps us read social policy better and that, as a corollary, 'social theory become more conspicuously problem-oriented and less conspicuously haughty' (p. 405). Thus we need to interrogate social theory with the 'failures' of policy practices. As Beilharz notes (p. 404), 'the problems of "radical" policy development lie mainly *outside* policy [or what is generally understood by that term], in the institutions (and their traditions) into which policy will, it is imagined, be inserted (Beilharz and Watts, 1986a)' (Beilharz, 1987:440). As I have said elsewhere, if the extent of resistance to the policy proposed in the 1984 report had been properly anticipated, as it could have been, namely the opposition between bureaucratically-based professionalism and democracy, then better use of the political process might have been made (Fulcher, forthcoming). As it was, the report was dumped on schools and moral panics ensued which could have been headed off in more astute negotiations in many arenas. Consistent with this misuse of the political process, the process of consulting constituencies was brief, taking place during the period in which the Review Committee sat making decisions, and somewhat expedient.

A discourse on integration without dominant themes of disability and resources failed to find a strong institutional base in the newly established Integration Unit in the Ministry, and present proposals are to reduce staffing and to 'lose' the unit in a new Social Justice Unit. While the Victorian ALP government has deployed a discourse on social justice as part of its platform, it is clear that government practices in many areas fail to produce this outcome. Moreover, the discourse bureaucrats deploy to regulate parents seeking to enrol a child described as disabled in a regular school draws on themes of disability, deficit, therefore extra resources. This discourse misleads parents seeking to enrol their child called disabled into a regular school, since resources are available but not in the right place: they are allocated to segregated settings.

How is it that parents have failed, as a group, to overcome these bureaucratic strategies? There are a number of reasons. First, parents generally negotiate as individuals with bureaucrats. And as Worthington notes, even the most articulate often fail to achieve their objective of integration (1987). Secondly, it seems likely that the majority of parents do not have available to them a discourse of democratism, as we might deduce from Brisenden's observations (the 'social world is steeped in the medical model of disability' (1986:174)) and Elkins' comments (1985:181). The introduction of parent advocates and advocacy 'in–service' programs (day-long seminar sometimes, which are run in some regional education offices) to teach parents how to negotiate their objectives or, in principle, rights, attests to this lack of the availablity of a democratic discourse. Thirdly, and consistent with the first point, parents as an agency have a weak institutional basis relative to teachers and bureaucrats: the Victorian Federation of State School Parents' Clubs has only three full-time paid officers (plus three part-time officers) and the recently formed Victorian Parents Advocacy Collective, which consists of representatives from various parent groups, has none.

In brief, the way the bureaucracy presents the resource issue and its use of bureaucratic delaying tactics undermines parents' ability to pursue their objectives (Fulcher, 1987). Bureaucrats talking about:

> shortages and about 'extra' allocations made in a time of economic restraint ... (the bureaucracy's) protracted procedures ... bewilder some parents: 'You will need an enrolment support group

(which may take a month to establish); then you may not apply for an aide or part of an aide until October even though we may not make a decision until the next school year has begun'. Faced with making a choice after the school year has begun, some parents keep their child in the segregated setting because he or she has been there for a couple of months and call it quits for [the] year! (Fulcher, 1987).

The practices which the bureaucracy deploys in this context also absorb huge amounts of resources: in one region, a committee met full-time for a fortnight to consider 383 applications for aides in regular schools. The salary costs of these committee members (possibly ten paid people on that committee with salaries each of $28,000 or more per year?), quite apart from the expense at school-level of organizing the writing of these applications and at regional level, of receiving and processing them, absorbed money which might otherwise have been spent on integration programs in schools. In addition, bureaucrats, taking into account the political effects of going against union positions, have retained the practice of allocating substantial monies, recurrent and capital, to segregated schools and units and have established, with the unions, practices such as delayed admission which deploy resource arguments. Thus bureaucratic practices, in various ways, exacerbate social conflict over resources: they constitute powerful political-economic conditions of the 1984 report by absorbing allegedly scarce resources and by their deployment of a resource discourse. Thus the politicization and bureaucratization of Victorian educational practices surrounding disability are clearly aspects of the same practices.

These decisions – to spend large amounts of money on the bureaucratic regulation of political disputes, to continue allocating large sums of money to the segregated sector, and adopting practices which reinforce resource arguments – are each economic and political decisions made *in* educational apparatuses for which, in this book's model, responsibility must be assigned to bureaucrats and, where relevant, to unions. Only via a very indirect connection, that bureaucracy necessarily increases as capitalism develops (Weber's fearful prediction), can it be assigned to capitalism and thus, as a number of accounts discussed earlier would argue, to a single level of political economic factors. The fact that a principal of a segregated school (Cobram Special Developmental School) managed to integrate all the school's students into regular schools so that the segregated school closed, and that some regular schools, both before and since the 1984 report, have been integrating students described as disabled in the way the report argues should happen, indicates there is no determinate connection between capitalism and bureaucracy and that there are conditions (which need theorizing) under which democratic practices may be achieved.

The counter-effective practices surrounding integration objectives which have emerged since the 1984 report are consistent, however, with the lack of democratic practice in other arenas in Australian social and political life. The resource position on integration adopted by teacher unions in Victoria is consistent with the laborist and economistic position Castles identifies in trade union practices in general, and with the general lack of a social democratic discourse in Australian political life compared with some European welfare states.

To criticize unions is, however, to challenge the orthodoxy of some educational arenas and to risk being identified with a rightist position.[27] But this would be to obscure the issues: social justice in the form of salary levels for teachers *vis-à-vis*, say, bureaucrats in the educational apparatus, is an objective which might be pursued separately from the social justice issue of a right of admission to regular schools for children called disabled. In this context, the real injustice may lie not between capital and wage labour or between administrators and teachers, but in some children providing the opportunity for teachers' unions to pursue their objectives relating to working conditions by deploying integration as an issue in, for instance, a log of claims predating the 1984 report, and in relating the working conditions of regular teachers closely to the working conditions another sector of teachers (special teachers) have historically acquired.

A social justice discourse was written into the Victorian APL 1982 election platform on education (*Primary and Secondary Education: What the ALP will do*) (and includes statements on disability, though its themes are somewhat muddled), and into the 1985 election platform (*Social Justice: the next 4 years*): this discourse has been seen as informing the 1984 report. But it is clear that this written policy has not made much of a reappearance in practice at other levels of state apparatuses. However, social justice, like any other discourse, should be closely examined for its themes rather than welcomed because it sounds like a democratic socialist discourse. In this context, the Director of the Integration Unit's statement that special schools 'also meet the objectives of [the Government's] Social Justice Policy' is interesting (B.W. Lamb, 29 November 1986:4) and Beilharz's analysis of other Victorian policy documents is timely (1987).

The rights theme in the 1984 report has a weak institutional basis, a basis which appears to lie only in the 1984 Equal Opportunity Act an avenue which only the most determined of parents pursue. The 1982 Freedom of Information Act appears to constitute a minor condition of the 1984 report. The failure in the wider Australian context of those called disabled to achieve an integral place in society (HRC, 1986a, 1986b; Bodna, 1987) and to be allocated, instead, one of dependence, poverty, and exclusion, attests to the weakness of rights issues in current Australian social and political life.

Disabling Policies?

In addition to the increasing bureaucratization and politicization of issues surrounding disability, it is clear that schools have responded differently to the 1984 report, and prior to it, concerning objectives surrounding integration. Schools have written, stated and enacted policies (classroom practices) on integration which may differ from the 1984 report. This is consistent with Rizvi *et al.*'s findings that schools responded differently to the Commonwealth Participation and Equity Program (1987). The findings in both this and Rizvi's work, that *policy is made at all levels*, contrast with the accounts discussed earlier which reduce social conditions of diverse kinds to the state of the economy or to associated ideological shifts.

The finding that policy is made at all levels of a state apparatus has extraordinarily serious implications for all but those who receive government written level policy in totally cynical terms. For one thing, it seriously questions the belief that a Westminster government system prevails in Australian political life. It is not the case that members of Parliament make political decisions and their departments implement them. The Victorian findings, both on integration and on PEP by Rizvi *et al.*, show that political decisions are made at all levels of the state apparatus and that to describe these findings as indicating 'poor implementation' of 'government policy' is convenient politically but misleading. This knowledge raises serious questions about government, social theory and about negotiating change in a way which, for instance, would reduce the marginalization, exclusion, and increasing bureaucratization and politicization which students called disabled have experienced in the Victorian educational apparatus, experiences which have been exacerbated by the 1984 report.

Finally, whether one takes the view that a social democratic project is hard to find in Australian political life or the view from certain Marxist positions which I have argued against, that the project has failed because of the state of the economy, or thirdly, the view that bureaucracy and its professionalism opposes democracy – hence the bureaucratic practices which characterize the Victorian educational apparatus significantly inhibit democratic practices in schools – each suggest a wider context where the precedents and present context for achieving democratic practices, such as those outlined in the 1984 report, are not encouraging.

Notes

1 For instance, Whitty sees curriculum development in Victoria, as internationally outstanding (Whitty, 1986), though this is clearly debatable, even within Whitty's frame of reference (see, for example, Kemmis, 1986). Kapferer (1987) sees the Blackburn report on curricuum for years 11 and 12 as setting an international standard for decommodifying education (though her 'evidence' appears to rest

on a simple or a theoretical reading of 'policy') and White (1984) sees the report as potentially more divisive socially.

2 The policies examined were for NSW (*Strategies and Initiatives for Special Education in New South Wales*, 1982), Tasmania (*A Review of Special Education*, 1983) and WA ('Changes to Services for Children in Need of Educational Support: statement of Education Department Policy', late 1984).

3 The review was carried out by Lyn Gow of the University of Wollongong. A discussion paper for the Commonwealth Schools Commission, drawing on the review process and outlining policy questions and options, was prepared by Gow and Fulcher (1986).

4 It is very similar to Booth's concept of integration. As the report notes, 'The Review's interpretation of integration draws on the work of the English commentators on the Warnock Report, Tony Booth. He defines integration in education as "a process of increasing children's participation in the educational and social life of comprehensive primary and secondary schools." Booth comments "Clearly this definition can be applied to all children, not only those currently regarded as having special needs. Most children could participate in education to a greater extent and it would be interesting to know whether schools are now more adept at responding to the needs and interests of children than they were ten years ago. That would be one criterion on which to judge whether the participation of children in education has increased though it would be exceedingly difficult to gather evidence about it." (1981:288–9).

5 While the notion of accountability is increasingly used in recent Australian policy documents it is rarely defined. Hayes suggests 'accountablity . . . at bottom . . . seems to involve the notion that representative democracy should be able to penetrate professions and institutions which up until now have enjoyed a legal or de facto power to govern themselves and to discipline their members free from outside scrutiny' (Hayes, 1984:2).

6 See chapter 3 in *Integration in Victorian Education* for my earlier 'structural' view of these conditions.

7 This was formerly the Department of Education and Youth Affairs, and was restructured following the re-election of the Hawke government in July 1987.

8 As Levin notes.

> The federal structure for governing education in Australia is headed by a Minister of Education [now Minister of Education, Employment and Training] who is appointed by the party in power and has a seat in Parliament. The Minister will change as the party in control changes. There is also a Secretary of Education, a top civil servant, who is the permanent head of the Department of Education. The Secretary of Education is responsible for administering funds for student aid, policymaking, and providing advice to the Minister.
>
> Labor government reforms in 1972 created a Schools Commission whose four full-time and six part-time members dispensed almost all specific purpose Commonwealth funds for elementary and secondary education, including funds for non-government schools (with the principal exception of funds for student aid). Although the Commission has separate statutory authority, it submits its budget to the Department of Education and to the Secretary of Education (Levin, 1985:229).

9 Hayes and Macalpine refer to legislation which predates the Karmel report (see their footnote 5) as part of the Karmel report's Renaissance (1986:34–5).

10 See the State Board of Education for a more detailed though somewhat different account (1987).
11 Commonwealth legislation which is not primarily concerned with education may provide conditions which affect educational policy practices on disability and integration in the Victorian educational apparatus. An indirect effect has occurred in the past where parents have chosen to receive the Handicapped Children's Allowance rather than send their child to a regular school. See HRC (1986a) on this. The Commonwealth Handicapped Persons Assistance Act has however been repealed by the Commonwealth Disability Services Act 1986.
12 Again, see the State Board of Education (1987).
13 Discussion with a spokesperson of the Board (February 1987). In '1984/85, the Board placed particular emphasis on educational programmes directed to reducing discrimination on the basis of disability' (Equal Opportunity Board *Eighth Annual Report 30th June 1985*, p. 1).
14 'Intellectually disabled people do not in themselves constitute a formidable political lobby group; and the voluntary organisations which represent their interests tend to be fragmented, and thus, easily divided and conquered by the shrewd bureaucrat and public servant. Of course, the elite of the community needs no Bill of Rights. But minority groups do – for the political process, unreviewed and unreviewable by the legal system, is a scant protector of the interests of vulnerable minorities' (Hayes and Macalpine, 1986:34).
15 See, for example, at the federal level, *Quality of Education in Australia* (April 1985) and *In the National Interest* (Commonwealth Schools Commission, April 1987a); at state level, *Better Schools in Western Australia: A Programme for Improvement* (Ministry of Education, Perth, 1987) and *Developing a Corporate Structure for the Education Portfolio* (Victorian Ministry of Education, 1986a).
16 See, for example, *Skills for Australians* (1987).
17 This research was carried out by third year sociology undergraduates in the Faculty of Arts in 1985.
18 As a policy adviser to the NSW Minister of Education pointed out (personal discussion February 1987).
19 See, for example, the President's Report to the Annual General Meeting, Melbourne, October 1987.
20 Elkins describes the influence of parents in decisions about their children as follows: 'Another dimension of disadvantage was that parents were often ignorant of their rights. They did not always know about services or financial assistance to which they were entitled, nor were they able to act as effective advocates for their disabled child in interaction with professionals or bureaucrats' (1985:181).
21 About one quarter of the Australian population lives under the poverty line (Miller, 1986:367).
22 *The VTU Journal*, May 8, 1985, 'An hour with the Director General'.
23 Student Services, n.d.; see Intgegration Policy (no date), Victorian Primary Principals Association, which also adds a new structure in the decision-making process, a School Resources Panel, in addition to the Enrolment Support Group. The policy on Enrolment Support Group membership is to have as regular members the principal, staff representative, School Council representative, and as coopted members, parent, parent advocate, Student Services personnel and grade coordinators. The Victorian Teachers Union framed their 1986 log of

claims as 'integration' issues, thus mobilizing their demand for resources within the debate on integration. The Victorian Secondary Teachers' Association and the Technical Teachers Union of Victoria incorporated, in their demands, students already enrolled in regular schools (VSTA *News*, 1985).

24 For example, *The Tech Teacher* No. 26, 1987, p. 3.
25 Figures supplied on the proportion of school-aged children enrolled in government schools in this Region are shown in Table 6.5 below.
26 Enrolment Support Group practices (now Integration Support Group) need to be researched in Victoria, along similar lines to Mehan's research in California.
27 However, Beilharz, an editor of the notably left journal *Thesis Eleven*, makes similar points on unions and other practices (1987).

Table 6.5   Regional Board x: Enrolments in government schools

February	1986		1987	
	nos.	%	nos.	%
Primary	40,874		41,257	
Special and	640	0.88	338	635 0.87
SDS			297	
Secondary	22,770		22,650	
Technical	7,710		7,189	
Postprimary	753		1,063	
	72,747		72,694	

Figures supplied verbally by an officer in the Region.
353 applications represents 0.9 per cent of the total primary school enrolment in February 1986.

References

Allen, G. chief executive, Ministry of Education, letters to *The Age*, Tuesday 3 November 1987.

Ashby, G., and Taylor, J. (1984) *Responses to Policies: review of Commonwealth Schools Commission Special Education Program*. Report to the Commonwealth Schools Commission, Canberra, October.

Australian Association of Special Education *Policy Resolutions*, adopted at the Annual General Meeting 3–4 September 1985.

Australian Association of Special Education, President's Report to the Annual General Meeting, Melbourne, Victoria, October 1987.

Australian Labor Party (1982) *Primary and Secondary Education: What the ALP will do*, February.

Barlow, K. (1986) 'The Commodification of Education – Public into Private?' paper given at the Australia and New Zealand Comparative and International Education Society Conference, December.

Beilharz, P. (1987) 'Reading Politics: Social Theory and Social Policy', *The Australian and New Zealand Journal of Sociology*, 23, 3, pp. 388–406.

Birch, I.K.F. (1986) 'The Courts as Education Policy-Makers in Australia', a paper presented to the American Education Research Association Meeting, San Francisco, 16–20 April.

Blackmore, J., and Spaull, A. (forthcoming) 'Australian Teacher Unionism: New Directions' in Boyd, W.C., and Smart, D. (Eds) *Educational Policy in Australia and America: Comparative Perspectives*, Lewes, Falmer Press, in press.

Bodna, B. (1987) *Finding the Way: The Criminal Justice System and the Person with Intellectual Disability*, Melbourne, Government Printer.

Booth, T. (1981) 'Demystifying integration', in Swann, W. (Ed) *The Practice of Special Education*, Oxford, Blackwell, in association with the Open University Press.

Boyd, W.L., and Smart, D. (Eds) (forthcoming) *Educational Policy in Australia and America: Comparative Perspectives*, Lewes, Falmer Press, in press.

Brisenden, S. (1986) 'Independent Living and the Medical Model of Disability', *Disability, Handicap and Society*, 1, 1, pp. 173–8.

Castles, F.G. (1985) *The Working Class and Welfare*, Sydney, Allen and Unwin.

Castles, F.G. (1987a) 'Thirty Wasted Years: Australian Social Security Development, 1950–1980, in Comparative Perspective', *Politics*, 22, 1, pp. 67–74.

Castles, F.G. (1987b) 'Trapped in an Historical Cul-de-Sac: The Prospects for Welfare Reform in Australia', in Saunders, P., and Jamrozik, A. (Eds) *Social Welfare in the late 1980s: Reform, Progress or Retreat?*, SWRC Reports and Proceedings No. 65, Social Welfare Research Centre, The University of New South Wales.

Changes to Services for Children in Need of Educational Support, Statement of Education Department Policy, Education Department of Western Australia (no date, but post March 1984).

Ciavallera, M. (1987) 'Democratization of Victorian Education Policy: towards a sociological account', a dissertation presented for the Degree of Bachelor of Arts (Honours) in the Department of Anthropology and Sociology at Monash University, November.

Commonwealth Department of Employment, Education and Training (1987) *Schooling in Australia: Statistical Profile No. 1*, Canberra, Australian Government Publishing Service, November.

Commonwealth of Australia (1987) *Commonwealth Programs for Schools: Administrative Guidelines for 1987*, Canberra, Canberra Printing and Publishing Co., January.

Commonwealth Schools Commission 1975 *Report for the Triennium 1976–78*, Canberra, June.

Commonwealth Schools Commission 1976 *Report: Rolling Triennium 1977–79*, Canberra, July.

Commonwealth Schools Commission 1978 *Report for the Trienniumn 1979–81*, Canberra, April.

Commonwealth Schools Commission (1985a) *Quality and Equality: Commonwealth Specific Purpose Programs for Australian Schools*, Canberra, November.

Commonwealth Schools Commission (1985b), *Discussion of some Issues Raised in Quality of Education in Australia,* Canberra Publishing and Printing Co., September.

Commonwealth Schools Commission (1985c) *Report of the Working Party on Commonwealth Policy and Directions in Special Education*, May.

Commonwealth Schools Commission (1987a) *In the National Interest: Secondary Education and Youth Policy in Australia*, Canberra Printing and Publishing Service, April.

Commonwealth Schools Commission (1987b) *Commonwealth Programs and Policy Development for Schools 1988*, Fyshwick, A.C.T., Canberra Printing and Publishing Co., May.

Connell, R.W., Ashenden, D., Kessler, S., and Dowsett, G.W. (1982) *Making the Difference: Schools, Families and Social Division*, Sydney, George Allen and Unwin.

Culley, L., and Demaine, J. (1983) 'Social Theory, Social Relations and Education', in Walker, S., and Barton, L. (Eds) *Gender, Class and Education*, Lewes, Falmer Press, pp. 161–72.

Demaine, J. (1981) *Contemporary Theories in the Sociology of Education*, Basingstoke, Macmillan.

Elkins, J. (1985) 'Disability and Disadvantage: Special Education in Australia – Past, Present and Future', *Melbourne Studies in Education*.

Equal Opportunity Board, *Eighth Annual Report 30th June 1985*, Melbourne, Government Printer.

Fulcher, G. (1986a) 'Australian Policies on Special Education: towards a sociological account', *Disability, Handicap and Society*, 1, 1, pp. 19–52.

Fulcher, G. (1986b) 'School Council policies on integration: obstruction or implementation of state level policy?', unpublished.

Fulcher, G. (1987) 'Bureaucracy takes round seven: round eight to commonsense?', *The Age*, 14 April.

Fulcher, G. (1988) 'Integration: inclusion or exclusion?', in Slee, R. (Ed) *Discipline and Schools: A Curriculum Perspective*, Macmillan Australia.

Fulcher, G. (1989) 'Disability: a social construction', in Lupton, G., and Najman, J. (Eds) *Sociology of Health and Illness: Australian Readings*, Macmillan Australia.

Fulcher, G. (forthcoming) 'The Politics of Integration Policy: its nature and effects' in Jones, N. (Ed) *Review of Special Education Needs*, Vol 3, Falmer Press (in press).

Goacher, B., Evans, J., Welton, J., Wedell, K., and Glaser, D. (1986) *The 1981 Education Act: Policy and Provision for Special Educational Needs*, a Report to the Department of Education and Science, University of London Institute of Education, typescript, October.

Gow, L., and Fulcher, G. (1986) Part 2, *Towards a Policy Direction on Integration*, discussion paper prepared for the Commonwealth Schools Commission, June 26.

Hayes, R. (1984) 'Legal Rights and Wrongs of Special Education', paper presented at the Australian Association of Special Education 9th Annual Conference, Sydney, 29 August to September.

Hayes, R., and Macalpine, S. (1986) 'A Lawyer's View of Special Education: Past, Present and Future', *The Australian Journal of Special Education*, 10, 2, pp. 33–9.

Hayes, S.C., and Hayes, R. (1982) *Mental Retardation: Law, Policy and Administration*, Sydney, The Law Book Company Limited.

Higher Education: a policy discussion paper, circulated by the Hon. J.S. Dawkins, M.P., Minister for Employment, Education and Training, Canberra, AGPS, December 1987.

Hindess, B. (1986) 'Actors and Social Relations', Wardell, M.L., and Turner, S.P. (Eds) *Sociological Theory in Transition*, Boston, Allen and Unwin.

Hindess, B. (1987) *Freedom, Equality and the Market: Arguments on Social Policy*, London, Tavistock Publications.

Hughes, P. (forthcoming) 'Reorganisation in Education in A Climate of Changing Social Expectations', in Boyd, W.L., and Smart, D. (Eds) *Education Policy in Australia and America: Comparative perspectives*, Lewes, Falmer Press, in press.

Huish, R. (1986) (Ed) *Integration – a place for everyone*, Melbourne Participation and Equity Program.

Human Rights Commission (1986a) *The Treatment of Disabled Persons in Social Security and Taxation Law*, Occasional Paper No. 11, Canberra, Australian Government Publishing Service.

Human Rights Commission (1986b) *Ethical and legal issues in the guardianship option for intellectually disadvantaged people*, Human Rights Commission Monograph Series No. 2, Canberra, Australian Government Publishing Service.

Integration in Victorian Education (1984) Report of the Ministerial Review of Educational Services for the Disabled, Melbourne, Government Printer (chair M.K. Collins).

Jamrozik, A. (1986) 'Social security and the social wage: priorities and options in social policy', in Jamrozik, A. (Ed) *Social Security and Family Welfare: Directions and Options Ahead*, SWRC Reports and Proceedings No. 61, Kensington Social Welfare Research Centre, University of New South Wales, pp. 9–41.

Jamrozik, A. (1987) 'Winners and Losers in the Welfare State: Recent trends and Pointers to the Future', in Saunders, P., and Jamrozik, A. (Eds) *Social Welfare in the late 1980s: Reform, Progress or Retreat?*, SWRC Reports and Proceedings No. 65, Social Welfare Research Centre, The University of New South Wales, June.

Jessop, B. (1982) *The Capitalist State: Marxist Theories and Methods*, Oxford, Martin Robertson.

Kapferer, J.L. (1987) 'Youth Policy and The State: Australia, Britain, Sweden', *Discourse*, 8, 1, pp. 1–24

Kemmis, S. (1986) 'Mapping Utopia: Towards a Socially Critical Curriculum', a talk given to the 20th Annual Meeting of the Geography Teacher's Association of Victoria, Monash University, August 10.

Kenway, J. (1987) 'Left right out: Australian education and the politics of signification', *Journal of Education Policy*, 2, 3, pp. 189–203.

Levin, B. (1985) 'Equal Educational opportunity for Children with Special Needs: The Federal Role in Australia', *Law and Contemporary Problems*, 48, 2, pp. 213–73.

Macintyre, S. (1985) *Winners and Losers: The Pursuit of Social Justice in Australian History*, Allen and Unwin Australia.

Macintyre, S. (1986) 'The Short History of Social Democracy in Australia', *Thesis Eleven*, 15, pp. 3–14.

Marginson, S. (1987) 'Free market education', *The Australian Universities' Review*, 30, 1, pp. 12–16.

Maslen, G. (1987) 'Anxiety and anguish pervade the Ministry', *The Age*, Tuesday 27 October.

Meares, L. (1986) 'What progress for disabled people?', *ASW Impact*, December, pp. 6–8.

Mehan, H. (1983) 'The role of language and the language of role', *Language in Society*, 12, pp. 187–211.

Miller, P. (1986) *Long Division: State Schooling in South Australian Society*, Adelaide, Wakefield Press.

Offe, C. (1984) *Contradictions of the Welfare State*, edited by John Keane, London, Hutchinson.

Quality of Education in Australia, (1985) Report of the Review Committee, Canberra, Australian Government Publishing Service, April (QERC Report).

Ramsay, P., Sneddon, D., Grenfell, J., and Ford, I. (1983) 'Successful and unsuccessful schools', *Australian and New Zealand Journal of Sociology*, 19, 2, pp. 292–304.

Rizvi, F., Kemmis, S., Walker, R., Fisher, J., and Parker, Y. (1987) *Dilemmas of Reform: An overview of issues and achievements of the Participation and Equity Program in Victorian Schools 1984–85*, Geelong, Deaking University, February.

Rutter, M., *et al.* (1979) *Fifteen Thousand Hours: Secondary Schools and their effects on children*, London, Open Books.

Schools in Australia, Report of the Interim Committee for the Australian Schools Commission, Australian Government Publishing Service, Canberra, May 1973 (Karmel Report).

Sheehan, C. (1986) *Special Education: legislation in New South Wales and Elsewhere*, Research Officer, Disability Advisory Council of New South Wales.

Skills for Australians (1987) circulated by The Hon J.S. Dawkins, Minister for Employment, Education and Training and The Hon. A.C. Holding, Minister for Employment and Youth Affairs, Canberra, Australian Government Publishing Service.

Smart, D. (forthcoming a) 'Reagan Conservatism and Hawke Socialism: Whither the Differences in the Education Policies of the US and Australian Federal Governments?', in Boyd, W.L., and Smart, D. (Eds) *Educational Policy in Australia and America: Comparative Perspectives*, Lewes, Falmer Press, chapter 2, in press.

Smart, D. (forthcoming b) 'The Hawke Labor Government and Public-Private School Funding Policies in Australia, 1983–86', in Boyd, W.L., and Smart, D. (Eds) *Educational Policy in Australia and America: Comparative Perspectives*, Lewes, Falmer Press, in press.

State Board of Education (1986) 'The Progress of Integration from the Perspective of Government and non-Government Special Schools in Victoria', a Report by the State Board of Education Task Force on Integration, Melbourne.

State Board of Education (1987) *Legislative changes to Implement the Integration of Students with Impairments, Disabilities or Problems in Schooling*, Advice to the Minister, Melbourne, February.

Stewart, D. (1986) *Workers' Compensation and Social Security: An Overview*, SWRC Reports and Proceedings No. 63, November.

Strategies and Initiatives for Special Education in New South Wales, (1982) A report of the Working Party on a Plan for Special Education in N.S.W., Government Printer, N.S.W., May.

Student Services (C.G., and C.S.) Response to the Report of the Ministerial Review of Educational Services for the Disabled 'Integration in Victorian Education', (no date) typescript.

Tasmania, Education Department (1983) *A Review of Special Education*, Government Printer, Tasmania, April.

The Tech Teacher, No. 24, 1987.

The VTU Journal, May 8, 1985, 'An Hour with the Director-General'.

Tomlinson, S. (1982) *A Sociology of Special Education*, London, Routledge and Kegan Paul.

Tschiderer, N.P. (1986) 'A Study to Identify the Nature of Integration at the Wonthaggi Primary School in 1986', research paper presented to the Faculty of Special Education, Melbourne College of Advanced Education, October, unpublished.

Varley, J., and Howard, S. (1985) 'Integration – what it's all about', *VSTA News*, March 20, Vol. 6, No. 5.

Victoria, Education Department (1983) *Enrolment and Staffing in Education Department Schools for the Disabled*, prepared for the Ministerial Review of Educational Services for the Disabled, Policy and Planning Unit, March.

Victoria, Education Department (1983) *Planning Report*.

Victoria, Education Department, *Compendium of Statistics (1985)*.

Victoria, Minister of Education (Robert Fordham), memorandum to Presidents of School Councils, Principals and staff of all schools, *Integration in Victorian Schools* (no date).

Victoria, Minister of Education (Ian Cathie) (1985) memorandum to Presidents of School Councils, School Principals and Staff Regional Directors of Integration, *Integration in Victorian Schools*, May 20.

Victoria, Ministerial Paper Number 2, *The School Improvement Plan* (1982).

Victoria, Ministerial Paper Number 3, *The State Board of Education* (1983).

Victoria, Ministerial Paper Number 4, *School Councils* (1983).

Victoria, Ministerial Paper Number 5, *Regional Education Boards* (1984).

Victoria, Ministerial Paper Number 6, *Curriculum Development and Planning in Victoria* (1984).

Victoria, Ministry of Education, Deputy Director General (M.K. Collins) memorandum to Presidents of School Councils, Schools Principals and staff, *Integration in Victorian Schools*, August 31, 1984.

Victoria, Ministry of Education, A/Director of Student Services (Alan R. Farmer), memorandum to Regional Directors of Education, OICS, Student Services (CG & CS) Centres, *Special School Placement Procedures*, 28 March 1985.

Victoria, Ministry of Education, Acting Chief Executive (M.K. Collins) memorandum to Executive Directors, Directors of Branches and Units, Regional Directors of Education, Principals of Schools, Presidents of School Councils, Officers-in-Charge of Student Services Centres, Teachers-in-Charge of Education Support Centres, *Guidelines for Schools: The Integration Teacher: Role Rationale and Responsibilities (Primary and Post Primary)*, (no date).

Victoria, Ministry of Education, *Compendium of Statistics 1986*.

Victoria, Ministry of Education (1986a) *Developing a Corporate Structure for the Education Portfolio*, a discussion paper from the Ministry Structures Project Team.

Victoria, Ministry of Education (1986b) Ministry Structures Project Team Report, *Volume 1, Schools Division, Volume 2, Portfolio, Volume 3, Appendices*, Melbourne, Government Printer.

Victoria, Ministry of Education (1986c) Ministry Structures Project Team Report *The Report in Outline*, Melbourne, Government Printer.

Victoria, Ministry of Education (1986d) The Government Decision on the Report of the Ministry Structures Project Team 1986, Melbourne, Government Printer.

Victoria, Ministry of Education (1986e) *Curriculum Guidelines for the Education of Students with Impairments, Disabilities or Problems in Schooling*, Curriculum Branch, May.

Victoria, Ministry of Education (1986f) Executive Memorandum No. 34 from the Acting Chief Executive (M.K. Collins) To Principals of Schools, Presidents of School Councils, OICs of Student Services Centres, Teachers-in-Charge of Education Support Centres, *Enrolment Support Group Guidelines for Regular Schools*, 13 March.

Victoria, Ministry of Education (1986g) memorandum to all members Senior Officers

Group Integration Committee from the Director, Integration Unit (B.W. Lamb), 29 April.

Victoria, Ministry of Education (1986h) *Taking Schools into the 1990s* (1986), A Proposal from the Ministry Structures Project Team, June.

Victoria, Ministry of Education (1986i) *Compendium of Statistics 1986*.

Victoria, Ministry of Education, B.W. Lamb, Director Integration, at a Conference of the Victorian Federation of State School Parents Clubs, 'Label Jars not People', 29 November 1986.

Victoria, Ministry of Education, General Manager (M.K. Collins), memorandum to Regional Directors of Education *Delayed Admission to School of Parent's Choice*, 19 January 1987.

Victoria, Ministry of Education, General Manager (School Division, M.K. Collins), Executive memorandum No. 144 to Regional Directors of Education, Principals of Schools, Presidents of School Councils, Officers-in-Charge of Student Services Centres, Teachers-in-Charge of Education Support Centres, *Integration Support Group Procedures for Regular Schools (Formerly Enrolment and Support Group Guidelines)*, 17 August 1987.

Victorian, ALP (1985) Education Platform, *Social Justice: The next 4 years*, Richmond, Industrial Printing and Publishing.

Victorian Ministerial Review of Postcompulsory Schooling (1985) (chair: J. Blackburn) 2 volumes, Melbourne, Government Printer.

Western Australia, Ministry of Education (1987) *Better Schools in Western Australia: A programme for improvement*, Perth, Western Australia.

White, D. (1984) 'Participating in Nothing. New Moves in Education', *Arena*, No. 68, pp. 79–90.

Whitty, G. (1986) 'Review article – recent American and Australian approaches to the sociology and politics of education', *Educational Theory* 36, pp. 81–5.

Worthington, J. (1987) 'Parents and Information, the What, the Why and the How: A Survey of Australian Parent Organisation', paper presented at the Australian Association of Special Education, 12th National Conference, Melbourne, October.

ACTS
Commonwealth of Australia
Handicapped Persons Assistance Act, 1974
Schools Commission Act, 1974
Disability Services Act, 1986
Victoria
Education Act, 1958, Victoria
Community Welfare Services Act, 1970
Education (Handicapped Children) Act, 1973, Victoria
Education (Special Development Schools) Act, 1976, no. 8918
Equal Opportunity Act, 1977
Equal Opportunity Act, 1984
Freedom of Information Act, 1982
Intellectually Disabled Persons' Services Act, 1986

Part Three
Comparisons

Chapter 7

Comparative issues

The idea that social justice concerns inform both US and English educational policy on disability or handicap (Stobart and Trickey, 1985), is both a one-sided reading of these policies and a limited view of where policy is made. Since policy is struggle (Introduction), there is always more than one concern or objective contending with others in its production (Figure 1). Chapters 4, 5 and 6 discuss these contending objectives in US and English national policy and in Victorian government policy. Secondly, since policy is political practice and politics characterizes all practices, policy is made at all levels in educational apparatuses. National policy may have wider effects on schools than, say, a local education authority's decisions, but this does not mean we should resort to a top-down model of policy filtering from government level through a state apparatus.

The assertion that policy is made at all levels is important theoretically and politically: we can use this model, rather than the 'gap' model, to theorize the contrary practices that have emerged in educational apparatuses following national level policy. The 'gap' model describes the failure of national or government policy as due to a 'gap' between policy and implementation: it is apolitical theorizing and it contains a reductionist model of politics (only government or politicians hold power). The model proposed here, that all practices are political, that policy is practice and occurs at all levels, made sense of policy practices in educational apparatuses and it raised comparative issues. This chapter discusses these comparative issues under five headings: competing objectives in national policy, government policy strategies and the construction of conditions at other levels, school practices and integration, wider institutional conditions, and debate about special educational policy.

Competing objectives in national policy

In at least four of the five places the book discusses, it is clear that historically, and currently, struggles between competing objectives have characterized government educational policy on disability or handicap, whether this policy is produced as a document, a report, or as legislation. Moreover, these struggles belong not just to disability or handicap but to educational practices in general. In Norway, educational practices have consisted of struggles between integration and segregation, despite the 'platform' that comprehensive schools have been a principle informing school practices for some time. Further, apart from the uneven establishment of 'comprehensive' schools in Norway, teaching practices in them vary in how far they integrate children already present in the regular classroom (Booth, 1983). Thus, and this is an important aside, *educational* integration is a matter separate from social and locational integration.

In North America, national policy took the form of legislative decisions. Public Law 94–142, The Education for All Handicapped Children Act, 1975, is widely regarded as mainstreaming law and as exemplifying and achieving educational reform. As chapter 4 discusses, legal strategies were deployed by advocates whose objective was to reform and remove the inequities in educational practices surrounding handicap, or 'special education'. But the law emerged as a complex composition of opposing themes and opposing objectives: it is informed by the overt politics of a theme of rights, by the covert politics of professionalism and by a medical discourse on handicap. These oppositions may not have been perceived by those advocating a legal strategy and by those who drafted the legislation: as Beilharz says, social theory allows us to know policy better than those who construct it (1987). But the presence of these oppositions is important. Identifying the struggles in a national policy document is a first analytical step in identifying the discourses and their objectives which were contested in national arenas which constructed (in this instance) the legislation. These struggles will be replayed in other arenas at other levels in the educational apparatus. That inequalities remain reaffirms this.

The Victorian government policy, initially a report called *Integration in Victorian Education* (1984), reveals a contest between democratism and professionalism. Professionalism has been the key strategy or discursive means which has been deployed historically by those who have sought to control educational practices surrounding disability, not only in Victoria, but also in England (Kirp, 1983), and in Norway (chapter 3), and perhaps less overtly in North America (chapter 4), and not only in relation to handicap, but generally. Democratization has been the historical struggle to open educational policy and discussion to public participation and debate: democratism has been the key discursive means deployed here. While democratism attained an uneasy dominance in the Victorian government report, the evidence suggests that professionalism has won this struggle in other educational arenas in Victoria (chapter 6).

English policy is not so easily categorized as to its contending discourses and contending objectives. While it was widely hailed as about reform and about integration, the Warnock Report and the 1981 Education Act, the key documents and decisions in English national level policy, are substantially dominated by professionalism, in particular by a medical version of professionalism, and by themes which belong properly, if at all, only to severe impairment. Yet the report is about 20 per cent of the school population or one in five children seen as likely to have special educational needs at some time in their school lives. While the notion of special educational needs was presented as a non-categorical approach to providing special education services the phrase retains the politics of a traditional discourse on disability and is ultimately defined as disability (see the 1981 Education Act). It is of course an extraordinarily political act to infer 20 per cent of the school population have an impairment, but this is the political logic underlying the notion of special educational needs. Moreover, as chapter 5 states, it is less clear, in English national policy, whether there was a serious struggle in the Warnock committee to reform 'special education' or whether the exercise was primarily a political one (as all policy making is, at least to some extent) whose objective was to contain the politics of educational practices surrounding disability. The rights theme in the Warnock report is very weakly articulated. Moreover, Warnock herself has said the Committee fudged integration as a matter of policy. English national policy also chose legislation to achieve its objectives. Chapter 5 argues that it is far from clear that the 1981 Education Act is about integration, despite a widely held view that it is. The 1981 Act contains a discourse on disability, professionalism and resources. Far from being enabling or advanced in thinking, it is reactionary when measured against alternate themes and objectives which characterize some school practices and the Open University courses on special education. It seems Tomlinson was accurate in saying that the 1981 Act represents more of the same (1985). In this sense, integration as a theme in the Warnock report (the 1981 Act is seen as Warnock legislation) makes only a brief appearance and is merely a new name for special education (see chapter 2 on this position on integration).

For Denmark, less literature was available, but it showed that a pedagogical discourse dominated statements by the Ministry of Education, as well as its decisions to research pedagogical issues surrounding integration. No contending objectives appeared in national level written policy; but the deployment of pedagogical themes, and assertions that children do not divide into two categories of handicapped and not handicapped, clearly aimed to eliminate a concern teachers might have with handicap and to replace it with a focus on children as pupils.[1] This suggests handicap has been a theme in the Danish educational apparatus and that it is likely that in Denmark also, there were struggles to establish pedagogy and teaching as the dominant theme in a discourse on integration. It is also significant, since it would reveal a contending objective, that Danish national written policy does not deploy professionalism as a theme and tactic. Other social actors might deploy such a discourse at other levels of the Danish educational apparatus. While the research evidence is limited it seems significant that government level policy does not legitimate this discourse and the associated struggles.

In sum, with the exception of Denmark, national educational policies on disability or handicap contain competing objectives. Struggles between an objective of meaningful integration and segregation (though, for political reasons, this is not explicit) clearly characterize national written policies in Norway, North America, Britain and Victoria (but see the discussion on English policy above). Danish national policy is consistent about its objective of educational integration, which also attains an uneasy dominance in North American national policy (PL 94–142) and Victorian government policy (*Integration in Victorian Education*). English national policy (the Warnock Report and the 1981 Education Act) is best read as containing a dominant objective to legitimize extensive practices of segregation, including an expansion of special education interpreted as a humanitarian professional concern.

Government policy strategies and the construction of conditions at other levels

In each of the five places discussed, government written policy represents the outcomes of political states of play in the arenas which produced the policy. Each policy proposes strategies which, conventionally, would be seen as directing 'implementation' of this policy and its dominant objective at other levels. In the model of policy in the Introduction, these government policies create conditions of policy practices at other levels.

North American government policy created significant legislative conditions which have instituted extensive, political-bureaucratic-administrative practices at SEA and LEA levels. These practices, where they are deployed in SEAs and LEAs (sometimes they are not), indicate a formal compliance with the law, PL 94-142, but the evidence from several positions which differ theoretically-politically, is that the law cannot achieve substantive educational aims which the advocates of reform clearly hoped to achieve via the notion of 'free appropriate education'. While the evidence suggests that a number of children called handicapped now receive educational services who did not prior to the law, and that some are in what might be called integrated settings, the evidence also shows a number of practices contrary to the law's dominant objective. It shows that though locational integration may occur educational integration is far from assured; that the 'due process' of a team constructing an Individualized Education Program cannot only not guarantee the outcome of a free appropriate education but that this procedural safeguard is not always followed; and that school level practices, such as the Californian Eligibility Placement Committee, are political practices in which the most powerful social actors deploy discourses (techniques of linguistic persuasion, is Mehan's term) to achieve their objectives over and above the 'rights' of parents.

From this, five issues emerge. One is that policy is made at all levels in the North American educational apparatus. Secondly, this legal strategy has clearly produced counter effects in the educational apparatus, in the sense of increased regulation. Thirdly, as mentioned, the research revealed practices contrary to the objectives of those who deployed legal strategies in an attempt to reform. Fourthly, the advocates of reform via legislation not only inadequately theorized the nature of decision making at other levels in the sense Mehan identifies (decisions at other levels do not conform to the rational model legislators appear to asume is how decisions are made (Mehan *et al.*, 1981)) but also because they either saw law as containing the exercise of power at other levels or they did not see policy, political practices, as occurring at other levels in the educational apparatus. Moreover, and fifth, North American government strategy contrasts with the Danish government level view which was that legislation for integration was an inappropriate means for an objective of educational integration.

English national policy also chose legislation to achieve its objectives. The evidence shows that increased regulation and politicization have followed the Warnock report and the 1981 Act, in that extensive, time-consuming reporting procedures (new political-bureaucratic-administrative practices) have emerged at LEA level, while it is clear that the issue of educational integration is not controlled by these legislative conditions. Moreover, the evidence shows practices at other levels contrary to an objective of even locational integration, in that children placed in the largest category, that of learning difficulties (the former ENS-M category), have been increasingly segregated (Swann, 1985). Clearly policy is made at all levels in the English educational apparatus.

Since it is far from clear whether English government level policy contained a dominant objective of educational integration, it cannot be claimed that the Act was an inappropriate strategy for this objective. It may well be that the objective of the most powerful social actors in arenas concerned with constructing the 1981 legislation was to legitimate both existing practices of extensive segregation and an increase in the control special education has exerted traditionally in the English educational apparatus. This is Tomlinson's view (1985).

Disabling Policies?

Government level integration policy in Victoria emerged first in the form of a report, *Integration in Victorian Education* (1984), and later in various memoranda (chapter 6). There have been counter effects following this report, and practices contrary to its objective of democratization and at least locational education: educational integration was not clearly addressed in the report. The category of 'integration child' has increased the numbers of children marginalized (Tschiderer, 1986). Their presence in regular classrooms, and that of others called disabled who seek to enter regular schools, has been made contingent on resources. A resource debate dominates discourse on integration in the Victorian educational apparatus. The new status of 'delayed admission' applied to children seeking to enter regular classrooms, on the basis that extra resources are necessary but not available, and the attempt to deploy this practice to suspend those already there, indicate the increased politicization of educational practices surrounding disability, and that policy is made at levels other than government: in this instance, in arenas where union representatives and senior bureaucrats were the most powerful social actors, and in schools. These policies have been made without the assistance of legislative conditions and despite the possibility that delayed admission practices are counter to the 1984 Equal Opportunity Act. In sum, a major effect of these practices in the Victorian educational apparatus constructed since the government's initial document has been to regulate more children more highly, to construct new forms of exclusion and to make it more difficult for those termed disabled to enter regular schools (Fulcher, 1987; The State Board of Education, 1987).

In Denmark, government level policy has neither adopted legislation on integration nor does it appear to have deployed extensive administrative regulation to achieve its objective. Its strategy contrasts with national or government level policy elsewhere and consists in instituting a pedagogical discourse and research projects about teaching practices. There was no evidence (though the research was limited) of extensive contrary practices at other levels. The statistics on, and written statements about, school practices suggest that Denmark is more advanced in locational and educational integration than are schools in the other educational apparatuses discussed.

What does the evidence in these educational apparatuses imply about legislation as a site of decision-making? The brief answer is that, as Hindess asserts, it is only one site of decision-making and that, in the North American case, it seems a counter-productive national level strategy where genuine *educational* reform is the objective. In both the English and the North American educational apparatuses, legislative decisions have constructed more politicized practices, increasing conflict and increasing political-bureaucratic-administrative practices surrounding handicap or disability at other levels. The dominant objective in PL 94–142 appears to be to mainstream children called handicapped and formerly excluded from school. The finding that extensive *regulation* in the sense of procedural compliance only, is a consequence of this law, and that substantive educational reform, in the sense of *educational* integration (as opposed to social and locational integration), is beyond the control which flows from legislative decisions, suggests that legislation may do more harm than good if reform is the objective. This was clearly the view the Danish government held.

Furthermore, the contrary practices Swann identifies in the English educational apparatus (increased segregation of children in the largest category) indicates that policy practices occur at all levels. The failure by Sheffield LEA to change existing class and gender exclusions from regular schooling, despite a clear objective to do so, also indicates inadequate social theorizing of political practices in this area.

The contrary practices in the Victorian educational apparatus show that powerful social actors are able to construct conditions of 'integration policy' at school level which can be easily deployed by those in schools who wish to block the entry of a child called disabled. In this instance political-bureaucratic-administrative practices at central levels in the educational apparatus appear to have at least as much effect as legislative conditions. Part of this effect derives from the fact that parents appear not to have available a democratic discourse: they appear to accept arguments about resources and 'expertise' (Fulcher, 1987). Moreover, the contrary practices and counter effects suggest that the Ministerial Review inadequately theorized policy making at other levels in the educational apparatus, that it failed to anticipate the extent to which there would be resistance to integrating those labelled disabled (though there is abundant evidence that those thus labelled are excluded from attaining their rights as citizens in other areas of Australian life) and that it failed to look at problems in the theory that participatory decision-making structures are a means to democratization.

School practices and integration

All four chapters showed that schools within each of these educational apparatuses differed in how far they integrated students described as disabled or handicapped. As the model in the Introduction proposes, schools are sites of decision-making which are relatively independent of wider institutional conditions, whether these are in or outside the educational apparatus (though the division of those outside and those in is only just defensible analytically). Thus, for instance, in England, Booth notes there are examples of children with severe impairments being integrated in regular schools. This occurs despite national level equivocal policy and counter-effects. In North America, teachers were identified as key policy makers (Noel and Fuller, 1985) and in Norway, Booth notes some schools included those called handicapped and some did not and, further, that teaching styles varied in how far they integrated children present in regular classrooms. In Victoria, too, some schools were successfully integrating children called disabled both before the 1984 report and after it, despite the conditions it created which could easily be deployed by those wishing to block the entry of children termed disabled to regular schools. The notable case of the closure of a Victorian rural Special Developmental School (seen as for children with severe impairments) well before the 1984 report, indicates the independence of school practices from government level written policy. It raises questions about the relevance of large-scale, political exercises such as the Warnock Committee and the Ministerial Review in Victoria.

The research also revealed some insights into conditions of successful integration. The American literature, in particular, identified conditions in schools which promote meaningful integration. Collegiality between teachers, commitment by teachers, as well as the staying power of the principal, are especially relevant (Biklen, 1985; Hargrove *et al.*, 1983). How instruction is delivered is crucial and this includes cooperative styles of teaching (Booth, 1983; Voelker Morsink *et al.*, forthcoming). Differences between school systems were noted as directly affecting the nature and consequence of special education programs. North American inner city schools, which Milofsky describes as 'administratively disrupted', undermine both the control and therapeutic aspects of special education practices since in these schools no one is administratively responsible. In contrast, suburban schools in North America made different use of special education practices. In Norway, geographical features meant the use of special education was contingent for some children on a range of factors, though it was noted that in the urban area of Oslo more use was made of special education.

Wider institutional conditions

As Beilharz notes, both the content of policy (by which he means government level written policy), and the institutions into which it is to be inserted, matter (1987). Both conditions in and outside educational apparatuses are implicated here. Thus the chapters on local practices examined these wider conditions in varying degree; that is, institutional conditions 'outside' educational apparatuses. Government level policies or strategies vary. Similarly, the wider institutional conditions of these policies vary.

Where egalitarianism and the welfare state are concerned, there is a widely held discourse that the Scandinavian countries are more egalitarian than other Western countries, that this egalitarianism is more widely agreed (consensual) and that, consistent with this, the treatment of those called handicapped is more humane than that in other welfare states. The evidence confirms and refutes aspects of this.

If social welfare expenditure is a useful indicator of the degree to which egalitarianism dominates in arenas concerned with social welfare, the Scandinavian countries perform better than North America, Britain and Australia and would thus appear to be more egalitarian in their social policies. But this does not mean that this egalitarianism is consensual at all levels of state apparatuses. In Norway, for example, struggles between exclusion and inclusion, or segregation and integration, have characterized educational practices surrounding handicap since the beginning of state schooling, and this still occurs. Nor are Scandinavian countries equally egalitarian. On a number of measures Denmark has been ahead of Sweden and Norway this century on social democratic policies, and on a recent example it remains ahead of Sweden (chapter 3). The dominance of egalitarianism in Scandinavian social policies has been attributed to the success of social democratic parties. This has derived from their having had a wider than working–class base and from their negotiating successfully with capitalists (Castles and McKinlay, 1979; Castles, 1985). The underlying theorizing here is that politics matter, not merely economics or class.

Consistent with these wider institutional conditions, school practices in Denmark appear ahead of other welfare states. Admittedly the research was limited compared with that for North America, Britain and Victoria. But the research on Denmark failed to reveal current struggles over handicap in government educational policy and the statistics on school practices and integration, which are much more specific than any available for North America, Britain and Victoria, suggest again, that school practices, consistent with government level policy, are more advanced than in the other places discussed. The research on Norway was also limited but this revealed, at government and at other levels of the educational apparatus, continuing struggles between integration and segregation, even where locational integration is concerned. It seems then that wider institutional conditions in Denmark are favourable to an objective of educational integration at whatever level this policy appears.

Given the consistency in Denmark which appears to hold between institutional conditions outside the educational apparatus (a better established egalitarianism?), conditions in the educational apparatus constructed by government level policy (pedagogy not handicap) and the statistics on locational integration and school practices, it seems plausible to suggest that the fate of schoolchildren called disabled is related to the wider society in which they go (or don't go) to school. Such connections seem plausible for

Victoria. In Australia generally, there is abundant evidence of a lack of democratic practice: this is also the case for schoolchildren called disabled in the Victorian educational apparatus, at least as much since the 1984 report as before it. Such connections are not however *determinate*: as Booth notes for England, there are instances of schools integrating children with severe impairments. Thus while school practices are, as common sense would suggest, both characteristic of and help to characterize their wider society, they also matter independent of these wider contexts. Individual schools can be democratic in a context which is generally undemocratic. Closures of special schools can occur despite initial community resistance. Again this might seem common sense but such possibilities seem denied by determinist theorizing of a broad-based Marxist kind. (This of course is an unsatisfactory category since Marxism has so many variants.)

Debate about special education policy

Some of the chapters on local practices looked at debate on educational policy and disability or handicap or, more widely, on educational practices more generally. The American literature was both specifically concerned with educational policy on handicap and more comprehensive in the theoretical-political positions it contained. Clearly the politics of educational policy on handicap in the US has been widely accepted and the central issue is strategies to achieve an objective of educational integration. The solutions vary according to theoretical bases: they range from suggestions to increase legal regulation and adopt behavioural criteria for performance at other levels consistent with federal laws, to a focus (which seems to be widely held) on styles of teaching. The debate included sociological theorizing which ranged from class structural to institutional practices accounts and included those which note the administrative bureaucratic nature of schools as a significant factor in the extent to which special education practices might be therapeutic, and social control.

In contrast, there is less critical, social and political theorizing in Australia on educational policy and almost none on special education. The debate on education policy is presently dominated by Marxist accounts of various sorts, perhaps reflecting the relatively new emergence of this theorizing in Australian debate compared with America or Britain. The evidence from the Victorian educational apparatus on decisions in the educational apparatus challenges these accounts. A significant theoretical contribution emerged from researchers at Deakin University, from Rizvi and his colleagues, who examined the response of schools and other levels in the educational bureaucracy to a Commonwealth government education policy. Their findings were that schools varied, that the education bureaucracy bureaucratized this program and consequently opposed the democratic objectives of the Commonwealth's written policy.

The theorizing and findings of Rizvi *et al.* were compatible with the idea that policy is made at all levels, not surprisingly since their theorizing implies this. This view can accommodate the notion that government level policy initiates conflict at other levels of a state apparatus (Offe's insight) but, in these educational policies, the extent of this appears to depend on how government theorizes the likely responses to 'their' policy (how they theorize the political processes): it will depend too, on their objectives, the discourses they deploy and thus legitimate. We can theorize this conflict in ways other than Offe's view that the role of 'state' policy is to initiate conflict at other levels and to reconcile, albeit temporally, the state's internal structural problems (1984). Policy struggles over, for instance, 'integration' are thus replayed in a range of arenas at a number of levels in the educational apparatus.

Notes

1 Warnock made similar statements but these coexist with opposing themes (1978) and this contrasts with the lack of opposing themes in the Danish Ministry of Education's written policy.

References

Beilharz, P. (1987) 'Reading Politics: Social Theory and Social Policy', *Australian and New Zealand Journal of Sociology*, 22, 3, pp. 388–406.

Biklen, D. (1985) 'Mainstreaming from Compliance to Quality', *Journal of Learning Disabilities*, 18, 1, pp. 58–61.

Booth, T. (1983) 'Policies Towards the Integration of Mentally Handicapped Children in Education', *Oxford Review of Education*, 9, 3, pp. 255–68.

Castles, F.G. (1985) *The Working Class and Welfare*, Sydney, Allen and Unwin.

Castles, F.C., and McKinlay, R.D. (1979) 'Public Welfare Provision, Scandinavia, and the Sheer Futility of the Sociological Approach to Politics', *British Journal of Political Science*, 9, pp. 157–71.

Fulcher, G. (1987) 'Bureaucracy takes round seven: round eight to commonsense?' *The Age*, 14 April.

Hargrove, E.C. *et al.* (1983) 'Regulation and Schools: The Implementation of Equal Opportunity for Handicapped Children', *Peabody Journal of Education*, 60, 4, pp. 1–126.

Integration in Victorian Education (1984) Report of the Ministerial Review of Educational Services for the Disabled, Melbourne, Government Printer, (Chair: M.K. Collins).

Kirp, D. (1983) 'Professionalization as a policy choice: British Special Education in Comparative Perspective', in Chambers, J.C. and Hartmann, W.T. (Eds)

Special Education Policies: Their History, Implementation and Finance, Philadelphia, Temple University Press, pp. 74–112.

Mehan, H. (1984) 'Institutional Decision Making' in Rogoff, B. and Lave, J. (Eds) *Everyday Cognition: Its Development in Social Context*, Cambridge, Massachusetts, Harvard University Press.

Mehan, H., Meihls, J.L., Hertweck, A., and Crowdes, M.S. (1981) 'Identifying handicapped students', in Bacharach, S.B. (Ed) *Organizational Behaviour in Schools and School Districts*, New York, Praeger, pp. 381–422.

Milofsky, C.D. (1986) 'Special Education and Social Control', in Richardson, J.G. (Ed) *Handbook of Theory and Research for the Sociology of Education*, New York, Greenwood Press, pp. 173–202.

Ministry of Education (1986) *Handicapped Students in the Danish Educational System*, a survey prepared for the IX international school psychology colloquium, Copenhagen, Ministry of Education, Special Education Section, August.

Noel, M.M., and Fuller, B.C. (1985) 'The Social Policy Construction of Special Education: The Impact of State Characteristics on Identification and Integration of Handicapped Children', *RASE*, 6, 3, pp. 27–35.

Offe, C. (1984) *Contradictions of the Welfare State*, edited by John Keane, London, Hutchinson.

Rizvi, F., Kemmis, S., Walker, R., Fisher, J., and Parker, Y. (1987) *Dilemmas of Reform: An overview of issues and achievements of the Participation and Equity Program in Victorian Schools 1984–85*, Geelong, Deakin University.

Special Educational Needs (1978) Report of the Committee of Enquiry into the Education of Handicapped Children and Young People, London, HMSO (Warnock Report).

State Board of Education (1986) 'The Progress of Integration from the Perspective of Government and non-Government Special Schools in Victoria', a Report by the State Board of Education Task Force on Integration, Melbourne.

Stobart, G., and Trickey, G. (1985) 'Mainstreaming – a lesson from America?' *The Times Educational Supplement*, 13.9.85, p. 4.

Swann, W. (1985) 'Is the integration of children with special needs happening?: an analysis of recent statistics of pupils in special schools', *Oxford Review of Education*, 11, 1, pp. 3–18.

Tomlinson, S. (1985) 'The Expansion of Special Education', *Oxford Review of Education*, 11, 2, pp. 157–165.

Tschiderer, N.P. (1986) 'A Study to Identify the Nature of Integration at the Wonthaggi Primary School in 1986', research paper presented to the Faculty of Special Education, Melbourne College of Advanced Education, October, unpublished.

Voelker Morsink, C., Chase Thomas, C., and Smith Davis, J. (forthcoming) 'Non-categorical Special Education Programs: Process and Outcomes', typescript.

ACTS

England
Education Act, 1981
US
The Education for All Handicapped Children Act, 1975
Victoria
Equal Opportunity Act, 1984

Part Four
Conclusions and an agenda

Chapter 8

Conclusions

The Introduction theorized policy as political practice, as representing the outcomes of political states of play in a particular arena, thus as struggle. This model derives from a wider view of social life, including what we call 'policy', as consisting of practical projects: all practices are struggles to achieve objectives; they are based in a social theory (however inaccurate) and they are simultaneously political and moral. They sustain or undermine existing relations and their institutional bases. Policy, it was argued, is made at all levels of the educational apparatus. This means that all practices in educational arenas, including teacher–parent encounters and teaching practices, are equally political practices, as is the lengthy production by committees of government level policy and the drafting of legislation. The model integrates educational practices of whatever kind, and dissolves the distinctions usually drawn between theory and practice, policy and practice or implementation. Implementation is an apolitical, administrative term for political practice at levels other than government decisions. Theorizing is a practical project: as an activity in academia, people engage in doing it, but this activity characterizes all social practices; moreover accurate theory is about actual practices: As Kurt Lewin puts it, 'There is nothing so practical as good theory' (cited by Fullan, 1987:1). The divisions in bureaucratic academia between educational 'policy', 'research' and 'theory', and in educational bureaucracies or state apparatuses between policy and implementation reflect the fragmentation which charaterizes the bureaucratic and politicized nature of struggles in late twentieth-century life. The divisions are themselves political constructs.

Policy, as the outcomes of political states of play in an arena, was also defined as objectives reached in that arena in the form of decisions, whether these are recommendations to be included in a report, or other directions for future action of whatever kind: whether to exclude a child or revise the curriculum, to apply for resources, etc.

The model was developed because existing theorizing of social policy, including education policy is problematic. It drew on the work of Offe (1984), Hindess (1986), Mehan (1984, etc.) and Culley and Demaine (1983), and it was used to examine educational practices surrounding disability or handicap in Norway, Denmark, California, England and Victoria. The evidence from these places was then used to interrogate the model, with a view to revising it if necessary. This is how social theories are both used to make sense of everyday life and are tested.

The research revealed nothing which refutes the model. In all five places, it is clear, for instance, that schools make their own policy practices surrounding handicap or disability and that there is a wide variation between schools within the one 'set' of wider institutional conditions. The complex interaction between government policy and its strategies, and institutional conditions at various levels and in a range of arenas in educational apparatuses, has been a major theme in the book.

Policy as struggle

The notion that policy, whether written, stated or enacted, as political practice, is struggle has a number of implications for 'reading', listening to, and observing policy practices. As Beilharz points out, in relation to written policy, we need to know the policy better than those who formulated it. Thus, if we read, listen to, or observe integration policy practices, it becomes clear that a whole range of practices get called integration that might often be called segregation. This is because the terms have no inherent meaning. They are names people give to their discourses which they deploy to achieve their objectives. It is the themes and the discursive means in these discourses which reveal objectives and the meaning of a particular use of integration. Are these themes those of disability and handicap, difference and loss, *or* those of teaching practices, curriculum and pedagogy? Do teachers deploy democratism or professionalism? These are opposing discursive means: they contain opposing themes and opposing means and they lead to different practices and different objectives. These tactics and their objectives have radically different consequences for those they teach. Some objectives surrounding integration are consistent with extensive practices of segregation.

Objectives and discursive means

Theorizing policy as political practice, thus as struggle around competing objectives, leads to the analysis of the discursive means people deploy to achieve their objectives. This is because discourse is both tactic (Macdonell) and theory which informs the social actor deploying that discourse on how to achieve those objectives: this is how this bit of the social world works, and therefore how I/we should go about achieving my/our aim.

Chapter 1 suggested professionalism and democratism were opposing discourses with opposing objectives for educational practices. And later chapters showed that professionalism has been a powerful tactic at various levels in some educational apparatuses for blocking a government level democratic policy on integration.

The critique of professionalism will be unpopular. But what has been claimed about professionalism? To work as a professional is to engage in a political process at a number of levels.[1] A key strategy *some* professionals adopt in this process is what can be called professionalism. Professionalism has a number of meanings but it has been used here to refer to a *discourse and its associated practices* which makes a claim to expert knowledge, which uses language to establish this claim of expertise. Secondly, that as discourse, thus tactic, professionalism has particular objectives. In some Western educational apparatuses professionalism has been deployed to control not only educational practices surrounding disability or handicap, but educational practices in general. This has been the case in Victoria, Britain and Norway, and (to a lesser extent, the evidence suggests) in North America, despite its inconsistency with the self-conscious democratism and the theme of rights which characterizes North American political discourse and, more recently, educational discourse.

There are two important caveats here. Firstly, not all professionals use professionalism: alternative discourses and practices are available, such as democratism. Secondly, professionalism is distinct from what can be called *technical competence.* This book does not argue against technical competence: quite the reverse, it argues for increased technical competence for teachers. In discussing professionalism it seeks to clarify the sometimes unacknowledged and unperceived, and sometimes abusive, use of power via professionalism. While professionalism presents itself as technical, its objective is control.

How professionalism works

Professionalism achieves it controls firstly through its use of language and secondly, because this discourse and its associated practices have two key institutional bases: bureaucracy and professional and paraprofessional training schools. I shall examine the issue of language first.

As both discourse theory (Macdonnell, 1986) and critical theory argue,

language constructs social reality, it 'is not natural or neutral but "loaded"'
(Tomlinson, 1987). How does professionalism mask its loaded language?

The language in the various versions of professionalism (educational,
medical, legal, etc.) typically includes phrases such as 'in the
patient's/child's/client's *best interests*'; 'appropriate' is a frequently occurring
theme, as is the notion of needs: for instance, special educational needs. These
issues are presented as beyond politics, as things on which an expert has
technical knowledge which then allows him/her to judge without bias and
as though such decisions are beyond moral debate.

But in a discourse about needs, a key political question is: Who defines
these needs? As Cooper puts it: 'people only see their needs in terms of the
services that they are offered and it is this institutional reality that defines
their awareness of their own needs' (1982:25). Professionals are part of
institutional reality and thus typically they, rather than the other, define needs.
Despite the apparent humanitarianism implict in the notion of needs, the
evidence suggests that where resource allocation has been made in welfare
states on the basis of 'need', groups so defined become marginal members
of society. Such marginality is consequent on this definition rather than
preceding it: this is evidenced in the increasing number of schoolchildren
labelled disabled or as having special educational needs who have been
consequently marginalized *following* the official introduction of these terms
(chapters 5 and 6). The theme of needs in discourses of professionalism
illustrates the way in which language is used as 'both the instrument and
object of power' (Codd, 1988:241).

As the Introduction noted, judgements and decisions in teaching include
a politics and morality: We'll teach *this* (curriculum), *here* (in special schools)
rather than *there* (in regular schools) in *this* way and to *this* category of students
(whom we label disabled and whom we assert have special educational needs).
The politics and morality inherent in these statements precede their
substantive, technical implications. Thus nothing follows technically, morally,
or politically, from the fact that a 13-year-old may not be able to read (see
the Introduction).

Education provides numerous examples of the inextricably political and
moral nature of its practices. Amongst the most contentious is the debate
about curriculum: what is to count as valued knowledge; a debate especially
topical in the English[2] and Victorian educational apparatuses.[3] Where
changes in curriculum policy are centrally imposed, as they currently are
in England, professionalism as the major tactic is less applicable to this
analysis, since this decision emanates from high level government arenas.
But in educational apparatuses where community involvement in curriculum
decisions have been government policy, and where teachers have deployed
professionalism to exclude others from taking part in these decisions, it is

applicable. Such a claim illustrates the exercise of power based on 'professionalism', the claim to *know* best. But knowledge is never neutral: it involves notions of desirable and undesirable, and if acted on without full consultation with those such action affects, it involves the use of power. The disputes about, for instance, correct procedures, whether in medicine or in teaching, are never merely technical, despite the introduction of technobabble[4] phrases such as 'appropriate': this distracts most people's attention from the moral judgement being made.

Professionalism produces linguistic constructs such as IEP (individualized educational program), ILU (independent living unit), 'learning difficulty,' SEN (special educational needs). These constructs obscure the politics embedded in this vocabulary. But their politics can be challenged. As Ian Parsons recently said, writing under the heading 'Making Simple Things Difficult: Some thoughts on the professionalisation of human services'.

> We need to return much more to real commonsense and human decency in understanding the needs and rights of people with intellectual disabilities. Do, for example, people really need 'social skills programmes' or do they just need chances to make friends? Do they need hydrotherapy or do they just need a swim? Do they need a level A2 CRU or just a decent place to live with a fair bit of help? (1988:3).

Further, the language of professionalism is embedded in, and constitutes, various versions of an individualistic gaze. The politics of the individualistic gaze are that they construct or interpret problems out of their wider social, political context. This is not to argue that such gazes have no relevance or contribution, rather that they contain the politics of those problems to those of 'private troubles' rather than identifying them as 'public issues': such an interpretation requires wider action than treating individuals.[5]

In medicine, this individualistic gaze takes the form of a 'clinical gaze',[6] in law, a 'judicial gaze',[7] and in education, a 'meritocratic gaze'. These gazes have their bases in institutional contexts. In education, the meritocratic gaze clearly finds an institutional base in educational apparatuses geared to assess, select and allocate students to different educational careers. This basis of selectivity protects the meritocratic gaze from serious challenge, at least in Australia,[8] although elsewhere, in the Scandinavian countries, it has been challenged by a discourse about comprehensive and inclusive schooling and by a focus on pedagogy rather than assessment and selection.

The effects of these gazes on those thus gazed upon is profound. The judicial gaze sees only *individual* culpability: as Lee and Raban note,

> We should hardly be surprised that a 'judicial gaze' can *only*

understand *individual* culpability, in just the same way as it reinforces the belief that everyone has an equal chance of legal remedy in a capitalist society. In other words, it reproduces inequality by treating unequals as if they had the same resources and power (1988:104).

The clinical gaze divides people into parts of a body and divorces the body's health/illness from its social context, thus systematically distracting the medical practitioner from developing a wider, more socially responsible discourse on health and illness beyond his or her individual patient. In education, the meritocratic gaze divides the school population into 'types' of children to be taught by different types of teachers and this deflects attention from the central issue in education, namely pedagogy.

Thus professionalism constructs its clients; in medicine as patients, not *people* with a body, and in education as children with alleged disabilities rather than as *pupils*.[9] In superimposing these definitions, professionalism subordinates and reconstructs those it thus defines and confines the definer to a limited view. In these effects, the language of professionalism is clearly political: it functions as the instrument of power. It operates via what Mehan (in his research in Californian schools) calls techniques of linguistic persuasion (1983).

More on how professionalism works: its institutional bases

Bureaucracy is a key institutional base of profession and it makes a threefold contribution. Firstly, as an hierarchical authority system based on the notion of experts, with allegedly technical spheres of competence and thus clearly defined areas of responsibility, it promotes professionalism. It provides a home – a key institutional base – for deploying discursive practices based on a notion of expertise. Secondly, and at the same time, it promotes a lack of responsibility: passing the buck is the colloquial phrase for this. This is a powerful tactic, manifest in delaying decisions (bureaucratic enquiries), withholding information, etc. (Fulcher, 1987). Thirdly, as the typical form of modern organization, whether this is a hospital, school, government department, or the judicial system, bureaucracy increasingly provides employment for professionals and paraprofessionals. This, of itself, encourages the trend in welfare state services to professionalize, and to deploy professionalism and this was the trend which Weber feared.

Vocational training institutions are also key institutional bases for professionalism. There are a number of reasons for this. As a generalization, occupational knowledge is presented in those institutions as a technical discourse so that the politics and morality inherent in medical/

educational/legal judgements are ignored. Moreover, given the competition between those who teach in these institutions to develop their own courses in their own specialities, this promotes fragmented knowledge and the notion of expertise in different areas. Often such institutions employ only practitioners from their own occupations, a practice which systematically works against broadening the curriculum beyond the vocational areas which belong to that occupation. From these training schools, newly qualified professional and paraprofessional workers emerge without understanding the politics of their occupational discourses.

In sum, professionalism has clear institutional bases: through its use of language, it compatibility with bureaucracy and its place in training schools. Given these bases, this analysis suggests a number of ways or means for challenging professionalism. This is taken up below.

Policy at all levels

The observation that schools, including teachers, make their own policy practices, and that teachers are highly powerful policy makers (Booth, 1983; Biklen, 1985; Noel *et al.*, 1985; Ysseldyke, 1986; Nevin and Thousand, 1987; Fulcher, 1988a; Voelker Morsink *et al.*, forthcoming), accords with commonsense knowledge and observation. But of course that happens. Some teachers do this and some do that. But they do not all create their policy practices under equal conditions, they do not do so under circumstances of their own choosing, as Marx and Engels put it (1970:58–9). Some conditions which teachers face encourage integration, some discourage it, but none are determining. Which institutional conditions are favourable and which directly encourage counter-effects is discussed in the section on institutional conditions in educational apparatuses and integration, and wider institutional conditions.

The argument that policy is made at all levels in the educational apparatus will be unpopular with various audiences. It will be disliked by sociologists who are attached to traditional structural frameworks which theorize social life and its historical development as the product of class struggle, and by sociologists who theorize state policy as a form of state action, and who thereby avoid the politics, and the detailed empirical work, of unearthing who makes decisions in various arenas and who should therefore take responsibility for them.[10]

It will be rejected by those who believe countries like Australia and Britain have Westminster type governments and that real power lies only with government in the sense of elected members of Parliament. These people are likely to decry the American political system, which is widely recognized as political in its administration, and are also unlikely to share the assumption, which is apparently widespread in Scandinavian countries, that practice at all levels in educational apparatuses are political, including counselling and curriculum. Those who retain a belief that a Westminster type system prevails in Australia, ignore the evidence. Bureaucrats, teacher union representatives, teachers as individuals, and educational psychologists make decisions in educational arenas which are significant in their own right and which are not determined by government written policy.

In the Victorian educational apparatus, bureaucrats together with representatives of teacher unions, have made political economic decisions which have sustained existing practices surrounding disability and extended the regulation of children tagged disabled. Bureaucrats, it seems, have also made such decisions in Norway (chapter 3), and such an interpretation makes sense of evidence of English practices since the Warnock Report and the 1981 Education Act; but at a distance of several thousand miles, the direct evidence was not readily available.[11] But in Norway and Victoria, political-economic decisions are made *in* the educational apparatus to retain an extensive array of segregated schools and thus the institutional basis for extensive practices of exclusion (Warnock, 1982; Booth, 1983; Fulcher, 1988a).[12] Similarly, other social actors make decisions which are political: this includes teachers, educational psychologists and whoever holds power in an educational arena, whether in committees or in an encounter between two people.

The model, because of the deductions it allows that teachers act politically as individuals, will also be rejected by union representatives whose job it is to present teachers as favourable on democratic policies, and thus as for, rather than against, practices which increase equality. But this is to confuse a legitimate union task, that of deploying a particular discourse in certain arenas, with the different empirical-theoretical task of looking at what teachers actually do in the classrooms and whether their decisions in various educational arenas are democratic in content, means and objective. To argue that this is always the case, is to argue that teachers in general are somehow outside the prejudices and discrimination which currently characterize the treatment of those called disabled in welfare states like North America, Britain and Australia. Teachers, like everyone else, are equally members of an unequal society and may contribute to, or undermine, this inequality. Evans (1986b) and Galloway and Goodwin (1987) make this point, somewhat more diplomatically. Broad-based Marxist theorists in Australia, such as Miller, Kenway, Kapferer, Barlow, avoid confronting this issue and its politics by locating their explanations of what is happening in educational apparatuses in wider 'social forces' such as the global crisis and restructuring of capital and 'social division'. The issue and its politics is got around, too, by Weberian theorists such as Mehan (chapter 4). But there is considerable evidence that teachers in some educational apparatuses have resisted integration: there are other issues here, however, which are taken up below.

Others will dislike the book because it presents educational practices as political and moral. These people may see teaching as basically technical: this is true at only one level. There are technical aspects of pedagogy, that is, techniques of teaching others; but pedagogic practice is embedded in the moral and political. Western educational apparatuses have created schools where age dominates what curriculum a child is exposed to and where age when a task is mastered is regarded as a critical indicator of normality. This practice systematically disadvantages those who go faster or more slowly than most of their classmates. It is part of practices which construct 'deviants', those with learning difficulties, etc.

It will also be disliked by the uncommitted, those who prefer to sit on political fences and to avoid confronting how their work as teachers sustains or undermines 'normal' and deviance-producing relations. This claim draws on the analysis put before, that integration, in the sense of teaching styles which encourage all children to be part of the social and educational lives of their peers in regular classrooms, is a curricular issue and that curriculum is a matter of politics, morality and substance (chapter 2): We'll teach *this* content, in *this* way, *here* (rather than there), with *these resources* and this is what we *ought* to do. The politics and morality in these statements precede their substantive, technical implications. The fact that decisions about curriculum may be made at central levels in the educational apparatus is consistent with the view that teachers also make political decisions about curriculum and children.

Theorizing policy as political practice, made at all levels in the educational apparatus, will be acceptable, in part, to Weberian sociologists such as Mehan. He argues that institutional practices, the routine enactment of these in schools, which comply, to a degree, with state level written policy such as federal law PL 94–142, construct student identities of handicap rather than attributes the student allegedly has. Thus for Mehan, both government level policy and institutional level practices are relevant in understanding how particular students acquire identities of handicap. But Mehan does not share the decision-making framework adopted here, nor therefore its morality and politics. Mehan prefers an organizational model of decision making, where responsibility lies with organizations, rather than with people. For Mehan the 'outcomes' in schools and for student identities which follow from PL 94–142, are to be understood not as 'decisions' or as deliberate choice but as the enactment of routines:

> As a consequence of this shift in perspective, organizational behaviour can be understood less as deliberate choice and more as end results, or as consequences of organizations functioning according to standard

operating procedures. For this case study, the shift in metaphor means that the placement of a student is more a function of organizational procedure than of organizational choice. The placement of a student in a special education program is not so much a decision made as it is an enactment of routines (1984:66).

The view that institutional practices construct student identities contains the morality that people act with integrity within the logic of their own situation and ought not to be held responsible for the outcomes of their actions, since these are not decisions, or deliberate choice, but the 'enactment of routines':

> Our daily observations, interviews, and discussions showed that educators were honest and genuinely concerned for the welfare of students in their charge; they were not trying to discriminate against any children. Nevertheless, special education services were made differently available to students in the district (Mehan *et al.*, 1981:390).

But as Hindess says, the assignment of responsibility is politically crucial (1986). Allocating responsibility to organizations not people is morally problematic and instances what Fuhrman calls sociology's problem in dealing with the moral and political (1986). It is thus politically and morally problematic to argue that people are not aware of the consequences of their actions in segregating a particular student nor of the overall consequences of contributing to a discriminatory system of separate education. It should, anyway, become less possible to adopt the view and discourse that segregation is 'in the child's best interests', given the mounting evidence and debate which Galloway and Goodwin have summarized (1987), given Swann's analysis (1985) and Tomlinson's arguments (1982, 1985), and given the arguments and evidence discussed here.

The institutional view is also empirically problematic: how are we to explain the closure of Cobram Special Development School by its principal, before the Victorian government policy, and initially against the local community's wishes, other than via a political struggle model? Thus as a struggle (won) to integrate. The alternatives an institutional practices framework offers either do not make sense (this outcome was hardly the enactment of routine practices) or must draw more widely on Weber's ideas, and argue the closure was achieved by a charismatic leader. This is an almost magical explanation.

Relativity and better policy

Some may say the book merely presents educational practices as relative and that pointing out the relativity of social arrangements does not take us very far politically. Hirst and Woolley are right in suggesting that:

> Sociological relativism, in showing that certain categories or institutions are neither necessary nor inevitable, that they depend on certain conditions and that things are ordered differently elsewhere ... refuses to take questions of policy, reform, and genuinely available alternatives seriously (Hirst and Woolley, 1982:97).

Relativity is only part of the book's themes. The book goes beyond the themes of relativism and attempts to show which social policy strategies and which institutional conditions are better able to achieve the intent of government policy writers where there has been a genuine desire to move from the inequities which have characterized educational practices surrounding disability or handicap in Western countries.

The comparative analysis has suggested which strategies and which institutional conditions are counter-productive for, and which encourage an objective of, meaningful integration. What can be concluded from the evidence in chapters 3, 4, 5 and 6?

Institutional conditions in educational apparatuses and integration

The research confirmed that in none of the five educational apparatuses discussed did constitutional, legislative, economic and political-bureaucratic-administrative conditions determine practices at other levels, in schools and in classrooms. This is not to say they had no effect.

A significant effect of legislative conditions in the US and in England has been to introduce new forms of regulations via extensive, time-consuming, administrative practices at other levels: SEA, LEA and school levels in the US and at LEA level in England. Increased regulation has followed Victorian government written policy, the 1984 report, without the assistance of legislation and has derived from negotiations between the most powerful social actors involved, the Minister, the unions and senior bureaucrats. The complex enrolment procedures for a child called disabled and the introduction of the status of 'delayed admission' for children discribed as disabled who seek to enter a regular school, but where the resources alleged necessary are not available, instance increased regulation. Thus in the US, England and Victoria, legislative decisions and/or political-bureaucratic-administrative decisions have constructed new forms of regulation. This regulation has increased the number of children who are marginalized and, in Victoria, has made contingent on resources, the presence of these children in regular classrooms. A resource struggle surrounding disability or special educational needs also occurs in the English educational apparatus and reference to the same struggle is made in the Danish Ministry's literature.

A major effect of increased regulation is to have politicized practices surrounding disability. In the US, the litigation following PL 94–142, and the extensive reporting procedures at SEA and LEA levels, illustrate this. The debate about parent rights in the English educational apparatus, where there are no conditions in or outside the educational apparatus for realizing such 'rights', also indicates politicization. In Victoria, delayed admission (including the attempt to use this procedure to suspend students already in regular schools) indicates politicization. Again, in Victoria, the emergence of advocacy courses to provide parents with a democratic discourse and better negotiation skills, may be a form of politicization rather than empowerment (see below). Thus encounters between parents and bureaucrats or teachers, where there is disagreement, are more politicized. This is a major effect, or consequence, of struggles since the 1984 Victorian report. Similarly, wider institutional conditions in Victoria provide almost no opportunity for the realization of parent rights, a dominant discourse in the 1984 report, beyond the 1984 Equal Opportunity Act, a means to their objectives few parents would take.

Further, the politicization and bureaucratization of educational practices is inconsistent with their democratization. This is a conclusion others have reached about practices in Victorian schools and at other levels in the educational bureaucracy, following another government policy, the Commonwealth Participation and Equity Program (Rizvi *et al.*, 1987). This is particularly significant in the Victorian context, since democratism predominated in the Victorian report. But the opposition between democratization, and politicization and bureaucratization, is relevant to government policy in England and the US.

A key issue arising from the politicization and increased regulation in the North American, British and Victorian educational apparatuses is the extent to which government level policy can achieve substantive educational change. Chapter 4 suggests that legislative decisions may achieve formal rationality (to use Weber's terminology), in the sense that the law is 'complied with', in a procedural sense (schools will carry out a search for 12 per cent as handicapped, for instance); but the evidence also suggests the law cannot achieve substantive rationality, or goals of the kind implied by the notion of free appropriate education (if, for the moment, we ignore the professionalism inherent in the notion of appropriate). The literature on English school practices revealed a child may be placed in a regular school (locational integration) but that social and educational integration do not necessarily follow. Booth reports similar occurrences in Norway's 'comprehensive' schools (chapter 3). This evidence suggests that *educational aims and educational reform are a matter for educators and are not achievable via the kind of decisions made at government level in the US in 1976, in England in 1978 and in 1981, and in Victoria in 1984.*

Of the government policy practices which encourage educational integration, the Danish Ministry of Education's approach is significant in a number of aspects. Legislating for integration it considered inappropriate and counterproductive, a view and a theoretical stance which seems accurate, given the failure of legislative strategies in the US and in England. In the US, the failure of legal strategies is acknowledged by their most ardent advocates (for example, Gerry, 1985). In England, Warnock, whose report underpinned the 1981 Education Act, admits 'we fudged integration as a matter of policy' (1978). This shows very clearly how a simple reading of that Act as integration legislation misunderstands its objectives. Legislation appears not to be a solution or a useful condition of *educational* reform in the sense of attempting to deal with key educational matters such as pedagogy and curriculum. Rather, the main effect of the US and English legislative decisions is regulation. Similar regulation followed the Victorian report. The evidence shows these policies have had no substantive program implications: they do not suggest to teachers how to integrate. Their major effect has been to regulate or control increased numbers of children.

The Danish Ministry of Education chose a different strategy. In Denmark, a process of consulting with people likely to be affected by proposals about integration took place over several years. In Victoria, in contrast, constituencies were consulted somewhat expediently and in a brief time span, during the Ministerial Review. The Danish view and understanding of the political process thus contrasts markedly with the understanding in the Victorian Review which itself reflected the view of the Victorian Labour government. Put differently, the social theory informing the Danish Ministry's strategies seems a more accurate view of how politics work and of how to make a government level policy succeed than the Ministerial Review's deployment and understanding of democratic consultation.

Finally, the Danish Ministry's written policy and its research projects have pedagogy and the notion that all children are firstly pupils, as central themes. These statements and the research focus have been deployed to remove handicap from being a theme in integration discourse. The research findings are disseminated in schools so that government policy practice endeavours to confront the curriculum practices and pedagogical issues which are central to an objective of meaningful integration. This contrasts with the absence of such research in Victoria, for instance, and with the attempt to legislate in PL 94–142 on educational intent and content, via 'a free appropriate education'. The US procedural safeguard, a team constructing an Individualized Education Program, cannot guarantee a free appropriate education will be the outcome of their decisions and not surprisingly, the meaning of free appropriate education is still in dispute.

In sum, three strategies or practices distinguish the Danish government level policy from government policies in North America, Britain and Victoria. These are the removal of legislation regulating children called handicapped, a more accurate view, understanding and successful use of the political process, and instituting a discourse on pedagogy and pupils at government level rather than one on disability and loss.

If the Danish achievement may be used as a measure, legal strategies in the US, and democratic-participatory strategies in Victoria, have been wrong directions for an objective of educational reform, an objective which appears to have been dominant in both these government policies. In the case of English government-level policy, there appear to be good reasons for seeing both the Warnock report and the 1981 Education Act as primarily political exercises, in the sense that the dominant objective here was to retain the status quo, the range of segregated practices and the balance of power between parents and educators, since rights, in the English policy, were strategically even more fictitious than in the Victorian context where strategies were recommended in the 1984 report in an attempt to realize these 'rights', despite unfavourable wider institutional conditions.

Finally, while we can make judgements about the appropriateness or not of government strategies according to their objective, favourable and unfavourable conditions do not determine whether meaningful integration occurs. There are instances in the Victorian educational apparatus (the closure of Cobram Special Developmental School; and see Huish (1986)) where successful integration has occurred both before, and despite the unfavourable conditions constructed at other levels in the educational apparatus following, the 1984 report. This raises the question of the *relevance* of major political exercises such as the Ministerial Review in Victoria for achieving *educational* reform.

In sum, the institutional bases of professionalism are clearly relevant to understanding counter effects and contrary practices. There are two key bases, the educational bureaucracy and those teacher training institutions where there are courses that promote the idea that those called disabled are different and require a separate pedagogy and a separate profession to teach them.

Wider institutional conditions

The evidence also suggests there are differences in the wider institutional conditions of government policy in each of the five places discussed. It is clear that in Denmark, institutional conditions outside the educational apparatus encourage an objective of meaningful integration. Denmark appears to have introduced democratic practices earlier than Sweden, Norway and other Western countries (Therborn *et al.*, 1978), and to have retained this position, despite the election of a non-socialist coalition government in the eighties (chapter 3).

These social democratic practices in Denmark contrast with the historical absence of a social democratic project in Australian political life (Castles, 1985), with the exception of government level policy in the Whitlam era (1972–75). (Though the extent to which this filtered through to arenas at other levels in state apparatuses is highly debatable, despite elegant, coherent, broad-based Marxist theorizing that a social democratic project in education has failed following the global economic crisis (chapter 6)).

The wider institutional conditions in Denmark thus contrast with those in North America, England and Australia. The US is 'a reluctant welfare state' (Jones, 1985:99, citing Mishra), there are views that the Thatcher government has gone a long way towards dismantling the welfare state in Britain and, opposingly, that regulation has become more covert: whichever view is more apt, the plight of those called disabled in Britain in 1987 remains desperate (Wicks, 1987:246). Australia has been the male wage-earner's welfare state (Castles, 1985); it performs relatively poorly on social welfare expenditure and in key social institutions including the Victorian educational apparatus there is a lack of democratic practice (Fulcher, 1989b). The failure of these recommended strategies and the emergence at other levels of practices contrary to those of the Victorian report, raise the question: What are the appropriate means to an objective of democratizing the educational apparatus?

Schools and conditions of integration

The research also confirmed that while wider institutional conditions, both in and outside educational apparatuses, help or hinder an objective of meaningful integration, or indicate the likelihood of this being a dominant objective in educational arenas, *schools also matter:* they, too, are sites where decisions are made which are not determined by these wider institutional conditions.

Clearly both conditions in schools and teaching practices for successful integration are critical factors in such an objective. Fullan, while working with an implementation model, discusses conditions for educational change, including the development of commitment (1987). While these issues are clearly central to educational integration, they have been outside the book's main question: What is the relationship between government level policy and school practices surrounding disability or handicap? The research here suggests policy practices in schools are critical factors and that for three at least of the five government level policies discussed, government level policy has detracted from, rather than supported, an objective of educational integration. Part of the counter-effects of government level policies lies in their failure to theorize (to understand the counter-effects of) the nature of integration or mainstreaming discourses which have disability or handicap as a central theme.

The finding that schools make their own policy practices within the one 'set' of institutional conditions has implications for achieving change in this area. It means that *teachers matter,* that human agency is the source of change, despite the degree of struggle with institutional conditions. The findings that four of the five government level policies produced counter-effects and contrary practices mean that human agency at government level also matters: the kind of policy government committees, for instance, produce on education practices surrounding the issues in integration either facilitates or hinders social actors and their objectives at other levels.

Theorizing disability, integration and mainstreaming

The theorizing offered on policy, disability, and integration and mainstreaming has also been an attempt to clarify firstly, the nature of this policy, secondly, the critical choice between integration discourses and thirdly, the consequences for an objective of educational integration of choosing discourses on disability and handicap. The aim here has been to contribute to different policy, to do it 'better' as Beilharz puts it (1987).

A major theme in the chapters on local practices has been the almost inevitable exclusion which follows from a discourse on disability or handicap in the context of seeking to remove historical inequities from special educational pratices. As Shapiro states, disasbility is inevitably about exclusion:

> the meaning of disability as a phenomenon is a matter of understanding the legitimized discursive practices that constitute disability. By monitoring a society's discursive practices, we discover the structural contribution to the meaning of phenomena ... to understand the meaning of disability ... is to describe its location in a field of discursive relations and thereby to locate those persons or groups of persons who control the responsibility prescriptions that attend and constitute the disabled role. Taken as a whole, the set of discursive practices in which the concept of disability is lodged

provides the rules of exclusion that constitute the meaning of disability (1981:87).

The implications of this are, firstly, that social relations surrounding disability are those of exclusion. Moreover, given disability's connection with exclusion, as Abberley (1987) argues, *disability is a political construct of oppression*. Chapter 1 has argued, however, that the oppression which results from being called disabled becomes clearer if we separate, in a way the literature on disability in general does not, impairment from disability, thus reserving impairment to refer to physical lesions from whatever source and disability as a procedural, therefore *political* construct. While the presumption is generally made whenever the term disability is used, that impairment is present, there is no necessary connection. Chapter 1 discussed the evidence for this. Abberley's social theory of disability is based on a social origin view of impairment and in a materialist theory of social life. The material basis of the distribution of impairment is a key idea here. He suggests that:

A theory of disability as oppression, then,

(1) recognises and, in the present context, emphasises the social origins of impairment;

(2) recognises and opposes the the social, financial, environmental and psychological disadvantages inflicted on impaired people;

(3) sees both (1) and (2) as historical products, not as the results of nature, human or otherwise;

(4) asserts the value of disabled modes of living, at the same time as it condemns the social production of impairment;

(5) is inevitably a political perspective, in that it involves the defence and transformation, both material and ideological, of state health and welfare provision as an essential condition of transforming the lives of the vast majority of disabled people (1987:17).

The discussion in chapter 1 showed that whether or not an impairment is present, disability is a term which can be used analytically to reveal those political procedures which occur when the imputation of impairment is made. Describing 20 per cent of all schoolchildren (chapter 5) as disabled, as the logic of special educational needs does, shows very clearly the oppressive nature of disability as a political construct. The presumption that an impairment is present in 'disability' underlies the themes of loss, difference, therefore marginal identity, therefore contingent presence: these themes construct the political logic which inheres in a discourse on disability and excludes the more appropriate themes of pedagogy and teaching practices.

Disabling Policies?

A discourse on disability is clearly the wrong choice where the objective
is meaningful integration. To move from exclusion, different themes and
different questions must replace this discourse. The relevant themes here
are those of teaching styles and the relevant questions should focus on solving
the problems which lead to exclusion.

A discourse on disability does not disappear through deploying the
notion of 'special educational needs'. As Tomlinson has noted (1982) and
as chapter 5 discusses, special educational needs is also a political construct.
Warnock now rejects it and argues that a focus on curriculum should replace
it (though we do not have to agree with her proposals for curriculum) (1982).
In addition, a discourse on need has been a key category in how welfare
states regulate certain sections of their citizenry. Given its association with
unmet need, the various critiques and evidence that such a category leads
to dependence and reliance on professionals (Borsay, 1986), the notion of
special educational needs is no advance on disability. As Fried argues
persuasively, the notion of 'need' oppresses those to whom it is applied. He
asks: 'What can we do in meeting human needs without condemning our
population to be passive recipients of bureaucratic humanitarianism', so
that we can remove them from 'the continual intervention of benevolent
despotism'? (1980:7, 16) He suggests, citing Freire, that an alternative to
the 'delivery of services' approach is that 'whatever program of action is
implemented on behalf of perceived human needs becomes a vehicle designed,
constructed and piloted by *those being served*. It is the alternative called
"empowerment"' (1980:8).

It is also clear that a discourse on disability is inconsistent with the central
issues in integration. As chapter 2 notes, *integration is basically about discipline
and control: it is not about disability.* But discipline is a curriculum matter rather
than about externally imposed control. It is the achievement of a discourse
on disability, even in the context of an objective some hold of meaningful
integration, to have deflected attention from the fact that *it is the failure in
the educational apparatus by those whose concern it should be, to provide an inclusive
curriculum, and to provide teachers with a sense of competence in such a curriculum,
which constructs the politics of integration.*

Since integration is a curriculum matter and since curriculum is a moral,
political and substantive issue (Fulcher, 1988a), it requires commitment on
the part of teachers to democratize and to include children formerly excluded
from their classrooms. The responsibility for this lies partly with teachers
and partly with their educators, that is, with those who have presented
professionalism to trainee teachers as though it were a technical discourse
only, whereas it is tactic, thus political and moral. The politics and morality
of professionalism, its opposition to democratic practice, have been obscured
and this has systematically undermined the democratization of educational

practices and the likelihood that trainee teachers will acquire the technical competence necessary for democratic practice. To say this is to pass judgement on those who train treachers, as well as teachers, and others who deploy professionalism. But all social theorists moralize: they differ in how explicit they make this. As Fuhrman notes:

> in spite of the attempts to rid moral and political concerns from sociological theory, a moral discourse remains buried within the project because it expresses an ethical telos, has underlying value interests, possesses a discourse impossible to separate from everyday moral discourse; and has moral effects in terms of social reform (1986:75).

The agenda for moving from the exclusion of those called disabled from regular schools lies, firstly, in instituting a discourse on pedagogy and teaching, in focusing on the central educational issues of an inclusive curriculum rather than regulation, in researching the bases of, and arguing for, commitment. Developing inclusive teaching styles, good pedagogic practice, is itself a major task.

Secondly, this agenda involves decoding professionalism for the moral retreat and political discourse it is.[13] While I have argued that professionalism is the opponent of democratism, I do not think this takes us necessarily in the direction of a debate about the *rights* of patients, students, clients, of whatever sort. The evidence discussed in this book on educational policy, comparative evidence across five educational apparatuses, is that a debate about rights, whether this takes place in a context where there is a constitutional basis for such rights, or where there is no such basis, as in Australia, appears merely to politicize issues. Enshrining these rights in legislation, as in the US, was also counterproductive: legalization of rights to an appropriate education appeared merely to achieve mere *compliance* with the law whilst leaving untouched, perhaps further out of reach, the substantive aims the legislation was designed to achieve. Good educational practice in the US and in Victoria, took place independently of either legislation or government documents and was achieved by those who knew what they were doing, that is, by people who were *technically competent.*

This means that those who teach in tertiary training institutions need to teach their students to be as technically competent as possible, since failures in technical competence are one reason for the resort to professionalism. Increased technical competence is clearly a solution in the politics of professionalism in education which, in England and in Victoria, has been deployed to block democratic policies. Thus an enhanced confidence in how to teach might encourage some teachers to adopt a more inclusive and democratic curriculum and so extend the range of children they'll include in their classroom. The distinction between technical competence (how to do substantive things) and professionalism (a discourse of persuasion) is critical.

Secondly, a way out of professionalism towards democratism cannot be achieved by pseudo-democratic means such as gestures by practitioners to provide clients with (partial) information.[14] It is in this context that the Freedom of Information Act in Victoria should, unfortunately, be understood. There are reports that bureaucratic procedures have been deployed to prevent access to 'information' which the law, in principle, guarantees access to. Herein, too, lies some of the reported failure of the Integration Support Groups in Victoria. Again, neither legalization nor increased regulation (tighter guidelines?) are an answer.

Rather, the answer to confronting professionalism lies in teaching intending workers about the nature of politics and its discourses. This has implications for the curriculum in both secondary schools and tertiary training institutes. Curriculum changes at these levels will help decode professionalism and, clearly, a prime task in all of this is to decode professionalism for the tactic it is, so that it can be recognized whenever and wherever it is deployed. This would help professional and paraprofessional workers out of contributing unwittingly to the increased regulation which is the present trend in welfare state services, as well as assist those who don't want to be regulated in this way.

But decoding professionalism is far from easy. For one thing, it presumes people understand political processes, including debate, and hence the difference between professionalism and democratism as discourse and practice. This is clearly not the case in general, and arguing for political understanding means changing and adding to aspects of the curriculum in both tertiary institutes and secondary schools. In secondary schools, it means introducing politics into the curriculum not in its present form, which (in Victoria) seems to be a course about the structure of Parliamentary institutions: it means teaching politics with a syllabus about power and how it is exercised in major institutions. This is an extremely controversial proposal, given the current debate from the right in Western countries, in business arenas and at high level in government, that education should respond more to the economy and produce people with labour force skills, presumably with unquestioning acceptance of labour force arrangements. But understanding politics as about power rather than, say, voting, is basic to assisting people to understand political discourses and thus to take a democratic position on decisions which affect them.

In tertiary institutes which train professionals and paraprofessionals, political discourse should also be a central part of the curriculum; this would include a critique of the position of professionals in the welfare state. Again, this is controversial. It would mean some systematic presentation of the debate about the welfare state and its politics, about the historical point this debate and the future of the welfare state has now reached, and the place of professionals and professionalism in all of this.

Finally, professionalism as tactic is self-defeating since, as Jamrozik notes, citing from a recent book on the welfare state, 'there simply can be no guarantee for the security of the self if it does not take into account the well-being of the other' (1988:27). Both bureaucracy and teacher training institutions, as key institutional bases of professionalism, are implicated here. The professionalism which characterizes educational practices in England and Victoria and it seems, in Norway and North America, too, indicates not merely a lack of democracy in educational apparatuses but a significant lack of democratic practice in a key social institution. This failure has educational roots. As Amy Gutmann argues, 'Our concern for democratic education lies at the core of our commitment to democracy' (1987:288–9). This takes us back then, to a concern with the curriculum.

Notes

1 The discussion of professionalism draws heavily on Fulcher (1989a).
2 Following the 1988 Education Reform Act.
3 The proposed Victorian Certificate of Education to replace the former Higher School Certificate as the final secondary schooling credential is relevant here.
4 Stan Cohen's term (1982).
5 On the distinction between 'public issues' and 'private troubles' see Wright Mills (1970:chapter 1).
6 Foucault's term (1973).
7 See Lee and Raban (1988).
8 Although there is a debate about inclusive styles of teaching and some work emerging from the Victorian Ministry of Education project teams on this.
9 The Danish Ministry of Education is notable for its stance here: children cannot be divided into those with handicaps and those without. Children are firstly pupils (Fulcher, forthcoming).
10 However, Offe, who theorizes state policy as controlling the production of wage labour and as reconciling structural problems internal to the state, nevertheless urges sociologists to understand implementation processes of state policy better than they presently do, so that they can help develop more socially just policy (1984).
11 Booth implies this is what happens in saying 'The Norwegians, as much as ourselves, are beset by bureaucratic absurdities over money' (1983:24).
12 Warnock notes with reference to Norway, 'There is a contradiction in a policy which gives heart-felt priority to desegregation, yet pours vast sums of money into special schools' (1982:59).
13 Fulcher (1989a) is the source for this section.
14 I thank Dr Bob Myers for drawing my attention to this.

References

Abberley, P. (1987) 'The Concept of Oppression and the Development of a Social Theory of Disability', *Disability, Handicap and Society*, 2, 1, pp. 5–20.

Barlow, K. (1986) 'The Commodification of Education – Public into Private?', paper given at the Australia and New Zealand Comparative and International Education Society Conference, December.

Beilharz, P. (1987) 'Reading Politics: Social Theory and Social Policy', *Australia and New Zealand Journal of Sociology*, 22, 3, pp. 388–406.

Biklen, D.P. (1985) 'Mainstreaming from Compliance to Quality', *Journal of Learning Disabilities*, 18, 1, pp. 58–61.

Booth, T. (1983) 'Policies Towards the Integration of Mentally Handicapped Children in Education', *Oxford Review of Education*, 9, 3, pp. 255–68.

Borsay, A. (1986) 'Personal Trouble or Public Issue': Towards a model of policy for people with physical and mental disabilities', *Disability, Handicap and Society*, 1, 2, pp. 179–95.

Castles, F.G. (1985) *The Working Class and Welfare*, Sydney, Allen and Unwin.

Codd, J.A. (1988) 'The construction and deconstruction of educational policy documents', *Journal of Education Policy*, 3, 3, pp. 235–47.

Cohen, S. (1985) *Visions of Social Control*, Cambridge, Polity Press.

Cooper, D. (1982) 'Deinstitutionalization in Psychiatry, Everyday Life and Democracy', *Thesis Eleven*, 5–6, pp. 20–31.

Culley, L., and Demaine, J. (1983) 'Social Theory, Social Relations and Education', in Walker, S., and Barton, L. (Eds) *Gender, Class and Education*, Lewes, Falmer Press, pp. 161–72.

Evans, R. (1986a) 'Children with learning difficulties: Context and consequences', paper presented at the Australian Association of Special Education 11th National Conference, Adelaide, October.

Evans, R. (1986b) 'Responding to Special Educational Needs: Perspectives on Professional Extension', paper presented at The Australian Association of Special Education Conference, Adelaide, October.

Foucault, M. (1973) *The Birth of the Clinic*, London, Tavistock Publications.

Fried, R. (1980) 'Empowerment vs Delivery of Services', New Hampshire State Department of Education, October.

Fuhrman, E.R. (1986) 'Morality, Self and Society: the Loss and Recapture of the Moral Self', in Wardell, M.L., and Turner, S.P. (Eds) *Sociological Theory in Transition*, Boston, Allen and Unwin, pp. 69–79.

Fulcher, G. (1987) 'Bureaucracy takes round seven: round eight to commonsense?', *The Age*, 14 April.

Fulcher, G. (1988a) 'Integration: inclusion or exclusion?', in Slee, R. (Ed) *Discipline and Schools: A Curriculum Perspective*, Macmillan Australia.

Fulcher, G. (1989a) 'The Politics of Professionalism: Its nature, bases and some ways out', *Proceedings* of the 9th Annual Congress of the Australian and New Zealand Association of Psychiatry, Psychology and Law, and 1st Joint Congress with the American Academy of Psychiatry and the Law, University of Melbourne, 27–30 October, 1988.

Fulcher, G. (1989b) 'Disability: a social construction' in Lupton, G., and Najman, J. (Eds) *Sociology of Health and Illness: Australian Readings*, Macmillan Australia, pp. 41–65.

Fulcher, G. (forthcoming) 'Integrate and Mainstream? Comparative issues in the politics of these policies', in Barton, L. (Ed) *Integration: Myth or Reality?*, Falmer Press (in press).

Fullan, M.G. (1987) 'Implementing Educational Change: What We Know', paper prepared for the World Bank seminars, Planning for the Implementation of Educational Change.

Galloway, D., and Goodwin, C. (1987) *The Education of Disturbing Children: Pupils with learning and adjustment difficulties,* New York, Longman.

Gerry, M.H. (1985) 'Policy development by state and local education agencies: the context, challenge, and the rewards of policy leadership, *RASE,* 6, 3, pp. 36–43.

Gutmann, A. (1987) *Democratic Education,* Princeton, New Jersey, Princeton University Press.

Hargrove, E.C. *et al.* (1983) 'Regulation and Schools: The Implementation of Equal Opportunity for Handicapped Children', *Peabody Journal of Education,* 60, 4, pp. 1–126.

Hindess, B. (1986) 'Actors and Social Relations' in Wardell, M.L., and Turner, S.P. (Eds) *Sociological Theory in Transition,* Boston, Allen and Unwin, pp. 113–26.

Hirst, P., and Woolley, P. (1982) *Social Relations and Human Attributes,* London, Tavistock Publications.

Huish, R. (1986) *Integration – a place for everyone,* Melbourne, Participation and Equity Program.

Jamrozik, A. (1987) 'The Viability of the Welfare State', a discussion paper presented at the Conference organized by the New Zealand Council on the Distribution of Income and Wealth in New Zealand, Wellington, 27–28 July.

Jamrozik, A. (1988) Review of Evers, A., Nowotny, H., and Wintersberger, H. (Eds) *The Changing Face of Welfare,* Aldershot, Hants, Gower Publishing Company, in *SWRC Newsletter,* No. 28, February, pp. 26–7.

Jones, C. (1985) *Patterns of Social Policy: An introduction to comparative analysis,* London, Tavistock Publications.

Kapferer, J.L. (1987) 'Youth Policy and The State: Australia, Britain, Sweden', *Discourse,* 8, 1, pp. 1–24.

Kenway, J. (1987) 'Left right out: Australian education and the politics of signification', *Journal of Educational Policy,* 2, 3, pp. 189–203.

Lee, P., and Raban, C. (1988) *Welfare Theory and Social Policy: Reform or Revolultion?* London, Sage Publications.

Macdonell, M. (1986) *Theories of Discourse: An Introduction,* Oxford, Basil Blackwell.

Marx, K., and Engels, F. (1970) *The German Ideology,* Part 1, edited by C.J. Arthur, New York, International Publications.

Mehan, H. (1983) 'The role of language and the language of role', *Language in Society,* 12, pp. 187–211.

Mehan, H. (1984) 'Institutional decision-making', in Rogoff, B., and Lave, J. (Eds) *Everyday Cognition: Its Development in Social Context,* Cambridge, Massuchusetts, Harvard University Press.

Mehan, H., Hertweck, A., and Crowdes, M.S. (1981) 'Identifying handicapped students', in Bacharach, S.B. (Ed) *Organizational Behaviour in Schools and Schools Districts,* New York, Praeger, pp. 381–422.

Miller, P. (1986) *Long Division: State Schooling in South Australian Society,* Adelaide, Wakefield Press.

Nevin, A., and Thousand, J. (1987) 'What the Research Says About Limiting or

Avoiding Referrals to Special Education', *Teacher Education and Special Education,* 9, 4, pp. 149–61.

Noel, M.M., Burke, P.J., and Valdeviesco, C.H. (1985) 'Educational Policy and Severe Mental Retardation', in Bricker, D., and Filler, J. (Eds) *Severe Mental Retardation: From Theory to Practice,* Lancaster PA, The Division on Mental Retardation of the Council of Exceptional Children, pp. 12–35.

Offe, C. (1984) *Contradictions of the Welfare State,* edited by John Keane, London, Hutchinson.

Parsons, I. (1988) 'Making Simple Things Difficult: Some thoughts on the professionalization of human services', *Star,* June/July.

Rizvi, F., Kemmis, S., Walker, R., Fisher, J., Parker, Y. (1987) *Dilemmas of Reform: An overview of issues and achievements of the Participation and Equity Program in Victorian Schools 1984–85,* Geelong, Deakin University.

Shapiro, M.J. (1981) 'Disability and The Politics of Constitutive Rules', in Albrecht, G.L. (Eds) *Cross-National Rehabilitation Policies,* Beverly Hills, California, Sage Publications, pp. 84–96.

Swann, W. (1985) 'Is the integration of children with special needs happening?: an analysis of recent statistics of pupils in special schools', *Oxford Review of Education,* 11, 1, pp. 3–18.

Therborn, G., Kjellberg, A., Marklund, S., and Ohlund, U. (1978) 'Sweden Before and After Social Democracy: A First Overview', *Acta Sociologica,* pp. 37–58.

Tomlinson, S. (1982) *A Sociology of Special Education,* London, Routledge and Kegan Paul.

Tomlinson, S. (1985) 'The Expansion of Special Education', *Oxford Review of Education,* 11, 2, pp. 157–65.

Tomlinson, S. (1987) 'Critical Theory and Special Education: "Is s/he a product of cultural reproduction, or is s/he just thick?"', *CASTME,* 7, 2, pp. 33–41.

Voelker Morsink, C., Chase Thomas, C., and Smith Davis, J. (forthcoming) 'Non-categorical Special Educational Programs: Process and Outcomes'.

Warnock, M. (1978) *Times Educational Supplement,* 25 May.

Warnock, M. (1982) 'Children with Special Needs in Ordinary Schools: Integration Revisited', *Education Today,* 32, 3, pp. 56–61.

Wicks, M. (1987) *A Future for All: Do We Need the Welfare State?* Harmondsworth, Penguin.

Wright Mills, C. (1970) *The Sociological Imagination,* Harmondsworth, Penguin.

Ysseldyke, J.E. (1986) 'Current U.S. Practice in Assessing and Making Decisions About Handicapped Students', *The Australian Journal of Special Education,* 10, 1, pp. 13–20.

ACTS

England
Education Act, 1981
Education Reform Act, 1988

Victoria
Freedom of Information Act, 1982

Index